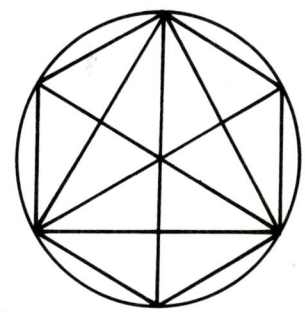

Participative Management: Concepts, Theory and Implementation

Edited by Ervin Williams
Department of Management
Georgia State University

Publishing Services Division
College of Business Administration
Georgia State University
Atlanta, Georgia
1976

Georgia State University is an equal educational
opportunity institution and an equal opportunity/
affirmative action employer.

Library of Congress Cataloging in Publication Data

Main entry under title:

Participative management.

    1. Employees' representation in management--Addresses,
essays, lectures. 2. Management--Addresses, essays,
lectures. I. Williams, Ervin, 1933-
HD5650.P333   658.31'52   76-13650
ISBN 0-88406-102-7

Published by:

Publishing Services Division
College of Business Administration
Georgia State University
University Plaza
Atlanta, Georgia 30303 U S A

658.3152
P 25

87248

Printed and bound in the United States of America

Cover Design by Fredd Chrestman

Contents

Preface

Very few subjects in the field of management have received as much attention in the last decade as participative management. Although several management styles have emerged, the predominate prescriptive advice given to administrators is to be supportive, consultative, or democratic. It is widely assumed that such behavior exhibited by the participative manager will yield high productivity and increased worker satisfaction. To what extent these assumptions are true and under what conditions is the subject of this book.

It has been stated that participative management is the most vital organizational problem of our time, and it is therefore astonishing that there have been so few investigations in this area and that the theoretical basis for these studies has been so meager. Participative techniques can be applied to a wide range of organizational activities, and one has to search a variety of sources to find articles of interest. The purpose of this book is to bring together in one source basic participative management theory, a broad range of research on the subject, and a number of methods and techniques to assist the practitioner in implementing participative management.

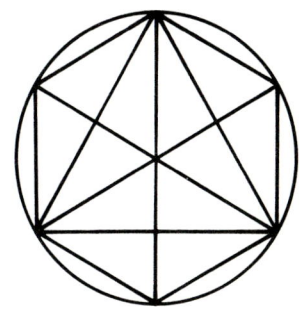

Part I
Participative Management: Concepts and Theory

Keith Davis is at Arizona State University. This article is reprinted with permission from Academy of Management Journal, *March 1968, pp. 27-38.*

Evolving Models of
Organizational Behavior

KEITH DAVIS

The affluent society of which John Kenneth Galbraith wrote a decade ago has become even more affluent.[1] There are many reasons for this sustained improvement in productivity, and some of them are advancing technology, available resources, improved education, and a favorable economic and social system. There is, however, another reason of key significance to all of us. That reason is management, specifically the capacity of managers to develop organizational systems which respond productively to the changing conditions of society. In recent years this has meant more complex administrative systems in order to challenge and motivate employees toward better teamwork. Improvement has been made by working smarter, not harder. An increasingly sophisticated knowledge of human behavior is required; consequently, theoretical models of organizational behavior have had to grow to absorb this new knowledge. It is these evolving models of organizational behavior which I wish to discuss; then I shall draw some conclusions about their use.

The significant point about models of organizational behavior is that the model which a manager holds normally determines his perception of the organizational world about him. It leads to certain assumptions about people and certain interpretations of events he encounters. The underlying model serves as an unconscious guide to each manager's behavior. He acts as he thinks. Since his acts do affect the quality of human relations and productivity in his department, he needs to be fully aware of the trends that are occurring. If he holds to an outmoded model, his success will be limited and his job will be harder, because he will not be able to work with his people as he should.

Similarly, the model of organizational behavior which predominates among the management of an organization will affect the success of that whole organization. And at a national level the model which prevails within a country will influence the productivity and economic development of that nation. Models of organizational behavior are a significant variable in the life of all groups.

Many models of organizational behavior have appeared during the last 100 years, and four of them are significant and different enough to merit further discussion. These are the autocratic, custodial, supportive, and collegial models. In the order mentioned, the four models represent a historical evolution of management thought. The autocratic model predominated 75 years ago. In the 1920s and 1930s it yielded ground to the more successful custodial model. In this generation the supportive model is gaining approval. It predominates in many organizations, although the custodial model probably still prevails in the whole society. Meanwhile, a number of advanced organizations are experimenting with the collegial model.

The four models are not distinct in the sense that a manager or a firm uses one and only one of them. In a week—or even a day—a manager probably applies some of all four models. On the other hand, one model tends to predominate as his habitual way of working with his people, in such a way that it leads to a particular type of teamwork and behavioral climate among his group. Similarly, one model tends to dominate the life of a whole organization, but different parts therein may still be pursuing other models. The production department may take a custodial approach, while supportive ideas are being tried in the office, and collegial ideas are practiced in the research department. The point is that one model of organizational behavior is not an adequate label to describe all that happens in an organization, but it is a convenient way to distinguish one prevailing way of life from another. By comparing these four models, we can recognize certain important distinctions among them.

THE AUTOCRATIC MODEL

The autocratic model has its roots deep in history, and certainly it became the prevailing model early in the industrial revolution. As shown in Figure 1, this model depends on power. Those who are in command must have the power to demand, "You do this—or else," meaning that an employee will be penalized if he does not follow orders. This model takes a threatening approach, depending on negative motivation backed by power.

In an autocratic environment the managerial orientation is formal, official authority. Authority is the tool with which management works and the context in which it thinks, because it is the organizational means by which power is applied. This authority is delegated by right of command over the people to whom it applies. In this model, management implicitly assumes that it knows what is best and that it is the employee's obligation to follow orders without question or interpretation. Management assumes that employees are passive and even resistant to organizational needs. They have to be persuaded and pushed into performance, and this is management's task. Management does the thinking; the employees obey the orders. This is the "Theory X" popularized by Douglas McGregor as the conventional view of management.[2] It has its roots in history and was made explicit by Frederick W. Taylor's concepts of scientific management. Though Taylor's writings show that he had worker interests at heart, he saw those interests served best by a manager who scientifically determined what a worker should do and then saw that he did it. The worker's role was to perform as he was ordered.

Under autocratic conditions an employee's orientation is obedience. He bends to the authority of a boss—not a manager. This role causes a psychological result which in this case is employee personal dependency on his boss whose power to hire, fire, and "perspire" him is almost absolute. The boss pays relatively low wages because he gets relatively less performance from the employee. Each employee must provide subsistence needs for himself and his family; so he reluctantly gives minimum performance, but he is not motivated to give much more than that. A few men give higher performance because of internal achievement drives, because they personally like their boss, because the boss is a "natural-born leader," or because of some other fortuitous reason; but most men give only minimum performance.

When an autocratic model of organizational behavior exists, the measure of an employee's morale is usually his compliance with rules and orders. Compliance is unprotesting assent without enthusiasm. The compliant employee takes his orders and does not talk back.

Although modern observers have an inherent tendency to condemn the autocratic model of organizational behavior, it is a useful way to accomplish work. It has been successfully applied by the empire builders of the 1800s, efficiency engineers, scientific managers, factory foremen, and others. It helped to build great railroad systems, operate giant steel mills, and produce a dynamic industrial civilization in the early 1900s.

Actually the autocratic model exists in all shades of gray, rather than the extreme black usually presented. It has been a reasonably effective way of management when there is a "benevolent autocrat" who has a genuine interest in his employees and when the role expectation of employees is autocratic leadership.[3] But these results are usually only moderate ones lacking the full potential that is available, and they are reached at considerable human costs. In addition, as explained earlier, conditions change to require new behavioral models in order to remain effective.

As managers and academicians became familiar with limitations of the autocratic model, they began to ask, "Is there a better way? Now that we have brought organizational conditions this far along, can we build on what we have in order to move one step higher on the ladder of progress?" Note that their thought was not to throw out power as undesirable, because power is needed to maintain internal unity in organizations. Rather, their thought was to build upon the foundation which existed: "Is there a better way?"

THE CUSTODIAL MODEL

Managers soon recognized that although a compliant employee did not talk back to his boss, he certainly "thought back"! There were many things he wanted to say to his boss, and sometimes he did say them when he quit or lost his temper. The employee inside was a seething mass of insecurity, frustrations, and aggressions toward his boss. Since he could not vent these feelings directly, sometimes he went home and vented them on his wife, family, and neighbors; so the community did not gain much out of this relationship either.

It seemed rather obvious to progressive employers that there ought to be some way to develop employee satisfactions and adjustment during production—and in fact this approach just might cause more productivity! If the employee's insecurities, frustrations, and aggressions could be dispelled, he might feel more like working. At any rate the employer could sleep better, because his conscience would be clearer.

Development of the custodial model was aided by psychologists, industrial relations specialists, and economists. Psychologists were interested in employee satisfaction and adjustment. They felt that a satisfied employee would be a better employee, and the feeling was so strong that "a happy employee" became a mild obsession in some personnel offices. The industrial relations specialists and economists favored the custodial model as a means of building employee security and stability in employment. They gave strong support to a variety of fringe benefits and group plans for security.

The custodial model originally developed in the form of employee welfare programs offered by a few progressive employees, and in its worst form it became known as employer paternalism. During the depression of the 1930s emphasis changed to economic and social security and then shortly moved toward various labor plans for security and control. During and after World War II, the main focus was on specific fringe benefits. Employers, labor unions, and government developed elaborate programs for overseeing the needs of workers.

A successful custodial approach depends on economic resources, as shown in Figure 1. An organization must have economic wealth to provide economic security, pensions, and other fringe benefits. The resulting managerial orientation is toward economic or material rewards, which are designed to make employees respond as economic men. A reciprocal employee orientation tends to develop emphasizing security.

FIGURE 1
Four Models of Organizational Behavior

	Autocratic	Custodial	Supportive	Collegial
Depends on:	Power	Economic resources	Leadership	Mutual contribution
Managerial orientation:	Authority	Material rewards	Support	Integration and teamwork
Employee orientation:	Obedience	Security	Performance	Responsibility
Employee psychological result:	Personal dependency	Organizational dependency	Participation	Self-discipline
Employee needs met:	Subsistence	Maintenance	Higher-order	Self-realization
Performance result:	Minimum	Passive cooperation	Awakened drives	Enthusiasm
Morale measure:	Compliance	Satisfaction	Motivation	Commitment to task and team

Source: Adapted from Keith Davis, *Human Relations at Work: The Dynamics of Organizational Behavior*, 3rd ed. (New York: McGraw-Hill, 1967), p. 480.

The custodial approach gradually leads to an organizational dependency by the employee. Rather than being dependent on his boss for his weekly bread, he now depends on larger organizations for his security and welfare. Perhaps more accurately stated, an organizational dependency is added atop a reduced personal dependency on his boss. This approach effectively serves an employee's maintenance needs, as presented in Herzberg's motivation-maintenance model, but it does not strongly motivate an employee.[4] The result is a passive cooperation by the employee. He is pleased to have his security; but as he grows psychologically, he also seeks more challenge and autonomy.

The natural measure of morale which developed from a custodial model was employee satisfaction. If the employee was happy, contented, and adjusted to the group, then all was well. The happiness-oriented morale survey became a popular measure of success in many organizations.

Limitations of the Custodial Model

Since the custodial model is the one which most employers are currently moving away from, its limitations will be further examined. As with the autocratic model, the custodial model exists in various shades of gray, which means that some practices are more successful than others. In most cases, however, it becomes obvious to all concerned that most employees under custodial conditions do not produce anywhere near their capacities, nor are they motivated to grow to the greater capacities of which they are capable. Though employees may be happy, most of them really do not feel fulfilled or self-actualized.

The custodial model emphasizes economic resources and the security those resources will buy, rather than emphasizing employee performance. The employee becomes psychologically preoccupied with maintaining his security and benefits, rather than with production. As a result, he does not produce much more vigorously than under the old autocratic approach. Security and contentment are necessary for a person, but they are not themselves very strong motivators.

In addition, the fringe benefits and other devices of the custodial model are mostly off-the-job. They are not directly connected with performance. The employee has to be too sick to work or too old to work in order to receive these benefits. The system becomes one of public and private paternalism in which an employee sees little connection between his rewards and his job performance and personal growth; hence he is not motivated toward performance and growth. In fact, an overzealous effort to make the worker secure and happy leads to a brand of psychological paternalism no better than earlier economic paternalism. With the psychological variety, employee needs are dispensed from the personnel department, union hall, and government bureau, rather than the company store. But in either case, dependency remains, and as Ray E. Brown observes, "Men grow stronger on workouts than on handouts. It is in the nature of people to wrestle with a challenge and rest on a crutch.... The great desire of man is to stand on his own, and his life is one great fight against dependency. Making the individual a ward of the organization will likely make him bitter instead of better."[5]

As viewed by William H. Whyte, the employee working under custodialism becomes an "organization man" who belongs to the organization and who has "left home, spiritually as well as physically, to take the vows of organizational life."[6]

As knowledge of human behavior advanced, deficiencies in the custodial model became quite evident, and people again started to ask, "Is there a better way?" The search for a better way is not a condemnation of the custodial model as a whole; however, it is a condemnation of the assumption that custodialism is "the final answer"—the one best way to work with people in organizations. An error in reasoning occurs when a person perceives that the custodial model is so desirable that there is no need to move beyond it to something better.

THE SUPPORTIVE MODEL

The supportive model of organizational behavior has gained currency during recent years as a result of a great deal of behavioral science research as well as favorable employer experience with it. The supportive model establishes a manager in the primary role of psychological support of his employees at work, rather than in a primary role of economic support (as in the custodial model) or "power over" (as in the autocratic model). A supportive approach was first suggested in the classical experiments of Mayo and Roethlisberger at Western Electric Company in the 1930s and 1940s. They showed that a small work group is more productive and satisfied when its members perceive that they are working in a supportive environment. This interpretation was expanded by the work of Edwin A. Fleishman with supervisory "consideration" in the 1940s[7] and that of Rensis Likert and his associates with the "employee-oriented supervisor" in the 1940s and 1950s.[8] In fact, the *coup de grace* to the custodial model's dominance was administered by Likert's research which showed that the happy employee is not necessarily the most productive employee.

Likert has expressed the supportive model as the "principle of supportive relationships" in the following words: *"The leadership and other processes of the organization must be such as to ensure a maximum probability that in all interactions and all relationships with the organization each member will, in the light of his background, values, and expectations, view the experience as supportive and one which builds and maintains his sense of personal worth and importance."*[9]

The supportive model, shown in Figure 1, depends on leadership instead of power or economic resources. Through leadership, management provides a behavioral climate to help each employee grow and accomplish in the interests of the organization the things of which he is capable. The leader assumes that workers are not by nature passive and resistant to organizational needs, but that they are made so by an inadequate supportive climate at work. They will take responsibility, develop a drive to contribute, and improve themselves, if management will give them half a chance. Management's orientation, therefore, is to support the employee's performance.

Since performance is supported, the employee's orientation is toward it instead of mere obedience and security. He is responding to intrinsic motivations in his job situation. His psychological result is a feeling of participation and task involvement in the organization. When referring to his organization, he may occasionally say "we," instead of always saying "they." Since his higher-order needs are better challenged, he works with more awakened drives than he did under earlier models.

The difference between custodial and supportive models is illustrated by the fact that the morale measure of supportive management is the employee's level of motivation. This measure is significantly different from the satisfaction and happiness emphasized by the custodial model. An employee who has a supportive leader is motivated to work toward organizational objectives as a means of achieving his own goals. This approach is similar to McGregor's popular "Theory Y."

The supportive model is just as applicable to the climate for managers as for operating employees. One study reports that supportive managers usually led to high motivation among their subordinate managers. Among those managers who were low in motivation, only 8 per cent had supportive managers. Their managers were mostly autocratic.[10]

It is not essential for managers to accept every assumption of the supportive model in order to move toward it, because as more is learned about it, views will change. What is essential is that modern managers in business, unions, and government do not become locked into the custodial model. They need to abandon any view that the custodial model is the final answer, so that they will be free to look ahead to improvements which are fitting to their organization in their environment.

The supportive model is only one step upward on the ladder of progress. Though it is just now coming into dominance, some firms which have the proper conditions and managerial competence are already using a collegial model of organizational behavior, which offers further opportunities for improvement.

THE COLLEGIAL MODEL

The collegial model is still evolving, but it is beginning to take shape. It has developed from recent behavioral science research, particularly that of Likert, Katz, Kahn, and others at the University of Michigan,[11] Herzberg with regard to maintenance and motivational factors,[12] and the work of a number of people in project management and matrix organization.[13] The collegial model readily adapts to the flexible, intellectual environment of scientific and professional organizations. Working in substantially unprogrammed activities which require effective teamwork, scientific and professional employees desire the autonomy which a collegial model permits, and they respond to it well.

The collegial model depends on management's building a feeling of mutual contribution among participants in the organization, as shown in Figure 1. Each employee feels that he is contributing something worthwhile and is needed and wanted. He feels that management and others are similarly contributing, so he accepts and respects their roles in the organization. Managers are seen as joint contributors rather than bosses.

The managerial orientation is toward teamwork which will provide an integration of all contributions. Management is more of an integrating power than a commanding power. The employee response to this situation is responsibility. He produces quality work not primarily because management tells him to do so or because the inspector will catch him if he does not, but because he feels inside himself the desire to do so for many reasons. The employee psychological result, therefore, is self-discipline. Feeling responsible, the employee disciplines himself for team performance in the same way that a football team member disciplines himself in training and in game performance.

In this kind of environment an employee normally should feel some degree of fulfillment and self-realization, although the amount will be modest in some situations. The result is job enthusiasm, because he finds in the job such Herzberg motivators as achievement, growth, intrinsic work fulfillment, and recognition. His morale will be measured by his commitment to his task and his team, because he will see these as instruments for his self-actualization.

SOME CONCLUSIONS ABOUT MODELS OF ORGANIZATIONAL BEHAVIOR

The evolving nature of models of organizational behavior makes it evident that change is the normal condition of these models. As our understanding of human behavior increases or as new social conditions develop, our organizational behavior models are also likely to change. It is a grave mistake to assume that one particular model is a "best" model which will endure for the long run. This mistake was made by some old-time managers about the autocratic model and by some humanists about the custodial model, with the result that they became psychologically locked into these models and had difficulty altering their practices when conditions demanded it. Eventually the supportive model may also fall to limited use; and as further progress is made, even the collegial model is likely to be surpassed. There is no permanently "one best model" of organizational behavior, because what is best depends upon what is known about human behavior in whatever environment and priority of objectives exist at a particular time.

A second conclusion is that the models of organizational behavior which have developed seem to be sequentially related to man's psychological hierarchy of needs. As society has climbed higher on the need hierarchy, new models of organizational behavior have been developed to serve the higher-order needs that became paramount at the time. If Maslow's need hierarchy is used for comparison, the custodial model of organizational behavior is seen as an effort to serve man's second-level security needs.[14] It moved one step above the autocratic model which was reasonably serving man's subsistence needs, but was not effectively meeting his needs for security. Similarly the supportive model is an effort to meet employees' higher-level needs, such as affiliation and esteem, which the custodial model was unable to serve. The collegial model moves even higher toward service of man's need for self-actualization.

A number of persons have assumed that emphasis on one model of organizational behavior was an automatic rejection of other models, but the comparison with man's need hierarchy *suggests that each model is built upon the accomplishments of the other.* For example, adoption of a supportive approach does not mean abandonment of custodial practices which serve necessary employee security needs. What it does mean is that custodial practices are relegated to secondary emphasis, because employees have progressed up their need structure to a condition in which higher needs predominate. In other words, the supportive model is the appropriate model to use *because* subsistence and security needs are already reasonably met by a suitable power structure and security system. If a misdirected modern manager should abandon these basic organizational needs, the system would quickly revert to a quest for a workable power structure and security system in order to provide subsistence-maintenance needs for its people.

Each model of organizational behavior in a sense outmodes its predominance by gradually satisfying certain needs, thus opening up other needs which can be better served by a more advanced model. Thus each new model is built upon the success of its predecessor. The new model simply represents a more sophisticated way of maintaining earlier need satisfactions, while opening up the probability of satisfying still higher needs.

A third conclusion suggests that the present tendency toward more democratic models of organizational behavior will continue for the longer run. This tendency seems to be required by both the nature of technology and the nature of the need structure. Harbison and Myers, in a classical study of management throughout the industrial world, conclude that advancing industrialization leads to more advanced models of organizational behavior. Specifically, authoritarian management gives way to more constitutional and democratic-participative models of management. These developments are inherent in the system; that is, the more democratic models tend to be necessary in order to manage productively an advanced industrial system.[15] Slater and Bennis also conclude that more participative and democratic models of organizational behavior inherently develop with advancing industrialization. They believe that "democracy is inevitable," because it is the only system which can successfully cope with changing demands of contemporary civilization in both business and government.[16]

Both sets of authors accurately point out that in modern, complex organizations a top manager cannot be authoritarian in the traditional sense and remain efficient, because he cannot know all that is happening in his organization. He must depend on other centers of power nearer to operating problems. In addition, educated workers are not readily motivated toward creative and intellectual duties by traditional authoritarian orders. They require higher-order need satisfactions which newer models of organizational behavior provide. Thus there does appear to be some inherent necessity for more democratic forms of organization in advanced industrial systems.

A fourth and final conclusion is that, though one model may predominate as most appropriate for general use at any point in industrial history, some appropriate uses will remain for other models. Knowledge of human behavior and skills in applying that knowledge will vary among managers. Role expectations of employees will differ depending upon cultural history. Policies and ways of life will vary among organizations. Perhaps more important, task conditions will vary. Some jobs may require routine, low-skilled, highly programmed work which will be mostly determined by higher authority and provide mostly material rewards and security (autocratic and custodial conditions). Other jobs will be unprogrammed and intellectual, requiring teamwork and self-motivation, and responding best to supportive and collegial conditions. This use of different management practices with people according to the task they are performing is called "management according to task" by Leavitt.[17]

In the final analysis, each manager's behavior will be determined by his underlying theory of organizational behavior, so it is essential for him to understand the different results achieved by different models of organizational behavior. The model used will vary with the total human and task conditions surrounding the work. The long-run tendency will be toward more supportive and collegial models because they better serve the higher-level needs of employees.

FOOTNOTES

1. John Kenneth Galbraith, *The Affluent Society* (Boston, Mass.: Houghton Mifflin, 1958).

2. Douglas McGregor, "The Human Side of Enterprise," in *Proceedings of the Fifth Anniversary Convocation of the School of Industrial Management* (Cambridge, Mass.: Massachusetts Institute of Technology, April 9, 1957). Theory X and Theory Y were later popularized in Douglas McGregor, *The Human Side of Enterprise* (New York: McGraw-Hill, 1960).

3. This viewpoint is competently presented in R.N. McMurry, "The Case for Benevolent Autocracy," *Harvard Business Review* (Jan.-Feb., 1958), pp. 82-90.

4. Frederick Herzberg, Bernard Mausner, and Barbara Synderman, *The Motivation to Work* (New York: John Wiley and Sons, 1959).

5. Ray E. Brown, *Judgment in Administration* (New York: McGraw-Hill, 1966), p. 75.

6. William H. Whyte, Jr., *The Organization Man* (New York: Simon and Schuster, 1956), p. 3.

7. An early report of this research is Edwin A. Fleishman, *"Leadership Climate" and Supervisory Behavior* (Columbus, Ohio: Personnel Research Board, Ohio State University, 1951).

8. There have been many publications by the Likert group at the Survey Research Center, University of Michigan. An early basic one is Daniel Katz et. al., *Productivity, Supervision and Morale in an Office Situation* (Ann Arbor, Mich.: The University of Michigan Press, 1950).

9. Rensis Likert, *New Patterns of Management* (New York: McGraw-Hill, 1961), pp. 102-103. (Italics in original.)

10. M. Scott Myers, "Conditions for Manager Motivation," *Harvard Business Review* (Jan.-Feb., 1966), p. 61. This study covered 1,344 managers at Texas Instruments, Inc.

11. Likert describes a similar model as System 4 in Rensis Likert, *The Human Organization: Its Management and Value* (New York: McGraw-Hill, 1967), pp. 3-11.

12. Herzberg *et. al., op cit.*

13. For example, see Keith Davis, "Mutuality in Understanding of the Program Manager's Management Role," *IEEE Transactions on Engineering Management* (Dec., 1965), pp. 117-122.

14. A.H. Maslow, "A Theory of Human Motivation," *Psychological Review* (L, 1943), pp. 370-396.

15. Frederick Harbison and Charles A. Meyers, *Management in the Industrial World: An International Analysis* (New York: McGraw-Hill, 1959), pp. 40-67. The authors also state on page 47, "The design of systems of authority is equally as important in the modern world as the development of technology."

16. Philip E. Slater and Warren G. Bennis, "Democracy Is Inevitable," *Harvard Business Review* (March-April, 1964), pp. 51-59.

17. Harold J. Leavitt, "Management According to Task: Organizational Differentiation," *Management International* (1962), No. 1, pp. 13-22.

Robert Tannenbaum is Professor of the Development of Human Systems, Graduate School of Management, University of California, Los Angeles. Warren H. Schmidt is Senior Lecturer in Behavioral Science, Graduate School of Management, University of California, Los Angeles. This article is reprinted with permission from Harvard Business Review, March-April 1958, pp. 115-121. Copyright ©1958 by the President and Fellows of Harvard College, all rights reserved.

How to Choose
a Leadership Pattern

ROBERT TANNENBAUM and WARREN H. SCHMIDT

○ "I put most problems into my group's hands and leave it to them to carry the ball from there. I serve merely as a catalyst, mirroring back the people's thoughts and feelings so that they can better understand them."

○ "It's foolish to make decisions oneself on matters that affect people. I always talk things over with my subordinates, but I make it clear to them that I'm the one who has to have the final say."

○ "Once I have decided on a course of action, I do my best to sell my ideas to my employees."

○ "I'm being paid to lead. If I let a lot of other people make the decisions I should be making, then I'm not worth my salt."

○ "I believe in getting things done. I can't waste time calling meetings. Someone has to call the shots around here, and I think it should be me."

Each of these statements represents a point of view about "good leadership." Considerable experience, factual data, and theoretical principles could be cited to support each statement, even though they seem to be

17

inconsistent when placed together. Such contradictions point up the dilemma in which the modern manager frequently finds himself.

NEW PROBLEM

The problem of how the modern manager can be "democratic" in his relations with subordinates and at the same time maintain the necessary authority and control in the organization for which he is responsible has come into focus increasingly in recent years.

Earlier in the century this problem was not so acutely felt. The successful executive was generally pictured as possessing intelligence, imagination, initiative, the capacity to make rapid (and generally wise) decisions, and the ability to inspire subordinates. People tended to think of the world as being divided into "leaders" and "followers."

New Focus

Gradually, however, from the social sciences emerged the concept of "group dynamics" with its focus on *members* of the group rather than solely on the leader. Research efforts of social scientists underscored the importance of employee involvement and participation in decision making. Evidence began to challenge the efficiency of highly directive leadership, and increasing attention was paid to problems of motivation and human relations.

Through training laboratories in group development that sprang up across the country, many of the newer notions of leadership began to exert an impact. These training laboratories were carefully designed to give people a first-hand experience in full participation and decision making. The designated "leaders" deliberately attempted to reduce their own power and to make group members as responsible as possible for setting their own goals and methods within the laboratory experience.

It was perhaps inevitable that some of the people who attended the training laboratories regarded this kind of leadership as being truly "democratic" and went home with the determination to build fully participative decision making into their own organizations. When ever their bosses made a decision without convening a staff meeting, they tended to perceive this as authoritarian behavior. The true symbol of democratic leadership to some was the meeting—and the less directed from the top, the more democratic it was.

Some of the more enthusiastic alumni of these training laboratories began to get the habit of categorizing leader behavior as "democratic" *or* "authoritarian." The boss who made too many decisions himself was thought of as an authoritarian, and his directive behavior was often attributed solely to his personality.

New Need

The net result of the research findings and of the human relations training based upon them has been to call into question the stereotype of an effective leader. Consequently, the modern manager often finds himself in an uncomfortable state of mind.

Often he is not quite sure how to behave; there are times when he is torn between exerting "strong" leadership and "permissive" leadership. Sometimes new knowledge pushes him in one direction ("I should really get the group to help make this decision"), but at the same time his experience pushes him in another direction ("I really understand the problem better than the group and therefore I should make the decision"). He is not sure when a group decision is really appropriate or when holding a staff meeting serves merely as a device for avoiding his own decision-making responsibility.

The purpose of our article is to suggest a framework which managers may find useful in grappling with this dilemma. First we shall look at the different patterns of leadership behavior that the manager can choose from in relating himself to his subordinates. Then we shall turn to some of the questions suggested by this range of patterns. For instance, how important is it for a manager's subordinates to know what type of leadership he is using in a situation? What factors should he consider in deciding on a leadership pattern? What difference do his long-run objectives make as compared to his immediate objectives?

RANGE OF BEHAVIOR

Exhibit 1 presents the continuum or range of possible leadership behavior available to a manager. Each type of action is related to the degree of authority used by the boss and to the amount of freedom available to his subordinates in reaching decisions. The actions seen on the extreme left characterize the manager who maintains a high degree of control while those seen on the extreme right characterize the manager who releases a high degree of control. Neither extreme is absolute; authority and freedom are never without their limitations.

Now let us look more closely at each of the behavior points occurring along this continuum:

The manager makes the decision and announces it. In this case the boss identifies a problem, considers alternative solutions, chooses one of them, and then reports this decision to his subordinates for implementation. He may or may not give consideration to what he believes his subordinates will think or feel about his decision; in any case, he provides no opportunity for them to participate directly in the decision-making process. Coercion may or may not be used or implied.

The manager "sells" his decision. Here the manager, as before, takes responsibility for identifying the problem and arriving at a decision.

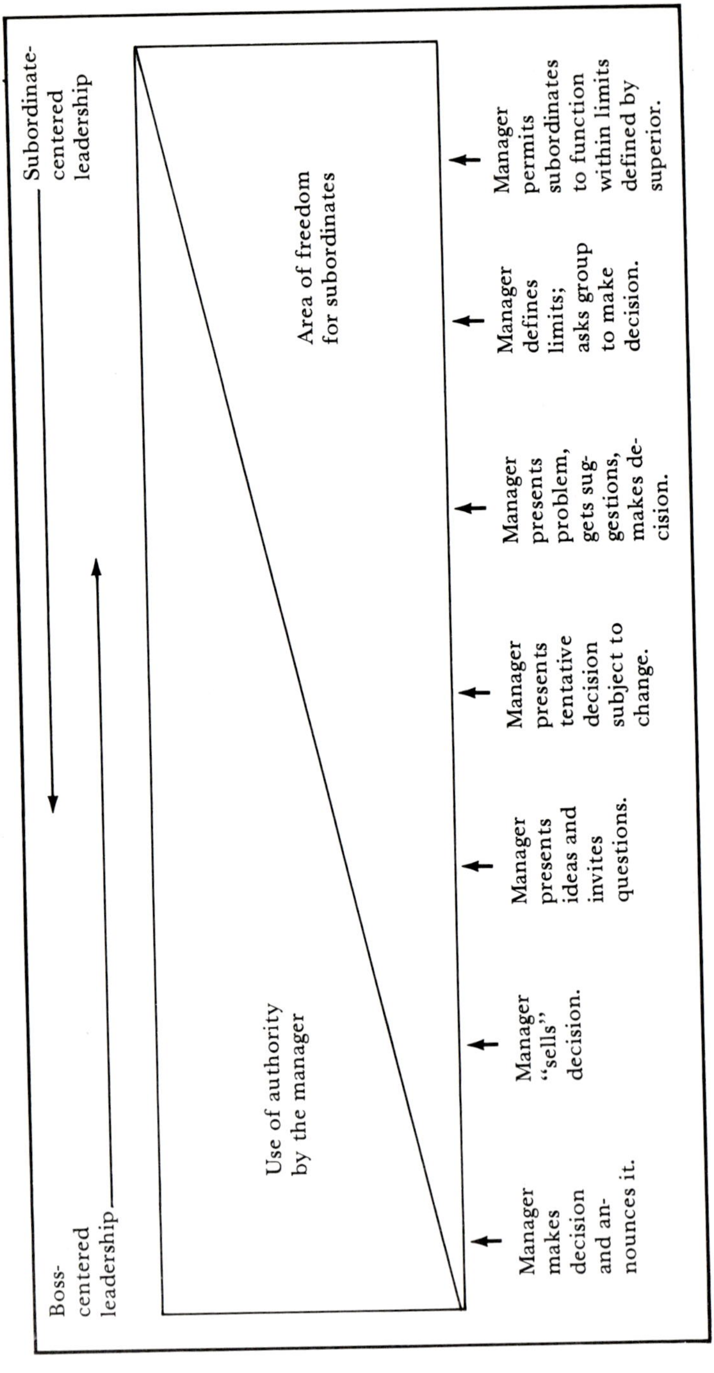

EXHIBIT 1
Continuum of Leadership Behavior

Boss-centered leadership ←———————————→ Subordinate-centered leadership

Use of authority by the manager

Area of freedom for subordinates

- Manager makes decision and announces it.
- Manager "sells" decision.
- Manager presents ideas and invites questions.
- Manager presents tentative decision subject to change.
- Manager presents problem, gets suggestions, makes decision.
- Manager defines limits; asks group to make decision.
- Manager permits subordinates to function within limits defined by superior.

However, rather than simply announcing it, he takes the additional step of persuading his subordinates to accept it. In doing so, he recognizes the possibility of some resistance among those who will be faced with the decision, and seeks to reduce this resistance by indicating, for example, what the employees have to gain from his decision.

The manager presents his ideas, invites questions. Here the boss who has arrived at a decision and who seeks acceptance of his ideas provides an opportunity for his subordinates to get a fuller explanation of his thinking and his intentions. After presenting the ideas, he invites questions so that his associates can better understand what he is trying to accomplish. This "give and take" also enables the manager and the subordinates to explore more fully the implications of the decision.

The manager presents a tentative decision subject to change. This kind of behavior permits the subordinates to exert some influence on the decision. The initiative for identifying and diagnosing the problem remains with the boss. Before meeting with his staff, he has thought the problem through and arrived at a decision—but only a tentative one. Before finalizing it, he presents his proposed solution for the reaction of those who will be affected by it. He says in effect, "I'd like to hear what you have to say about this plan that I have developed. I'll appreciate your frank reactions, but will reserve for myself the final decision."

The manager presents the problem, gets suggestions, and then makes his decision. Up to this point the boss has come before the group with a solution of his own. Not so in this case. The subordinates now get the first chance to suggest solutions. The manager's initial role involves identifying the problem. He might, for example, say something of this sort: "We are faced with a number of complaints from newspapers and the general public on our service policy. What is wrong here? What ideas do you have for coming to grips with this problem?"

The function of the group becomes one of increasing the manager's repertory of possible solutions to the problem. The purpose is to capitalize on the knowledge and experience of those who are on the "firing line." From the expanded list of alternatives developed by the manager and his subordinates, the manager then selects the solution that he regards as most promising.[1]

The manager defines the limits and requests the group to make a decision. At this point the manager passes to the group (possibly including himself as a member) the right to make decisions. Before doing so, however, he defines the problem to be solved and the boundaries within which the decision must be made.

An example might be the handling of a parking problem at a plant. The boss decides that this is something that should be worked on by the people involved, so he calls them together and points up the existence of the problem. Then he tells them:

> "There is the open field just north of the main plant which has been designated for additional employee parking. We can build underground or surface multilevel facilities as long as the cost does not

exceed $100,000. Within these limits we are free to work out whatever solution makes sense to us. After we decide on a specific plan, the company will spend the available money in whatever way we indicate."

The manager permits the group to make decisions within prescribed limits. This represents an extreme degree of group freedom only occasionally encountered in formal organizations, as, for instance, in many research groups. Here the team of managers or engineers undertakes the identification and diagnosis of the problem, develops alternative procedures for solving it, and decides on one or more of these alternative solutions. The only limits directly imposed on the group by the organization are those specified by the superior of the team's boss. If the boss participates in the decision-making process, he attempts to do so with no more authority than any other member of the group. He commits himself in advance to assist in implementing whatever decision the group makes.

KEY QUESTIONS

As the continuum in Exhibit 1 demonstrates, there are a number of alternative ways in which a manager can relate himself to the group or individuals he is supervising. At the extreme left of the range, the emphasis is on the manager—on what *he* is interested in, how *he* sees things, how *he* feels about them. As we move toward the subordinate-centered end of the continuum, however, the focus is increasingly on the subordinates—on what *they* are interested in, how *they* look at things, how *they* feel about them.

When business leadership is regarded in this way, a number of questions arise. Let us take four of especial importance:

Can a boss ever relinquish his responsibility by delegating it to someone else? Our view is that the manager must expect to be held responsible by his superior for the quality of the decisions made, even though operationally these decisions may have been made on a group basis. He should, therefore, be ready to accept whatever risk is involved whenever he delegates decision-making power to his subordinates. Delegation is not a way of "passing the buck." Also, it should be emphasized that the amount of freedom the boss gives to his subordinates cannot be greater than the freedom which he himself has been given by his own superior.

Should the manager participate with his subordinates once he has delegated responsibility to them? The manager should carefully think over this question and decide on his role prior to involving the subordinate group. He should ask if his presence will inhibit or facilitate the problem-solving process. There may be some instances when he should leave the group to let it solve the problem for itself. Typically, however, the boss has useful ideas to contribute, and should function as an additional member of the group. In the latter instance, it is important that he indicate clearly to the group that he sees himself in a *member* role rather than in an authority role.

How important is it for the group to recognize what kind of leadership behavior the boss is using? It makes a great deal of difference. Many relationship problems between boss and subordinate occur because the boss fails to make clear how he plans to use his authority. If, for example, he actually intends to make a certain decision himself, but the subordinate group gets the impression that he has delegated this authority, considerable confusion and resentment are likely to follow. Problems may also occur when the boss uses a "democratic" facade to conceal the fact that he has already made a decision which he hopes the group will accept as its own. The attempt to "make them think it was their idea in the first place" is a risky one. We believe that it is highly important for the manager to be honest and clear in describing what authority he is keeping and what role he is asking his subordinates to assume in solving a particular problem.

Can you tell how "democratic" a manager is by the number of decisions his subordinates make? The sheer *number* of decisions is not an accurate index of the amount of freedom that a subordinate group enjoys. More important is the *significance* of the decisions which the boss entrusts to his subordinates. Obviously a decision on how to arrange desks is of an entirely different order from a decision involving the introduction of new electronic data-processing equipment. Even though the widest possible limits are given in dealing with the first issue, the group will sense no particular degree of responsibility. For a boss to permit the group to decide equipment policy, even within rather narrow limits, would reflect a greater degree of confidence in them on his part.

DECIDING HOW TO LEAD

Now let us turn from the types of leadership that are possible in a company situation to the question of what types are *practical* and *desirable*. What factors or forces should a manager consider in deciding how to manage? Three are of particular importance:

Forces in the manager.
Forces in the subordinates.
Forces in the situation.

We should like briefly to describe these elements and indicate how they might influence a manager's action in a decision-making situation.[2] The strength of each of them will, of course, vary from instance to instance, but the manager who is sensitive to them can better assess the problems which face him and determine which mode of leadership behavior is most appropriate for him.

Forces in the Manager

The manager's behavior in any given instance will be influenced greatly by the many forces operating within his own personality. He will, of course, perceive his leadership problems in a unique way on the basis of his background, knowledge, and experience. Among the important internal forces affecting him will be the following:

(1) *His value system.* How strongly does he feel that individuals should have a share in making the decisions which affect them? Or, how convinced is he that the official who is paid to assume responsibility should personally carry the burden of decision making? The strength of his convictions on questions like these will tend to move the manager to one end or the other of the continuum shown in Exhibit 1. His behavior will also be influenced by the relative importance that he attaches to organizational efficiency, personal growth of subordinates, and company profits.[3]

(2) *His confidence in his subordinates.* Managers differ greatly in the amount of trust they have in other people generally, and this carries over to the particular employees they supervise at a given time. In viewing his particular group of subordinates, the manager is likely to consider their knowledge and competence with respect to the problem. A central question he might ask himself is: "Who is best qualified to deal with this problem?" Often he may, justifiably or not, have more confidence in his own capabilities than in those of his subordinates.

(3) *His own leadership inclinations.* There are some managers who seem to function more comfortably and naturally as highly directive leaders. Resolving problems and issuing orders come easily to them. Other managers seem to operate more comfortably in a team role, where they are continually sharing many of their functions with their subordinates.

(4) *His feelings of security in an uncertain situation.* The manager who releases control over the decision-making process thereby reduces the predictability of the outcome. Some managers have a greater need than others for predictability and stability in their environment. This "tolerance for ambiguity" is being viewed increasingly by psychologists as a key variable in a person's manner of dealing with problems.

The manager brings these and other highly personal variables to each situation he faces. If he can see them as forces which, consciously or unconsciously, influence his behavior, he can better understand what makes him prefer to act in a given way. And understanding this, he can often make himself more effective.

Forces in the Subordinate

Before deciding how to lead a certain group, the manager will also want to consider a number of forces affecting his subordinates' behavior. He will want to remember that each employee, like himself, is influenced by many personality variables. In addition, each subordinate has a set of expectations about how the boss should act in relation to him (the phrase "expected behavior" is one we hear more and more often these days at discussions of leadership and teaching). The better the manager understands these factors, the more accurately he can determine what kind of behavior on his part will enable his subordinates to act most effectively.

Generally speaking, the manager can permit his subordinates greater freedom if the following essential conditions exist:

- If the subordinates have relatively high needs for independence. (As we all know, people differ greatly in the amount of direction that they desire.)
- If the subordinates have a readiness to assume responsibility for decision making. (Some see additional responsibility as a tribute to their ability; others see it as "passing the buck.")
- If they have a relatively high tolerance for ambiguity. (Some employees prefer to have clear-cut directives given to them; others prefer a wider area of freedom.)
- If they are interested in the problem and feel that it is important.
- If they understand and identify with the goals of the organization.
- If they have the necessary knowledge and experience to deal with the problem.
- If they have learned to expect to share in decision making. (Persons who have come to expect strong leadership and are then suddenly confronted with the request to share more fully in decision making are often upset by this new experience. On the other hand, persons who have enjoyed a considerable amount of freedom resent the boss who begins to make all the decisions himself.)

The manager will probably tend to make fuller use of his own authority if the above conditions do *not* exist; at times there may be no realistic alternative to running a "one-man show."

The restrictive effect of many of the forces will, of course, be greatly modified by the general feeling of confidence which subordinates have in the boss. Where they have learned to respect and trust him, he is free to vary his behavior. He will feel certain that he will not be perceived as an authoritarian boss on those occasions when he makes decisions by himself. Similarly, he will not be seen as using staff meetings to avoid his decision-making responsibility. In a climate of mutual confidence and respect, people tend to feel less threatened by deviations from normal practice, which in turn makes possible a higher degree of flexibility in the whole relationship.

Forces in the Situation

In addition to the forces which exist in the manager himself and in his subordinates, certain characteristics of the general situation will also affect the manager's behavior. Among the more critical environmental pressures that surround him are those which stem from the organization, the work group, the nature of the problem, and the pressures of time. Let us look briefly at each of these:

Type of Organization. Like individuals, organizations have values and traditions which inevitably influence the behavior of the people who work in them. The manager who is a newcomer to a company quickly discovers that certain kinds of behavior are approved while others are not. He also discovers that to deviate radically from what is generally accepted is likely to create problems for him.

These values and traditions are communicated in many ways—through job descriptions, policy pronouncements, and public statements by top executives. Some organizations, for example, hold to the notion that the desirable executive is one who is dynamic, imaginative, decisive, and persuasive. Other organizations put more emphasis upon the importance of the executive's ability to work effectively with people—his human relations skills. The fact that his superiors have a defined concept of what the good executive should be will very likely push the manager toward one end or the other of the behavioral range.

In addition to the above, the amount of employee participation is influenced by such variables as the size of the working units, their geographical distribution, and the degree of inter- and intra-organizational security required to attain company goals. For example, the wide geographical dispersion of an organization may preclude a practical system of participative decision making, even though this would otherwise be desirable. Similarly, the size of the working units or the need for keeping plans confidential may make it necessary for the boss to exercise more control than would otherwise be the case. Factors like these may limit considerably the manager's ability to function flexibly on the continuum.

Group Effectiveness. Before turning decision-making responsibility over to a subordinate group, the boss should consider how effectively its members work together as a unit.

One of the relevant factors here is the experience the group has had in working together. It can generally be expected that a group which has functioned for some time will have developed habits of cooperation and thus be able to tackle a problem more effectively than a new group. It can also be expected that a group of people with similar backgrounds and interests will work more quickly and easily than people with dissimilar backgrounds, because the communication problems are likely to be less complex.

The degree of confidence that the members have in their ability to solve problems as a group is also a key consideration. Finally, such group variables as cohesiveness, permissiveness, mutual acceptance, and commonality of purpose will exert subtle but powerful influence on the group's functioning.

The Problem Itself. The nature of the problem may determine what degree of authority should be delegated by the manager to his subordinates. Obviously he will ask himself whether they have the kind of knowledge which is needed. It is possible to do them a real disservice by assigning a problem that their experience does not equip them to handle.

Since the problems faced in large or growing industries increasingly require knowledge of specialists from many different fields, it might be inferred that the more complex a problem, the more anxious a manager will be to get some assistance in solving it. However, this is not always the case. There will be times when the very complexity of the problem calls for one person to work it out. For example, if the manager has most of the background and factual data relevant to a given issue, it may be easier for him to think it through himself than to take the time to fill in his staff on all the pertinent background information.

The key question to ask, of course, is: "Have I heard the ideas of everyone who has the necessary knowledge to make a significant contribution to the solution of this problem?"

The Pressure of Time. This is perhaps the most clearly felt pressure on the manager (in spite of the fact that it may sometimes be imagined). The more that he feels the need for an immediate decision, the more difficult it is to involve other people. In organizations which are in a constant state of "crisis" and "crash programming" one is likely to find managers personally using a high degree of authority with relatively little delegation to subordinates. When the time pressure is less intense, however, it becomes much more possible to bring subordinates in on the decision-making process.

These, then, are the principal forces that impinge on the manager in any given instance and that tend to determine his tactical behavior in relation to his subordinates. In each case his behavior ideally will be that which makes possible the most effective attainment of his immediate goal within the limits facing him.

LONG-RUN STRATEGY

As the manager works with his organization on the problems that come up day by day, his choice of a leadership pattern is usually limited. He must take account of the forces just described and, within the restrictions they impose on him, do the best that he can. But as he looks ahead months or even years, he can shift his thinking from tactics to large-scale strategy. No longer need he be fettered by all of the forces mentioned, for he can view many of them as variables over which he has some control. He can, for example, gain new insights or skills for himself, supply training for individual subordinates, and provide participative experiences for his employee group.

In trying to bring about a change in these variables, however, he is faced with a challenging question: At which point along the continuum *should* he act?

Attaining Objectives

The answer depends largely on what he wants to accomplish. Let us suppose that he is interested in the same objectives that most modern managers seek to attain when they can shift their attention from the pressure of immediate assignments:

1. To raise the level of employee motivation.
2. To increase the readiness of subordinates to accept change.
3. To improve the quality of all managerial decisions.
4. To develop team work and morale.
5. To further the individual development of employees.

In recent years the manager has been deluged with a flow of advice on how best to achieve these longer-run objectives. It is little wonder that he is often both bewildered and annoyed. However, there are some guidelines which he can usefully follow in making a decision.

Most research and much of the experience of recent years give a strong factual basis to the theory that a fairly high degree of subordinate-centered behavior is associated with the accomplishment of the five purposes mentioned.[4] This does not mean that a manager should always leave all decisions to his assistants. To provide the individual or the group with greater freedom than they are ready for at any given time may very will tend to generate anxieties and therefore inhibit rather than facilitate the attainment of desired objectives. But this should not keep the manager from making a continuing effort to confront his subordinates with the challenge of freedom.

CONCLUSION

In summary, there are two implications in the basic thesis that we have been developing. The first is that the successful leader is one who is keenly aware of those forces which are most relevant to his behavior at any given time. He accurately understands himself, the individuals and group he is dealing with, and the company and broader social environment in which he operates. And certainly he is able to assess the present readiness for growth of his subordinates.

But this sensitivity or understanding is not enough, which brings us to the second implication. The successful leader is one who is able to behave appropriately in the light of these perceptions. If direction is in order, he is able to direct; if considerable participative freedom is called for, he is able to provide such freedom.

Thus, the successful manager of men can be primarily characterized neither as a strong leader nor as a permissive one. Rather, he is one who maintains a high batting average in accurately assessing the forces that determine what his most appropriate behavior at any given time should be and in actually being able to behave accordingly. Being both insightful and flexible, he is less likely to see the problems of leadership as a dilemma.

FOOTNOTES

1. For a fuller explanation of this approach, see Leo Moore, "Too Much Management, Too Little Change," *Harvard Business Review*, January-February 1956, p. 41.

2. See also Robert Tannenbaum and Fred Massarik, "Participation by Subordinates in the Managerial Decision-Making Process," *Canadian Journal of Economics and Political Science*, August 1950, pp. 413-418.

3. See Chris Argyris, "Top Management Dilemma: Company Needs vs. Individual Development," *Personnel*, September 1955, pp. 123-134.

4. For example, see Warren H. Schmidt and Paul C. Buchanan, *Techniques that Produce Teamwork* (New London, Arthur C. Croft Publications, 1954); and Morris S. Viteles, *Motivation and Morale in Industry* (New York, W.W. Norton & Company, Inc., 1953).

Dr. Patchen is Professor of Sociology, Purdue University, West LaFayette, Indiana. He has authored numerous articles and reports in the field of social psychology. His present research interests relate to public opinion, social conflict, and organizational processes. He is also a Lecturer in psychology at the University of Michigan.

The ideas presented in this paper were developed in collaboration with Craig W. Allen. Work on the paper was done under grant MH4514 from the National Institutes of Health. The paper was prepared for the Seminar on the Social Science of Organizations held at the University of Pittsburg under the sponsorship of the Ford Foundation.

Participation in Decision-Making and Motivation: What Is the Relation?

MARTIN PATCHEN

Much has been said and written about member "participation" in organizations. Participation in decision-making has been seen by many as a key to releasing energies and enthusiasms which ordinarily lie dormant. And a number of experiments, surveys and case histories—especially in industry—have demonstrated that various forms of participation can bring marked, even dramatic, improvement in motivation.[1]

Yet even investigators sympathetic to the idea of promoting member participation note evidence that democratic procedures are not always effective in eliciting enthusiasm and hard work.[2] Moreover, despite all that has been written on the subject, it is still not entirely clear why and how we should expect participation in decision-making to affect motivation to work.

It has been pointed out by some that participation in decision-making by organization members in setting organizational goals can result in objective changes in an organization's goals and in the means of reaching those goals.[3] This result is emphasized by those who, like McGregor, believe that organizations should create conditions "such that the members of the organization can achieve their own goals *best* by directing their efforts toward the success of the enterprise."[4] One possible effect of participative management is, thus, the creation of organizational goals which fit the needs and goals of its members.

While this practical result of member participation is potentially important, most of the reported cases in which member participation has led to more member effort have not seemed to involve important differences in the nature of the decisions arrived at. For example, in the now-classic study by Coch and French,[5] those employees who helped plan the changes in production methods in a pajama factory did not create practical conditions that were different from those met by their co-workers who merely received instructions about the changes. Yet production was far better in the participating groups. There seems to be something in the nature of the participatory process itself which leads to increased motivation. What is that something?

Some observers have emphasized the effects of member participation on the personal growth of individuals and on their "self-actualization." Thus, Argyris says:

> ... we defined the function of leadership as helping the individual to obtain optimum self-actualization and the organization to fulfill its objectives. If we accept this proposition, then it follows logically that "employee-centered" or "democratic" leadership fulfills primarily the individual's needs.[6]

It has also been noted that insofar as employee participation gets members to cooperate and work together, it can contribute to group cohesiveness. Thus, Likert points out that, "The leader develops his subordinates into a working team with high group loyalty by using participation and other kinds of group leadership practices...."[7] While this effect of group participation can be important, it is clear that group cohesiveness and loyalty will not in itself result in high work motivation. It is well known that group norms can, instead, pressure the individual to restrict his output.

The explanation of the effects of participation which perhaps appears most frequently is that participation in decision-making somehow gets people "involved" with the goals and work of the organization.

Hood expresses this basic idea when he says, "People support what they help create."[8]

Likert states, "Since the goals of the group are arrived at through group decisions, each individual group member tends to have a high level of ego identification with the goals because of his involvement in the decisions."[9]

Vroom, attempting to explain the effects of participation on motivation in terms of a formal theory of motivation, states the following assumptions: (1) Persons derive satisfaction from successfully carrying out decisions in which they have participated; (2) the more an individual has influence on a joint decision, the more satisfaction he obtains from its successful execution; (3) the motives for independence and power-equality are satisfied by the successful execution of joint decisions.[10]

While the general notion that participation leads to "involvement" has a ring of truth about it, the underlying process remains rather fuzzy. Does the individual work for the organization's goals because they are now "his" and because he will feel a sense of personal success or failure when the goals are reached or not reached? If so, does this assume that he must feel that what he does will have a direct and substantial effect on the over-all success of the organization? Or does he get intrinsic satisfaction from carrying out decisions that he has helped shape—regardless of whether he feels that what he personally does will have a marked impact on larger events? If so, it remains unclear just why he should derive such satisfaction.

In short, the whole process by which participation in decision-making can result in increased motivation needs further examination. This paper attempts to clarify the process. The ideas proposed are largely theoretical and need further empirical testing. It is hoped that they will have some value in stimulating thought about the subject.

We suggest that participation by organization members in decision-making may lead to increased motivation for two primary reasons.
1. Participation may create the opportunity for the individual to get a sense of *personal achievement* from reaching goals in his work.
2. Participation may lead to *identification* with the organization, which makes the individual more sensitive to *social pressures* from organization members.

The rest of this paper will be devoted to a closer examination of each of these mechanisms and their implications.

PARTICIPATION AND MOTIVATION FOR ACHIEVEMENT

To clarify the relation between participation in decision-making and the motivation for achievement, we must first consider the general conditions that produce motivation for achievement. For this purpose, we will use a goals-means framework. This general approach, derived from general psychology[11] has been used previously in industrial situations by Georgopoulos and associates[12] and discussed by Robert Kahn.[13]
We would assume that:

Motivation to work hard in order to get feelings of achievement	= f	Extent to which achievement in specific work is an important goal	X	Extent to which effort in work situation is perceived as leading to achievement for the individual

(Note: f stands for "is a function of"; X means "multiplied by.")

Following this general statement, the next step is to predict to the two terms on the right of this equation. Let us first consider "the extent to which achievement in specific work situations is an important goal."

We would assume that the extent to which achievement in work is a goal depends in part from a relatively fixed personality attribute, "need for achievement." This need has been conceptualized and measured by McClelland, Atkinson and their co-workers.[14] Given the general need for achievement, the formulation assumes, further, that the individual does not wish to achieve equally in every area of life. Achievement is most important in those roles which form an important part of the person's self-image. The man whose self-image is that of a fine athlete will care most about achieving in athletics. The more important the person's work role is in his self-image, the more important achievement in the work situation will be.[15]

Given both the personality need for achievement and a focusing of this need in the work area, the individual may still be little motivated if he fails to accept specific goals in the work situation as his own. For example let us take a carpenter who has a high need for achievement (basic personality) and whose role as a carpenter is an important part of his self-image. Suppose he is building a partition between two rooms, and he is told to make it 8 feet high and to finish in 10 hours. He may believe that the partition would look better if it were 7 feet high, and that he needs 12 hours to do the job right; moreover, he may feel that he should finish a cabinet he started before he starts on the partition. Despite his high basic achievement motivation and centrality of his role of carpenter to his self-image, he may have little effective motivation for achievement that day.

Here is where one aspect of "participation" comes in. One way to get our carpenter to accept the specific work goals as his own is to give him a voice in setting these goals. We might, for example, ask him how long he thinks he should spend on building the wall and whether he should start on it now or finish the cabinet first.

We may formalize this discussion somewhat by stating the following equation:

Extent to which achievement of specific work goals is important	= f	General need for achievement	X	Extent to which need for achievement is tied to work (importance of work role in self-concept)

$$X \quad \text{Extent to which specific work goals are accepted as important part of work role}$$

$$\uparrow$$

Part in setting work goals affects this

WILL EFFORT LEAD TO FEELINGS OF ACHIEVEMENT?

We need next to try to account for variations in the extent to which effort in the work situation is perceived as leading to achievement. The theory of achievement motivation, as stated by McClelland and Atkinson, views this motivation as the wish to live up to a given standard of excellence. This standard is always, directly or indirectly, one which involves comparisons with one's fellows. One is doing better than his co-workers. Or one is achieving an objective standard—say a bowling score of 200—which is reached by only the more gifted people. In the industrial situation, the standards may be objective quality standards or time standards (e.g., meeting deadlines), which permit the individual to compare his performance to that of others, or may involve a more subjective ranking against co-workers.

Closely related to the need for standards of excellence in the work situation is the need for the individual to provide feedback to the organization on his performance. An example of lack of feedback occurs in an engineering organization with which we are acquainted. Some engineers prepare drawings which go to a "checker," who makes any necessary corrections, but rarely tells the original designer what, if any, changes were required. Plainly the original engineer cannot long strive to live up to a standard of engineering excellence if he never finds out how he is doing.

A further organizational requirement comes directly from the theory of need for achievement. This is the requirement that the individual's work provide a moderate degree of difficulty. Experiments have established that persons with high need for achievement will choose situations where the probability of success is considerably less than one, yet not too small.[16] It should be expected that people with high need for achievement will respond best to job situations which provide something of a challenge to their abilities. It should be noted, on the other hand, that people with lower needs for achievement, and particularly those who fear failure, have been found to prefer situations where success is fairly certain (or so unlikely as not to cause concern when missed). However, even people who fear failure will probably be stimulated to greater effort (or not immobilized by anxiety) by situations in which there is a small probability of failure (say 1 in 10) than in routine jobs where success is entirely certain all the time.

Another necessary ingredient to provide opportunities for achievement is placing in the individual's own hands, a large measure of control over the means to reach the goals in his work situation. Unless a person feels that he is personally responsible for his job performance, he cannot feel achievement in reaching some goal. The individual's control may result in part from actual autonomy—that is, of having responsibility delegated to him. He can also enjoy a measure of control indirectly through being able to influence the actions of superiors and subordinates. Delegation of authority to lower levels and the according of greater influence to lower levels have, of course, been an important part of the concern with "participation." We see here another of the specific ways in which participation may have its effects—i.e., on the perceived opportunities for achievement. We may formalize the discussion of the extent to which effort is seen as leading to achievement as follows:

Perceived p that effort will objectively result in achievement	= f	Clear standard of good performance (involving social comparisons)	X	Feedback on performance	X	Difficulty of reaching goals

$$\text{X} \quad \begin{array}{l}\text{Control over means of}\\\text{reaching goals}\end{array}$$

(Note: p in the first part of the formula indicates "probability.")

For the present purposes of considering the effects of participation, there are several major points which this analysis brings to our attention. One is that insofar as "participation" involves some control by the individual over the goals for his *own* work and over the means of reaching these goals, it can be expected to increase motivation for achievement. The second major point is that participation, in itself, will *not* lead to high motivation for achievement. Other conditions—general need for achievement, importance of work role to the self-concept, clear standards of and feedback about performance, and moderate difficulty in the work are also necessary.

PARTICIPATION AND IDENTIFICATION WITH THE ORGANIZATION

We turn now to an examination of the relation between participation and "involvement" or "commitment" to the organization and its work.

We suggest that the basic phenomenon here is that when an individual participates in decisions that affect a group or organization to which he belongs, he comes to identify more with this organization. By identification we mean, following Daniel Miller,[17] that his role in the organization is an important and valuable part of his self-concept. The reason his organizational role has become a more important part of his self-concept is that, by virtue of participating in decision-making (attending meetings, being asked for his opinion, having his ideas considered and perhaps accepted, interacting with important people in the organization, etc.), the individual acquires a *higher status* in the organization. He is, by virtue of participating in decision-making, a more important member of the organization than he would otherwise be.

Notice that the meaning of participation here is somewhat different from that used in connection with motivation for achievement. In that context, we considered "participation" as it involved control over the goals and means for one's own particular job. In the present context of the relation of participation to organizational identification, the individual's voice in decisions that affect the whole organization—or at least parts of it—are most relevant. It is his part in such decision-making which is most likely to increase his sense of status in the organization and thus lead his organizational role to become a more important part of his self-concept (identification).[18]

It should be noted, also, that there are often many levels or sub-units in an organization. To the extent that the individual's participation is in affairs of a sub-unit rather than of the larger organization, we would expect him to identify with the sub-unit.

We may formalize the discussion so far, as follows:

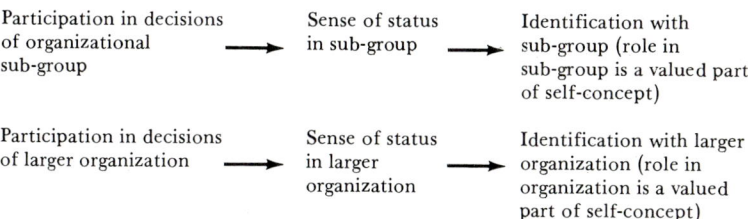

| Participation in decisions of organizational sub-group | → | Sense of status in sub-group | → | Identification with sub-group (role in sub-group is a valued part of self-concept) |
| Participation in decisions of larger organization | → | Sense of status in larger organization | → | Identification with larger organization (role in organization is a valued part of self-concept) |

But why should identification with the organization or organizational sub-unit lead a person to work hard? One possible explanation is that the individual thereby comes to accept the organization's goals as his own and thus works hard to achieve what are now "his" goals. However, on the basis of informal interview data from several large organizations, we reject this explanation. People we have interviewed just don't seem to feel this way. While they may in principle subscribe to the goals of the larger organization, such goals are clearly beyond their personal attainment. And while they may recognize the abstract argument that if everyone does his own job well the over-all goal will be reached, such a hope does not appear to be an effective motivator. (In an organization whose members were joined primarily because of their devotion to its goals—e.g., a religious or charitable organization—the hope of contributing to reaching the goals may be an effective motivator.)

We suggest, instead, that identification with the organization can lead to higher motivation to do the organization's work primarily because it makes the individual more susceptible to social pressures from organization members. Let us see why this should be so. Identification, as conceived here, means that the individual's role in the organization is an important part of his self-image. It is important that he be not only technically a member of the organization, but that he be a good and respected member. For example, for a young Marine who identifies with the Marine Corps, it is not enough merely that he be legally a Marine; he must live up to what "being a Marine" means. If he does not, he will not get much psychological benefit from thinking of himself as "a Marine, but a bad one." So too in other organizations, the person who values his organizational role will wish to be accepted as a full-fledged "good" occupant of his role. Because he identifies with the organization, because his organizational role is important to him, he is vulnerable to pressures from organizational representatives who say, in effect: It is right and proper for a man in your organizational role to work hard for organizational objectives.

At this point, it is important to consider *where* in the organization the pressures for good performance may come from. Such pressures may, of course, come from the officials of the larger organization. To the extent that he identifies with the organization as a whole, desire for approval by such persons may be an effective motivator.

But there is much research that points up the importance of the social pressures which come from individuals' immediate peer groups.[19] How is participation related to such pressures? We may first note that participation in decision-making may take place primarily within the immediate work group rather than with a larger organization—as where there are meetings of a supervisor with his group of subordinates. In this kind of situation, active participation by the individual may raise his status within the immediate work group and so, by our previous reasoning, lead him to value his role in that group more (identify with that group). Participation in the affairs of the immediate work group can thus help to build group loyalty and make the individual more susceptible to group pressures.

But what direction will these pressures take? Will the immediate work group encourage its members to work for the goals of the larger organization? This will be determined, in part, by the extent to which the group members, either individually or as a unit, are able to participate in making decisions which affect the larger organization. If they do participate in this way, their sense of status and importance in the larger organization will be high. The individual members will, therefore, identify with the organization. They will, as a result, be susceptible to pressures of approval and disapproval from organizational officials. Moreover, given these individual needs, a group norm of good performance is likely to arise which adds greatly to the pressures for effective performance.

The process described in this discussion may be formalized as follows:

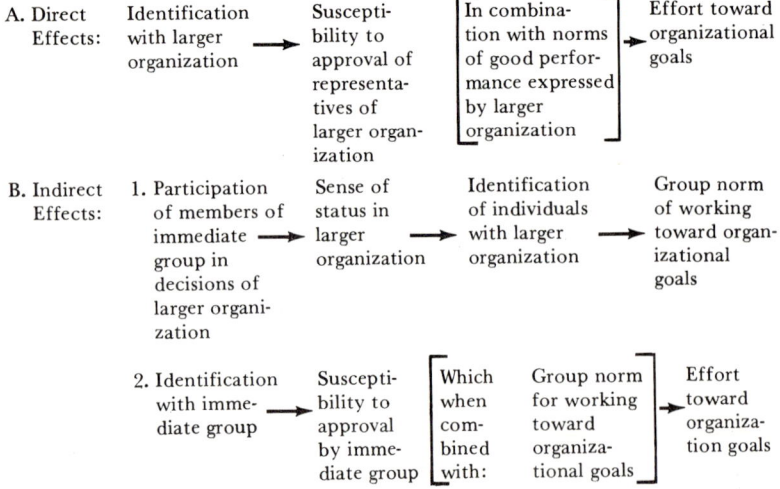

A. Direct Effects: Identification with larger organization → Susceptibility to approval of representatives of larger organization → [In combination with norms of good performance expressed by larger organization] → Effort toward organizational goals

B. Indirect Effects: 1. Participation of members of immediate group in decisions of larger organization → Sense of status in larger organization → Identification of individuals with larger organization → Group norm of working toward organizational goals

2. Identification with immediate group → Susceptibility to approval by immediate group → [Which when combined with: Group norm for working toward organizational goals] → Effort toward organization goals

At this point, the entire discussion of how participation relates to organizational identification and to social pressures needs to be put in a larger context. This context is that of the general need for approval by others. Using again a goal-means analysis parallel to that used for the need for achievement, we would hypothesize the following relationship:

Motivation to work hard in order to be approved by the group	= f	Extent to which acceptance by organizational unit is a goal	X	Extent to which doing a good job is perceived to lead to approval

Now where does the previous discussion concerning participation in decision-making fit in? First, we have seen that participation affects the first term on the right of the equation—i.e., the extent to which acceptance by the organizational unit is a goal. Participation does this by leading to identification with the unit. It is, however, important to note that participation is only one factor which may affect the importance of being accepted and approved by a group. Personality factors, such as the general need for affiliation, doubtless enter in. Also other organizational factors like the similarity of organization members in age, race and ethnic background; the prestige of the organization; and the power of the organization or sub-units to dispense rewards and punishments can be important. There are, in fact, a number of investigations in the literature which consider various sources of member attraction to groups.[20] Participative decision-making should be seen in this larger context, as one important variable which can indirectly influence the extent to which approval by the group is a goal.

Secondly, our previous analysis has indicated that participative methods can affect the second term on the right of the last equation—i.e., the extent to which doing a good job is perceived to lead to approval by group members. The reasoning was that groups whose members participate—singly or as a unit—in affairs of the larger organization, will develop norms which approve good performance in support of the larger organization. Here, too, we must see participatory decision-making as only one factor—though an important one—which can influence group norms. Other factors include the amount of reward that group members believe they will derive from helping the organization.[21]

IDENTIFICATION AND THE NEED FOR ACHIEVEMENT

A further aspect of the relation of participation to organizational identification may be noted now. We have argued that participation in decision-making leads the individual to identify with the organization—i.e., for his organizational role to become a more valued part of his self-concept. But in discussing motivation for achievement, we noted that the importance of the work role to the self-concept affects whether achievement motivation will be directed toward work activity. Here, then, is another way in which participation may affect motivation. By making his work role more important to him, it can increase his motivation for personal achievement.

CONCLUSION

Our analysis presented has attempted to explain the effects of participation on motivation in terms of two primary processes. One involves the need for personal achievement. The other involves identification with an organizational unit and a consequent increase in susceptibility to social pressures. This approach points to relations among a number of important phenomena often considered separately—especially participation, self-concept, organizational identification, and group norms. It also links the thinking about participation to the extensive literature on need for achievement and on social pressures and considers the impact of participation arrangements in the context of other factors which affect the need for achievement and the need for approval. It should be kept in mind that many of these theoretical ideas need further empirical testing.

FOOTNOTES

1. See Coch, L., & French, J.R.P., Jr., "Overcoming resistance to change," *Human Relations*, 1948, *1*, 512-532; Whyte, W.F., *Money and Motivation*, New York: Harper & Brothers, 1955; Argyris, C., *Personality and Organization*, New York: Harper & Brothers, 1957; Vroom, V.H., *Some Personality Determinants of the Effects of Participation*, Unpublished doctoral dissertation, University of Michigan, 1958; Likert, R., *New Patterns of Management* (New York: McGraw-Hill, 1961).

2. See Argyris, *op. cit.*, pp. 200-205; also, Mann, F.C. & Vroom, V.H., "Leadership, Authoritarianism, and Employee Attitudes," *Personnel Psychology*, 1960, *13*, No. 3.

3. Likert, *op. cit.*, p. 99.

4. McGregor, D., *The Human Side of Enterprise* (New York: McGraw-Hill, 1969), Chap. 4.

5. Coch & French, *op. cit.*

6. Argyris, *op. cit.*, p. 192.

7. Likert, *op. cit.*, p. 101.

8. Hood, R., "Effective Employee and Community Relations," *Business Relations Department*, Chamber of Commerce, 1956, p. 6.

9. Likert, *op. cit.*, p. 111.

10. Vroom (1958), *op. cit.*

11. Tolman, E.C., *Purposive Behavior in Animals and Man* (New York: Appleton-Century-Crofts, 1949).

12. Georgopoulos, B.S., Mahoney, G.M. & Jones, N.W., Jr., "A Path-goal Approach to Productivity," *Journal of Applied Psychology*, 1957, *6*, pp. 345-353.

13. Kahn, R.L., "Human Relations On The Shop Floor," in E.M. Hugh-Jones (Ed.), *Human Relations and Modern Management* (Amsterdam, Netherlands: North Holland Publishing Company, 1958).

14. McClelland, D.C., Atkinson, J.W., Clark, R.A., & Lowell, E.L. *The Achievement Motive* (New York: Appleton-Century-Crofts, Inc., 1953).

15. In developing these ideas, we have been influenced by Daniel Miller's discussions of the self-image, in his unpublished manuscript, *Identity, Situation, and Social Interaction: The impact of social structure on motivation.*

16. Atkinson, J.W. (Ed.) *Motives in Fantasy, Action, and Society* (Princeton: D. Van Nostrand Company, 1958).

17. Miller, D., *op. cit.*

18. If a major effect of participation is through its effect on the individual's sense of status and importance in the organization, it follows that other means of increasing status—e.g., promotion—can have the same ultimate effect on motivation. It is, in fact, the general experience of those familiar with organizations that motivation to work for organization goals is higher at upper status levels. The present theoretical approach permits us to explain this phenomenon in precisely the same way as we explain the effects of participation.

19. See, for example, Seashore, S.E., *Group Cohesiveness in the Industrial Work Group*, Survey Research Center Monograph Series No. 14, 1955.

20. Cartwright, D. & Zander, A., *Group Dynamics*, (Evanston, Illinois: Row, Peterson & Company, 1953), Part II.

21. See Seashore, *op. cit.*, and Patchen, M., Supervisory methods and group performance norms, Survey Research Center, University of Michigan, March 1962.

Raymond E. Miles is an Associate Professor in the School of Business Administration, University of California, Berkeley, and Associate Research Economist and Acting Associate Director of the Institute of Industrial Relations there. J.B. Ritchie is Assistant Professor in the Department of Organizational Behavior, Brigham Young University, Provo, Utah. Copyright © 1971 *by the Regents of the University of California. Reprinted from* California Management Review, *Vol. XIII, No. 4, pp. 48-56 by permission of the Regents.*

Participative Management:
Quality vs. Quantity

RAYMOND E. MILES and J.B. RITCHIE

Just as other vintage theoretical vehicles have demonstrated amazing durability on the academic stage, the theory of participative management has shown a remarkable facility for holding the spotlight of debate in the management literature. For this and other theories, however, it should be noted that it is often clever direction and staging, rather than substance, which sustains audience interest.

Having signaled this caveat, we must admit to some feeling of trepidation as we suggest another inquiry into this now middle-aged set of concepts. We do so, however, because we believe some of the recent findings from our continuing research on the process and effects of participation justify further examination of this theory. We should add that our research and its implications are unlikely to do much to resolve the polemics between those who view participation as the solution to all organizational ailments and those who consider it a humanistic palliative which threatens the moral fiber of managerial prerogatives. Nevertheless, we feel our findings may prove valuable to the much larger group for whom the concept of participation is neither panacea nor plague, but simply confusing.

In our view, a prime source of confusion surrounding the concept of participation is its *purpose*. We noted this confusion a few years ago, drawing from our research the conclusion that most managers appeared to hold at least two different "theories" of participation. One of these, which we labeled the *Human Relations* model, viewed participation primarily as a means of obtaining cooperation—a technique which the manager could use to improve morale and reduce subordinate resistance to his policies and decisions. The second, which we labeled the *Human Resources* model, recognized the untapped potential of most organizational members and advocated participation as a means of achieving direct improvement in individual and organizational performance. Predictably, managers viewed the *Human Relations* model as appropriate for their subordinates while wanting their superior to follow the *Human Resources* logic.[1]

Our recent research draws attention to a closely related, and probably equally important, source of confusion involving the *process* of participation. Our earlier descriptions of the purpose of participation under the Human Relations and Human Resources models implied that it is not only the degree of participation which is important, but also the nature of the superior-subordinate interaction. Upon reflection, the notion that both the quality and quantity of participation must be considered seems patently obvious. Rather surprisingly, however, the quality variable in the participative process has been infrequently specified in management theory, and even more rarely researched.

The lack of specific focus in theory or research on the quality aspect of the participative process has led, in our view, to the promulgation of a simple "quantity theory of participation," a theory which implies only that some participation is better than none and that more is better than a little. Clearly, a concept which, whether intended or not, appears to lump all participative acts together in a common category ignores individual and situational differences and is therefore open to a variety of justified criticisms. It is just such a simplified view that allows its more vitriolic critics to draw caricatures extending the participative process to include a chairman of the board consulting with a janitor concerning issues of capital budgeting—the sort of criticism which brings humor to journal pages but contributes little to our understanding of participation.

Recognizing these key sources of confusion, our current studies have been aimed at increasing our understanding of the process of participation under the Human Relations and Human Resources models. Specifically, we have attempted, within a large sample of management teams, to identify and measure the amount of superior-subordinate consultation and a dimension of the quality of this interaction—the superior's attitude which reflects the degree to which he has confidence in his subordinates' capabilities. (Our research approach and findings are described in a later section.) As indicated, in our theoretical framework both the quantity and quality of participation are important determinants of subordinate satisfaction and performance. For these analyses, we have focused on the impact of these variables, both separately and jointly, on the subordinate's satisfaction with his immediate superior. Our findings, we believe, clarify the role which quality plays in the participative process and add substance to the Human Relations-Human Resources differentiation.

In the following sections we explore further the concepts of quantity and quality of participation, integrate these into existing theories of participative management, and examine the implications of our research for these theories and for management practice.

THE QUALITY CONCEPT AND MANAGEMENT THEORY

A simple, and we believe familiar, example should assist us in firmly integrating the quantity-quality variables into the major theories of participative management and perhaps demonstrate, in part at least, why we are concerned with this dimension. Most of us have had the following experience:

An invitation is received to attend an important meeting (we know it is important because it is carefully specified as such in the call). A crucial policy decision is to be made and our views and those of our colleagues are, according to the invitation, vital to the decision.

Having done our homework, we arrive at the meeting and begin serious and perhaps even heated discussion. Before too long, however, a light begins to dawn, and illuminated in that dawning light is the fact that the crucial decision we had been called together to decide . . .

With a cynical, knowing smile, the typical organization member completes the sentence by saying "had already been made." It is helpful, however, to push aside the well-remembered frustration of such situations and examine the logic of the executive who called the meeting and the nature of the participative process flowing from his logic.

We can easily imagine (perhaps because we have frequently employed the same logic) the executive in our example saying to himself, "I've got this matter pretty well firmed, but it may require a bit of selling—I'd better call the troops in and at least let them express their views." He may even be willing to allow some minor revisions in the policy to overcome resistance and generate among his subordinates a feeling of being a part of the decision.

PURPOSES OF PARTICIPATION

Clearly defined in our example and discussion is the tight bond between the purpose of participation and the quality of ensuing involvement. And, underlying the purpose of participation is the executive's set of assumptions about people—particularly his attitudes concerning the capabilities of his subordinates.

Three theoretical frameworks describe this linkage between the manager's basic attitudes toward people and the amount and kind of consultation in which he is likely to engage with his subordinates. It is worth a few lines to compare these theory systems and to apply them to our example. Listed chronologically, these frameworks are:

- The Theory X-Theory Y dichotomy described by the late Douglas McGregor,[2]
- The System I, II, III, IV continuum defined by Rensis Likert,[3]
- Our own Traditional, Human Relations, Human Resources classification.[4]

TERMINOLOGY

We have been criticized for referring to an essentially autocratic (nonparticipatory) style of management as traditional. Such a style is no longer traditional in the sense that it is prescribed, taught, or openly advocated by a majority of modern managers. Our research suggests that most managers consider such a style to be socially undesirable and few will admit adherence to it in concept or practice.

Nevertheless, we would argue that many if not most of our institutions and organizations are still so structured and operated that this style is alive and well today in our society. Many schools, hospitals, labor unions, political parties, and a substantial number of business enterprises frequently behave, particularly at the lower levels, in a manner which can only be described as autocratic. Thus even though their policy statements have been revised and some participative trappings have been hung about, the main thrust of their activity is not greatly changed from what it was twenty, thirty, perhaps even fifty years ago—they behave in a traditional manner toward the structure and direction of work. Further, the assumptions of the Traditional model are, in our view, still widely held and espoused in our society—the rhetoric has improved, but the intent is the same. These assumptions seem to us still to be a part of our "traditional" approach to life. If our views are accurate, Traditional model is therefore still an appropriate tag.

McGregor's Theory X, Likert's System I, and our Traditional model describe autocratic leadership behavior coupled with tight, unilateral control, and little or no subordinate participation in the decision process. Theory X and the Traditional model explicitly delineate the superior's assumptions that most people, including subordinates, are basically indolent, self-centered, gullible, and resistant to change and thus have little to contribute to the decision-making or control process. Focusing more on descriptive characteristics and less on an explicit set of assumptions, Likert's System I manager is pictured only as having no confidence or trust in his subordinates. At the other extreme, Theory Y, System IV, and our Human Resources model define a style of behavior which involves subordinates deeply in the decision process and emphasizes high levels of self-direction and self-control. Again, both Theory Y and the Human Resources model make the logic underlying such behavior explicit—that most organization members are capable of contributing more than demanded by their present jobs and thus represent untapped potential for the organization, potential which the capable manager develops and invests in improved performance. A System IV superior is described simply as one having complete confidence and trust in subordinates in all matters. In between these extremes fall Likert's Systems II and III and our Human Relations model. Systems II and III describe increasing amounts of subordinate participation and self-control, as their superior's attitudes toward them move from "condescending" to "substantial, but not complete" confidence and trust. Our Human Relations model views the superior as recognizing his subordinates' desire for involvement but doubting their ability to make meaningful contributions.

THEORY AND MANAGEMENT PRACTICE

Comparing these frameworks with our example, it is clear that the executive calling the meeting was not operating at the Theory X, System I, Traditional end of the participative continuum. Had he followed the assumptions of these models, he would simply have announced his decision, and if a meeting were called, use it openly to explain his views. Similarly, it seems doubtful that our executive was following the Theory Y, System IV, or Human Resources models. Had he been, he would have called the meeting in the belief that his subordinates might make important contributions to the decision process and that their participation would possibly result in constructing a better overall policy. He would have had confidence and trust in their ability and willingness to generate and examine alternatives and take action in the best interest of the organization.

Instead, the meeting in the example and those from our own experience seem to be defined almost to the letter by our Human Relations logic and the behavior described in Likert's Systems II and III. The casual observer, and perhaps even the more naive participant, unaware of the reasoning of the executive calling the meeting, might well record a high level of involvement during the session—participation high both in quantity and quality. Most of the participants, however, would be much less charitable, particularly about the meaningfulness of the exercise. They would sense, although the guidance was subtle, that at least the depth of their participation was carefully controlled, just as they would be equally alert to the logic underlying the meeting strategy.

ALTERNATIVE THEORIES

Having described varying degrees of quantity and quality of participation flowing from alternative theories of management, and having attempted to link to a common experience through our meeting example, it is not difficult to conjecture about the relationships between these variables and subordinate satisfaction. We would expect subordinate satisfaction to move up and down with both the quantity and the quality of participation, and there is already some evidence, with regard to the amount of participation, at least, that it does. Thus, we would expect, particularly within the managerial hierarchy, that their satisfaction would be lowest when both quantity and quality of participation were lowest—as the Traditional model is approached—and highest when both quantity and quality are high—when participation moves toward the type described in the Human Resources model.

Predicting satisfaction under the Human Relations model is less easy. If the superior's behavior is blatantly manipulative, we might expect satisfaction to be quite low despite high participation. But, if the superior's logic were less obvious, even to himself, we might expect his subordinates to be somewhat pleased to be involved in the decision process, even if their involvement is frequently peripheral.

We cannot precisely test the impact of these models on subordinate satisfaction, but our recent research does provide some evidence with regard to these conjectures, and it is therefore appropriate that we briefly describe the method of our investigation and look at some of our findings.

RESEARCH APPROACH

The findings reported here were drawn from a broader research project conducted among management teams (a superior and his immediate subordinates) from five levels in six geographically separated operating divisions of a west coast firm.[5] The 381 managers involved in the study ranged from the chief executive of each of the six divisions down through department supervisors.

From extensive questionnaire responses we were able to develop measures of the three variables important to these analyses: *quantity of participation, quality of participation,* and *satisfaction with immediate superiors.* Our measure of quantity of participation was drawn from managers' responses to questions concerning how frequently they felt they were consulted by their superior on a number of typical department issues and decisions.[6] This information allowed us to classify managers as high or low in terms of the amount of participation they felt they were allowed. For a measure of the quality of this participation, we turned to the responses given by each manager's superior. The superior's attitudes toward his subordinates—his evaluation of their capabilities with regard to such traits as judgment, creativity, responsibility, perspective, and the like—were analyzed and categorized as high or low compared to the attitudes of other managers at the same level. Finally, our satisfaction measure was taken from a question on which managers indicated, on a scale from very satisfied to very dissatisfied, their reactions to their own immediate superiors.

FINDINGS

The first thing apparent in our findings, as shown in each of the accompanying figures, is that virtually all the subjects in our study appear reasonably well satisfied with their immediate superiors. This is not surprising, particularly since all subjects, both superiors and subordinates, are in managerial positions. Managers generally respond positively (compared to other organization members) on satisfaction scales. Moreover, supporting the organization's reputation for being forward looking and well managed, most participants reported generally high levels of consultation, and superiors' scores on confidence in their subordinates were typically higher than the average scores in our broader research.

Nevertheless, differences do exist, differences which, given the restricted range of scores, are in most instances highly significant in statistical terms. Moreover, they demonstrate that both the quantity and the quality of participation are related to managers' feelings of satisfaction with their immediate superiors.

As shown in Figure 1, the quantity of participation achieved is apparently related to managers' feelings of satisfaction with their superiors. (The taller the figure—and the smaller the numerical score—the more satisfied is that group of managers.) Managers classified as low (relative to the scores of their peers) in terms of the extent to which they are

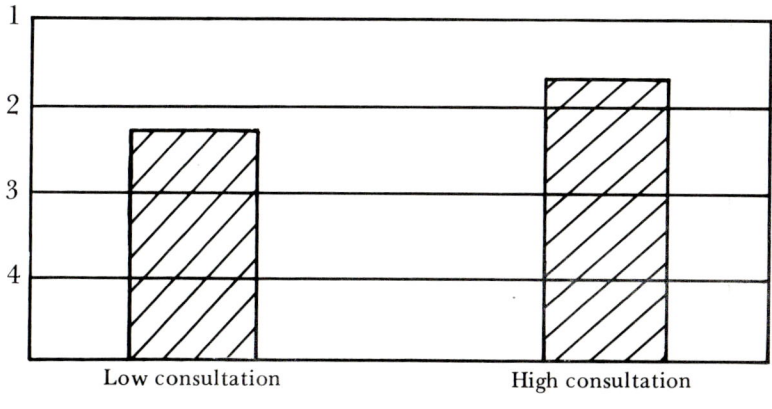

FIGURE 1
Amount of Superior Consultation
and Subordinate Satisfaction

1 Very Satisfied	3 Somewhat Satisfied	4 Dissatisfied
2 Satisfied	Somewhat Dissatisfied	5 Very Dissatisfied

FIGURE 2
Superior's Confidence in Subordinates
and Subordinate Satisfaction

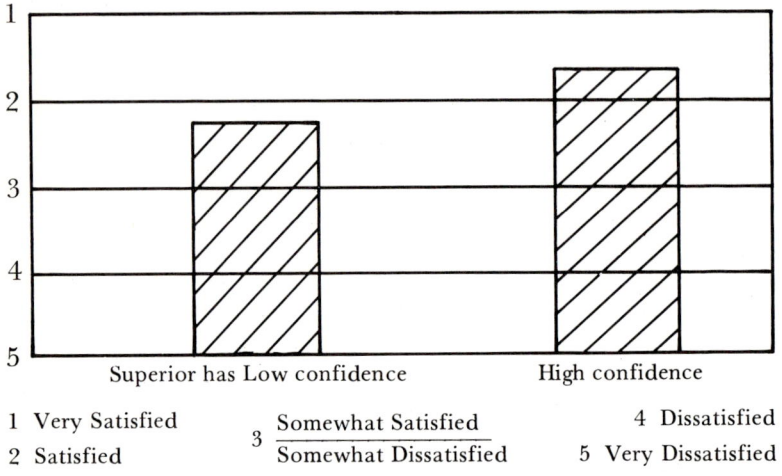

1 Very Satisfied

2 Satisfied

3 Somewhat Satisfied / Somewhat Dissatisfied

4 Dissatisfied

5 Very Dissatisfied

consulted by their superiors are less well satisfied than those classified as high on this dimension. The difference in the average satisfaction score for these groups is statistically significant. The average satisfaction score for the low consultation group (2.13) falls between the satisfied and the so-so (somewhat satisfied-somewhat dissatisfied) categories. For the high consultation group, the score (1.79) falls between the satisfied and the highly satisfied categories.

A slightly stronger pattern of results is apparent when managers are regrouped in terms of the amount of confidence which their superiors have in them (Figure 2). Managers whose superiors have relatively high trust and confidence scores are significantly more satisfied (1.72) than are their colleagues (2.16) whose superiors have relatively lower scores on this dimension.

Finally, our results take on their most interesting form when managers are cross-classified on both the quantity and quality dimensions of participation. As shown in Figure 3, the progression in satisfaction is consistent with our theoretical formulation. Especially obvious is the comparison between managers classified as low both in amount of consultation received and the extent to which their superior has confidence in them (2.26) and managers who are rated high on both variables (1.55). Of interest, and relevant to our later discussion, managers whose superiors have high confidence in them but who are low in amount of participation appear slightly more satisfied (1.95) than their counterparts who are high in amount of participation but whose superiors are low in terms of confidence in their subordinates (2.05).

FIGURE 3

Effects of Amount of Consultation and Superior's Confidence in Subordinates on Subordinate Satisfaction

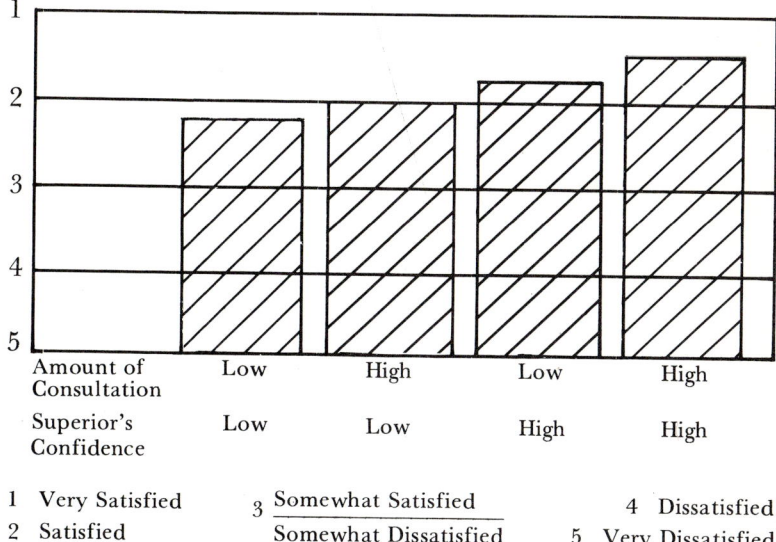

Amount of Consultation	Low	High	Low	High
Superior's Confidence	Low	Low	High	High

1 Very Satisfied	3 Somewhat Satisfied	4 Dissatisfied
2 Satisfied	Somewhat Dissatisfied	5 Very Dissatisfied

LINKING FINDINGS TO THEORY

The bulk of our findings, particularly as illustrated in Figure 3, thus appear to support our conjectures. Managers who least value their subordinates' capabilities and who least often seek their contributions on department issues have the least well satisfied subordinates in our study. It would probably be incorrect to place the Traditional (Theory X, System I) label on any of the managers in our sample, yet those who, relative to their peers, lean closest to these views do so with predictable results in terms of subordinate satisfaction.

Similarly, managers who, relative to their peers, are both high in their respect for their subordinates' capabilities and who consult them regularly on departmental issues also achieve the expected results. Precise labeling is again probably inappropriate, yet managers whose attitudes and behavior are closest to the Human Resources (Theory Y, System IV) model do in fact have the most satisfied subordinates.

Further, those managers who consult their subordinates frequently but who have little confidence in their ability to make a positive contribution to department decision-making, and who thus fall nearest to our Human Relations model, have subordinates who are more satisfied than those under the more Traditional managers but are significantly less satisfied than the subordinates of Human Resources managers.

The majority of our findings support the major formulations of participative management theory, but they also suggest the need for elaboration and clarification. This need is brought to attention by the total pattern of our findings, and particularly by the results for one of our categories of managers—those high in superiors' confidence but relatively low in participation. Recall that, while the differences were not large, this group had the second highest average satisfaction score in our sample—the score falling between that of the Human Relations (high participation, low superior confidence) group and that of Human Resources (high on each) group. Moreover, for the two groups characterized by high participation, there is substantially higher satisfaction for those whose superior reflects high confidence in his subordinates. Clearly, any theory which focused on the amount of participation would not predict these results. Rather, for these managers at least, the quality of their relationship with their superiors as indicated by their superiors' attitude of trust and confidence in them appears to modify the effects of the amount of participation.

IMPLICATIONS FOR THEORY

The quality dimension of the theory of participative management has not been fully developed, but its outlines are suggested in our own Human Resources model and in McGregor's Theory Y framework. McGregor stressed heavily the importance of managers' basic attitudes and assumptions about their subordinates. In expanding on this point,[7] he suggested that a manager's assumptions about his subordinates' traits and abilities do not bind him to a single course of action. Rather, he argued that a range of possible behaviors are appropriate under Theory Y or Human Resources assumptions—a manager with high trust and confidence in his subordinates could and should take into account a variety of situational and personality factors in deciding, among other things, when and how to consult with them. Extending this reasoning, one can even imagine a Theory Y or Human Resources manager actually consulting with his subordinates less often than some of his colleagues. Nevertheless, the nature and quality of participation employed by such a manager, when it occurs, would presumably be deeper and more meaningful, which would be reflected in high levels of subordinate satisfaction and performance.

This view of the superior-subordinate interaction process, emphasizing as it does the quality of the interaction rather than only the amount, can be employed to answer three of the more pervasive criticisms of participative management. These criticisms—each of which is probably most accurately aimed at the simple quantity theory of participation—focus on the inappropriateness of extensive consultation when the superior is constrained by time, technology, and his own or his subordinate's temperament.

THE TIME CONSTRAINT

"In a crisis, you simply do not have time to run around consulting people." This familiar explication is difficult to debate, and in fact, would receive no challenge from a sophisticated theory of participation. In a real building-burning crisis, consultation is inappropriate, and unnecessary. A crisis of this nature is recognized as such by any well informed subordinate and his self-controlled cooperation is willingly supplied. The behavior of both superior and subordinate in such a situation is guided by the situation and each may turn freely and without question to the other or to any available source of expertise for direction or assistance in solving the problem at hand.

Many crises, however, do not fit the building-burning category, and may be much more real to one person, or to one level of management, than to those below him. Our experience suggests that managers may not be nearly as bound by their constraints as they frequently claim to be, or if they are constrained, these limits are either known in advance or are open to modification if circumstances demand. Rather, in many instances it appears that managers employ the "time won't permit" argument primarily to justify autocratic, and at least partially risk-free behavior. If he succeeds, the credit is his; if he fails, he can defend his actions by pointing out that he had no time to explore alternatives.

Such self-defined, or at least self-sustaining, crises are most frequently employed by the manager with a Human Relations concept of participation—one who views participation primarily as a means of obtaining subordinate cooperation and who focuses mainly on the amount of formal involvement required. The crisis itself can be employed in place of participation as the lever to obtain cooperation and there is clearly no time for the sort of routine, frequently peripheral consultation in which he most often indulges.

Conversely, the manager with high trust and confidence in his subordinates' capabilities, the Human Resources manager, is less likely to employ time constraints as a managerial tactic. In real crises he moves as rapidly as the situation demands. He is, however, more likely, because of his normal practices of sharing information with his subordinates, to have a group which is prepared to join him in a rapid review of alternatives. He is unconcerned with involvement for the sake of involvement and thus his consultation activities are penetrating and to the point. His subordinates share his trust and feel free to challenge his views, just as he feels free to question their advice and suggestions openly.

THE TECHNOLOGY BARRIER

"Look, I've got fifteen subordinates scattered all over the building. What do you expect me to do—shut down the plant and call a meeting every time something happens?" This argument is obviously closely linked to the time constraint argument—technology is a major factor in determining the flow and timing of decisions. Similarly, it too flows from a Human Relations-quantity oriented view of participation.

A good manager obviously does not regularly "stop the presses" and call a conference. He has confidence in his subordinates' abilities to handle problems as they appear and to call him in when the problem demands his attention. This confidence is, however, reinforced by joint planning, both one-to-one and across his group of subordinates, before the operation gets under way. Having agreed in advance on objectives, schedules, priorities, and procedures, involvement on a day-to-day basis may be minimal. The manager in this instance does not seek participation to obtain cooperation with his views. Both the manager and his subordinates view the regularly scheduled work planning and review sessions as important because they result in well considered solutions to real problems.

THE TEMPERAMENT BARRIER

"I'm simply not the sort who can run around to his subordinates asking them how things are going—it's just not my style." The manager who made this statement did so somewhat apologetically, but there was little for him to be apologetic about. He had a high performing group of subordinates, in whom he placed high trust and confidence, who were in turn highly satisfied with their boss. Further, while he did not seek their views on a variety of routine departmental matters, and his subordinates did not drop in to his office to chat, he freely shared all departmental information with them and on a regular basis worked with his subordinates in coordinating department plans and schedules. In addition, he practiced a somewhat formal but effective form of management by objectives with each of his subordinates.

This manager and, unfortunately, many of the more outspoken critics of participative management, tend to feel that consultation must be carried out in a gregarious, back-slapping manner. Joint planning is a decision-making technique, and not a personality attribute. Extreme shyness or reserve may be an inhibiting factor, but is not an absolute barrier. Trust and confidence in subordinates can be demonstrated as effectively, if not more effectively, by action as by words.

Similarly, as suggested earlier, the manager who holds a Human Resources view of participation acknowledges personality and capability differences among his subordinates. He feels a responsibility to the organization and to his subordinates to assist *each* to develop continuously his potential for making important contributions to department performance. He recognizes that individuals move toward the free interchange of ideas, suggestions, and criticisms at different paces. However, by demonstrating his own confidence in his subordinates' capabilities and in their potential, he tends to encourage more rapid growth than other managers.

CONCLUDING COMMENTS

Our continuing research on the purpose and process of participative management has, in our view, contributed additional support for the

Human Resources theory of participation. It has emphasized that when the impact on subordinates is considered, the superior's attitude toward the traits and abilities of his subordinates is equally as important as the amount of consultation in which he engages.

This not-so-startling finding allows expansions and interpretation of modern theories of participation to counter criticisms which may be properly leveled at a simple quantity theory of participation. However, although our findings have obvious implications for both theory and management behavior, they too are open to possible misinterpretation. It is possible to read into our findings, as some surely will, that subordinate consultation may be neglected, that all that matters is that the superior respect his subordinates.

Such a philosophy—tried, found wanting, and not supported by our findings—is embodied in the frequent statement that "all you need to do to be a good manager is hire a good subordinate and turn him loose to do the job as he sees fit." Such a philosophy, in our view, abdicates the superior's responsibility to guide, develop, and support his subordinates. The most satisfied managers in our sample were those who received high levels of consultation from superiors who valued their capabilities. It is our view that effective participation involves neither "selling" the superior's ideas nor blanket approval of all subordinate suggestions. Rather, it is most clearly embodied in the notion of joint planning where the skills of both superior and subordinate are used to their fullest.

Our findings emphasize the importance of attitudes of trust and confidence in subordinates, but they do not indicate their source. It is possible, but unlikely, that those superiors in our sample who reported the highest levels of trust and confidence in their subordinates did so because their subordinates were in fact of higher caliber than those of their colleagues. Within our large sample of managers, several indicators—education, age, experience, for example—suggest that managers' capabilities are roughly evenly distributed across levels and divisions within the organization.

Another possible reason for differences in superiors' attitudes on this dimension is that they are caused by interaction with subordinates, rather than being a determinate of the nature of this interaction. That is, the manager who attempts consultation which is highly successful increases his confidence in his subordinates and thus develops broader involvement. This seems to be a highly plausible explanation which has implications for management development. In fact, there is growing evidence that managers who experiment with participative techniques over lengthy periods do develop both a commitment to such practices and additional trust in their subordinates.

FOOTNOTES

1. See Raymond E. Miles, "Human Relations or Human Resources?" *Harvard Business Review* (July-August 1965), p. 149.

2. See Douglas McGregor, *The Human Side of Enterprise* (New York, McGraw-Hill, 1960); and *The Professional Manager* (New York, McGraw-Hill, 1967).

3. See Rensis Likert, *New Patterns of Management* (New York, McGraw-Hill, 1961); and *The Human Organization* (New York, McGraw-Hill, 1967).

4. See Raymond E. Miles, "The Affluent Organization," *Harvard Business Review* (May-June 1966), p. 106; and Raymond E. Miles, Lyman W. Porter, and James A. Craft, "Leadership Attitudes Among Public Health Officials," *American Journal of Public Health* (December 1966), p. 1990.

5. Other findings from this research are reported in L.V. Blankenship and Raymond E. Miles, "Organization Structure and Management Decision Behavior," *Administrative Science Quarterly* (June 1968), p. 106; and in Karlene Roberts, Blankenship, and Miles, "Organizational Leadership, Satisfaction, and Productivity: A Comparative Analysis," *Academy of Management Journal* (December 1968), p. 401.

6. For more detailed analysis of these data see J.B. Ritchie and Raymond E. Miles, "An Analysis of Quantity and Quality of Participation as Mediating Variables in the Participative Decision Making Process," *Personnel Psychology* (in press).

7. Douglas McGregor, *The Professional Manager* (New York, McGraw-Hill, 1967), p. 79.

Stane Mozina and Janez Jerovsek are professors of sociology in Yugoslavia. Arnold Tannenbaum and Rensis Likert are directors of the Institute for Social Research at the University of Michigan. This article is *reprinted with permission from* European Business, *Autumn 1970, pp. 60-68.*

Testing a Management Style

STANE MOZINA, JANEZ JEROVSEK,
ARNOLD S. TANNENBAUM, and RENSIS LIKERT

When knights in tales of the Middle Ages wore either white or black, the colors were loaded with meaning. Today, words such as "control" and "participation" are loaded. Some think of participation as an exotic importation from America, as foreign to European soil as the Indians Columbus brought back with him. Control, on the other hand, often seems inherently European. Often the order-giving, supervision, and punishment it involves appear to be as firmly implanted on the Continent as Gothic cathedrals.

However, and this may be stating the obvious, the management styles in America based on participation are also valid on this side of the Atlantic. This article describes how we proved it in Yugoslavia. And we maintain that what is good for Yugoslavia is good for . . .

The theory of management we are discussing is based on a different idea of control and of how to obtain it. Control is more than merely giving orders and checking to see whether they have been carried out. In fact, participation can often bring about a system of control much more substantial and effective than that in a traditional industrial bureaucracy.

We hold that managers who head the most successful organizations employ a style of leadership, creating a system of management different from those of managers of less successful organizations. This style is based precisely on the principle of control by participation. In detail, our theory says *the successful managers foster an atmosphere of support so that members working in the organization feel a sense of personal worth and importance,* and the "supportive" leader is concerned as much with people as with the job itself. He is sensitive to the needs and feelings of his subordinates, he respects and trusts his personnel, he is receptive to their ideas and suggestions, and he has a sincere interest in their welfare.

In his *New Patterns of Management,* Rensis Likert classified various styles of management into four systems. Systems One, Two, and Three are generally characterized by high pressure and surveillance of employees, tight budget and work standards. System Four was described as follows:

> The social system here is made up of interlocking work groups with a high degree of group loyalty among the members and favorable attitudes and trust between superiors and subordinates. Sensitivity to others and relatively high levels of skill in personal interaction and the functioning of groups are also present. These skills permit effective participation in decisions on common problems. Participation is used, for example, to establish organizational objectives which are satisfactory integration of the needs and desires of all members of the organization and of persons functionally related to it. High levels of reciprocal influence occur, and high levels of total coordinated influence are achieved in the organization. Communication is efficient and effective. There is a flow from one part of the organization to another of all the relevant information important for each decision and action. The leadership in the organization has developed what might well be called a highly effective social system for interaction and mutual influence.

This participative approach to management implies a system of control or influence different from that in the traditional organization, but it is not a permissive or a laissez-faire system, as some stereotypes of participative management suggest. Through their participation in supportively led, highly cohesive, overlapping groups, organization members at all levels engage in the influence process. *The result is more, not less control than is usually found in organizations.*

THE NEED FOR A SENSE OF PERSONAL WORTH

Evidence for the validity of this model has been found in a number of American industrial and business organizations but the model should apply broadly to organizations in other countries too. We expected it to have validity in Yugoslavia for two reasons. First, the "principle of supportive relations," upon which the model is based, has very wide if not universal applicability. The need for a sense of personal worth or importance is shared by people in most cultures, although, obviously, the means for enhancing this sense of worth will vary among cultures. Second, as Yugoslav social scientists, the two last authors were struck by how well System Four described some of the social and psychological characteristics of the legally and administratively defined system of self-management in Yugoslavia.

These characteristics were not considered explicitly in the formal definition of the Yugoslav system. Nevertheless, they are becoming salient in discussions within Yugoslavia about how the system should work and how its favorable effects would be achieved. The legal, representative system of worker's self-management will work to the extent that it implies participation not only in formal policy-making bodies but also in the *daily interactions* of members and leaders.

Therefore, if the System Four theory really works as it seems to in many American organizations, it should also work in Yugoslavia—despite the manifest differences between Yugoslavia and the United States. The results of the two exploratory studies in Yugoslav organizations provided some evidence concerning the applicability of the theory in Yugoslavia.[1]

Yugoslavia is a socialist land although its political and economic life differ from those in other communist countries. Since the industrial system in Yugoslavia is based on the principle of collective ownership, industry belongs to all the people, rather than to the state. The technical distinction between collective and state ownership has an important consequence in Yugoslavia, namely, the system of self-management in which "workers' councils," elected by the members of each organization, are delegated authority for all major policy decisions within the organization.

This system of self-management, in which broad policy-making power resides with the councils, requires a certain decentralization in the Yugoslav economy. Industrial organizations do not have to meet centrally determined production quotas; rather, they compete in an open market and have considerable discretion to determine their production and marketing. They may invest, expand, and raise the wages of their members—providing they have the necessary funds either through loans or from retained earnings.

FREEDOM TO CHOOSE A MANAGEMENT STYLE

Most of the control exercised over plants by Belgrade is limited to the granting or withholding of bank loans and the levying of taxes. Thus the managers have a certain autonomy to manage as they wish. This means they can also choose (even if only unconsciously) their management style.

Figure 1 illustrates the major elements of the leadership styles generally chosen. In this chart, *management practice is seen as the cause of prevailing attitudes, motives and behaviors in the organization which, if favorable, result in high levels of performance and other criteria of effectiveness.*

In order to investigate our theory, we selected ten pairs of industrial organizations, each pair containing a high-performing and a low-performing organization. The organizations within each pair had comparable types of products, technology, amounts of capital investment, market conditions, opportunities for credit, degrees of modernity and locations (rural-urban). The more successful plants were slightly larger (average size 871) than the less successful (average size 751). While the latter has suffered some decline in manpower in the last three years, the former has experienced some growth. The more successful plants also have a slightly higher proportion of professional personnel than the less successful.

Two criteria, listed as the end results in Figure 1, were employed in selecting the more successful and less successful plants: (1) net profit, which reflects overall performance including productivity, sales, and costs, and (2) average wages and salaries of all employees, a criterion related to gross profit. Figure 2 shows the levels averaged separately by the more successful and less successful plants. These data come from company records.

Through questionnaires administered to the five leading managers and the five leading members of the workers' council in each plant, we found

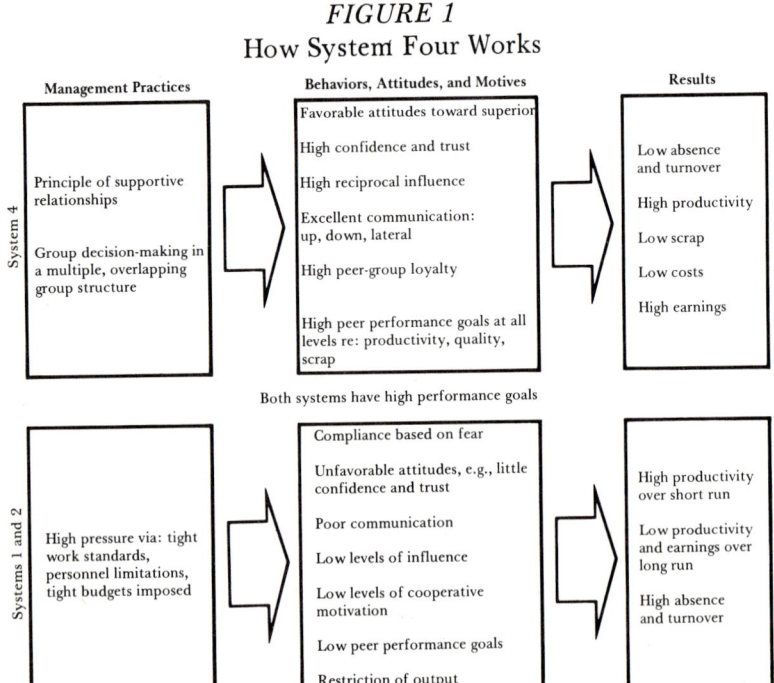

FIGURE 1
How System Four Works

From R. Likert, *The Human Organization*, New York: McGraw-Hill, 1967.

that the attitudes and opinions bear out the superiority of the more successful enterprises as indicated in the performance records.

For example, in answer to the question *"From time to time changes in policies, procedures, and equipment are introduced by the management. How often do these changes lead to better ways of doing things?"* 92 percent of the respondents in the more successful plants agreed that the changes led to improvements always or most of the time. Only 72 percent in the less successful plants answered in this way.

A second question asked how efficiently seven categories of employees (from unskilled workers to engineers and economists) used their working time. Employees in all categories in the more successful plant were judged to use their time more efficiently than those in the less successful plant. In the more successful plants the employees were judged to spend on the average between 70 to 90 percent of their time efficiently compared to between 50 to 70 percent in the less successful plants.

When respondents were asked whether or not they were considering quitting the enterprise, 11 percent in the more successful plants compared to 51 percent in the less successful plants replied that they had thought of leaving their enterprise. In fact, company statistics indicate an average

---

FIGURE 2
How the More Successful and Less Successful Plants
Stand on Profit and Employee Income

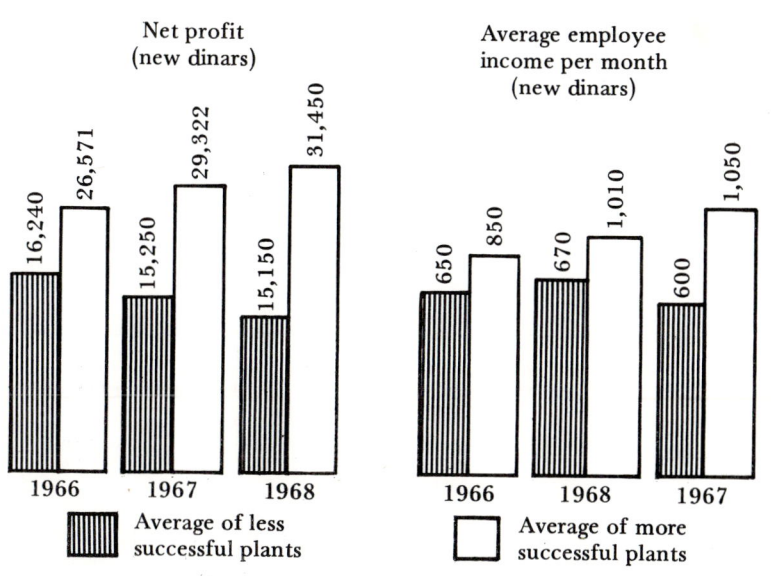

yearly turnover in 1968 of 60 persons in the more successful plants compared to 143 in the less successful.

SUCCESS FROM ONE PATTERN OF BEHAVIOR

There are many other questions about how the firms are managed. Figure 3 reproduces the model of questions that indicate the general leadership style of a firm. Usable as a general check list, this set of questions touches on a range of management practices and their corresponding

FIGURE 3
The Four Styles of Leadership—Their Characteristics

	System 1	System 2	System 3	System 4
Leadership				
1. How much confidence is shown in subordinates?	None	Condescending	Substantial	Complete
2. How free do they feel to talk to superiors about job?	Not at all	Not very	Rather freely	Fully free
3. Are subordinates' ideas sought and used, if worthy?	Seldom	Sometimes	Usually	Always
Motivation				
4. Is predominant use made of (1) fear, (2) threats, (3) punishment, (4) rewards, (5) involvement?	1, 2, 3, occasionally 4	4, some 3	4, some 3 and 5	5, 4, based on group set goals
5. Where is responsibility felt for achieving organization goals?	Mostly at top	Top and middle	Fairly general	At all levels
Communication				
6. What is the direction of information flow?	Downward	Mostly downward	Down and up	Down, up, and sideways
7. How is downward communication accepted?	With suspicion	Possible, with suspicion	With caution	With open mind
8. How accurate is upward communication?	Often wrong	Censored for boss	Limited accuracy	Accurate
9. How well do superiors know problems faced by subordinates?	Know little	Some knowledge	Quite well	Very well
Interaction				
10. What is the character of interaction?	Little, always with fear and distrust	Little, usually with some condescension	Moderate, often fair amount of confidence and trust	Extensive, high degree of confidence and trust
11. How much cooperative teamwork is present?	None	Relatively little	Moderate amount	Very substantial throughout organization
Decisions				
12. At what level are decisions formally made?	Mostly at top	Policy at top, some delegation	Broad policy at top, more delegation	Throughout but well integrated

Figure 3 continued

	System 1	System 2	System 3	System 4
13. What is the origin of technical and professional knowledge used in decision-making?	Top management	Upper and middle	To a certain extent throughout	To a great extent throughout
14. Are subordinates involved in decisions related to their work?	Not at all	Occasionally consulted	Generally consulted	Fully involved
15. What does the decision-making process contribute to motivation?	Nothing, often weakens it	Relatively little	Some contribution	Substantial

Goals

	System 1	System 2	System 3	System 4
16. How are organizational goals established?	Orders issued	Orders issued with some chance to comment	Orders issued after discussion	Group action (except in crisis)
17. How much covert resistance to goals is present?	Strong resistance	Moderate resistance	Some resistance at times	Little or none

Control

	System 1	System 2	System 3	System 4
18. How concentrated are review and control functions?	Highly at top	Relatively high at top	Moderate delegation to lower levels	Quite widely shared
19. Is there an informal organization resisting the formal one?	Yes	Usually	Sometimes	No—same goals as formal
20. What are cost, productivity, and other control data used for?	Policing, punishment	Reward and punishment	Reward, some self-guidance	Self-guidance, problem solving

motives and attitudes. Our theory says one pattern of behavior will lead to more successful performances within the firm.

Figure 4 is the answer to the questions in Figure 3—at least as far as the firms in Yugoslavia are concerned. This table shows the results based on the check list of questions within the ten more successful and ten less successful plants. (The headings in Figure 3 were not included in the questionnaire.)

The data in Figure 4 were obtained from the five leading managers and the five leading members of the workers' council in each plant.

The results are a simple average of the measures obtained from all respondents in the more successful and less successful plants respectively. (All respondents were similar in age, education, and seniority of Party membership.) They show that the two groups of plants clearly differ in their leadership practices and in the social and psychological systems resulting from these practices. Even though the results for each plant do not appear in Figure 4 separately, an analysis of these data reveals *that each successful plant is closer to the "System 4" model than is its less successful counterpart*, a result that would occur by chance less than once in a thousand times.

Discussions with managers in the successful and unsuccessful plants illustrate some of the differences suggested in Figure 4. *Managers in the more successful plants have different attitudes toward personnel than do those in the less successful plants.* As one manager in a less successful plant put it, "Those who are not satisfied with our company can leave."

Given such an attitude, management is likely to have difficulty in keeping good personnel and this leads to a vicious cycle. Because good personnel leave, the organization performs poorly, and because of poor performance there is an apparent need for pressure and emphasis on discipline—which are reasons why good personnel leave. This is an especially serious problem with professional personnel.

"Discipline and order" are among the major requirements for organizational success, according to one manager in a less successful plant. Another manager in a less successful plant complained of "many problems with supervision, control, and discipline."

Ironically, the more successful plants, where there is less manifest emphasis on order and discipline, are in fact more orderly and disciplined. These plants—more than the less successful ones—appear to have more effective control over behavior in actual operations.

HOW THE ROOTS OF CONTROL SPREAD

In response to the question "How much influence do the following groups have on what goes on in your plant?" we determined how much *actual* control there is. We compared this to the ideal control. The latter

FIGURE 4

Where the More Successful and Less Successful Plants Fall in the Systems Line-up

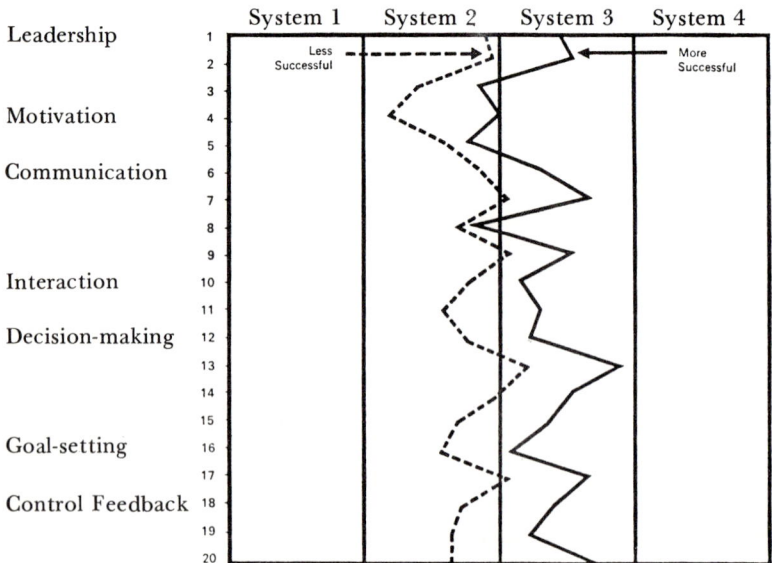

was obtained in answer to the questions "How much influence *should* the following groups have on what goes on in your plant?" Although differences in actual control between the more successful and less successful plants are not dramatic, they follow the direction predicted by the theory. In addition, nine out of the ten pairs showed that the more successful plants exercised a greater amount of control or influence than the less successful. Such a pattern of results would occur less than once in a hundred times by chance.

Moreover, the more and less successful groups differ not only in the amount of control, but also in the manner in which this control is exercised. As the data in Figure 4 indicate, control in the more successful plants is exercised thus. Compared to the less successful plants, there is:

1. Greater confidence by superiors in subordinates
2. More freedom felt by subordinates to talk to their superiors
3. More frequent seeking and use of subordinates' ideas
4. Use of involvement rather than threats
5. Mutual confidence and trust, rather than condescension by superiors and fear by subordinates
6. Greater participation by subordinates in decisions related to their work
7. Productivity, cost and other accounting data used by departments for self-guidance rather than by top management for punitive purposes.

The employees in the more successful plants also felt motivated to control themselves through:

—widespread feeling of responsibility for achieving the goals of the organization
—mutual expectations that each person will do his job well and help others
—cooperative attitudes to achieve goals, rather than covert resistance to them and restriction of output.

The differences in control in the two sets of plants and how that control is exercised are obvious. We asked the question "To what extent is the work of employees from unskilled workers to professional staff checked through supervision?" Respondents answered on a three-point scale, from "too much" to "too little." With the exception of one pair of plants, a greater percentage of those in the less successful plants felt the burden of being supervised weighing down on them.

Not so surprisingly, however, the results of the curves we plotted show that supervision does not mean more control. Even though certain traditional forms of control, such as checking, are more prevalent in the less successful plants, the total amount of actual control is not increased. It is the more successful plants, with apparently less complicated supervision, that end up having the greater amount of control. We checked these differences between the more and less successful plants.

ORDER-GIVING CAN BE USELESS

Thus, the participative organization need not be a purely permissive system. On the contrary, these data, as well as data from a number of American studies, suggest that the participative organization may be characterized by a system of control that is more effective than in the highly supervised organization.

Control should be viewed as involving any means through which the behavior of persons is affected in intended ways. Unless the intended effects on behavior are achieved, control cannot be said to exist, regardless of how much order giving is involved. Thus while supervisors in the Likert System Two may exert a good deal of pressure, the employees may feel resentment and resistance and "too much supervision." This is exactly what happened to those in the less successful plants in this study.

On the other hand, supervisors may exercise substantial control by eliciting cooperation through supportiveness and the development of favorable attitudes, and through the use of groups and peer influence. This is the key to leadership in System Four.

As a corollary, participative management is often thought of as "power equalization." The power equalization hypothesis argues, firstly, that participation implies equalizing the power of groups in an organization and, secondly, that this equalization is the basis of organizational effectiveness. However, this is not necessarily the case.

The power equalization view assumes there is a fixed amount of power or control in an organization. Increasing the control exercised by one group (for example, workers) decreases that exercised by another (for example, managers). The data of this study and of others suggest that *it is possible for managers to increase the control they exercise* (and the control exercised by lower levels as well) *by sharing some of their decision-making authority with lower levels.*

Thus we find our respondents in the more successful plants compared to those in the less effective plants reporting (in Figure 4) that subordinates more often participate in decisions related to their work. Likewise, superiors seek and make use of subordinates' ideas. Yet in these more effective plants managers are not less influential, and actual power (control) is not more equalized among the various hierarchical groups than it is in the less effective plants.

That the total amount of power or control in an organization is not fixed but actually varies is of basic importance. When administrators assume, as they often do, that there is a fixed amount of control, they create for themselves a serious problem in understanding supervisor-subordinate relationships and in functioning effectively as supervisors.

A manager is not likely to try to enhance the control exercised by subordinates if he thinks that his own amount of control will be reduced. Rather, he will act in ways to limit the control of others. For example, he will restrict the information he provides to subordinates or he will oppose their ideas and suggestions. He may also apply coercion in trying to get subordinates to follow his orders. Because such managerial behavior often creates resistance, the manager may succeed not only in limiting the control exercised by others, but in limiting his own control as well.

Variations in total amount of control can be seen in everyday situations—friendships, marital relations, as well as supervisory/subordinate interactions. Compare a friendship between two persons with a mere acquaintanceship. Acquaintances meet occasionally and know one another only superficially. These persons have few if any mutual obligations or expectations. Accordingly, they control one another very little. If this acquaintanceship evolves into a friendship, however, interaction becomes more frequent and expectations and obligations develop. One friend will ask and expect things of the other, and the other will comply. In many friendships compliance is reciprocal, although it need not be. But the strength of a friendship is marked by the amount of influence that the participants have with one another. A strong friendship, marriage, or group of any kind is characterized by a high total amount of control or influence.

Superiors and subordinates need not be friends, but they do establish relations involving expectations and obligations and implying control, whether unilateral or involving some degree of reciprocity.

While we have argued for the value of participative management, we would like to point out that, as opposed to what some think, participation does not mean power equalization. Equality of power is not practicable in most contemporary large-scale industrial organizations. *Furthermore, there is a distinction between power and decision-making.* Decision-making implies power or control only when the decisions *made* are *carried out.* Because decisions are not always carried out, or are only imperfectly expedited, the actual distribution of power does not always correspond to the distribution of decision-making.

AN UNLIMITED PIE OF POWER

Managers would do well to remember the notion of an expanding power pie, analogous (in some ways) to the expanding economic pie. Like the economic one it has basic practical implications. The anticipated effects of economic action, for example, are viewed quite differently by planners under the assumption of a fixed economic pie than they would be under the assumption of a variable pie. The choice of an economic policy is therefore likely to be quite different under one assumption than under the other. Similarly, many social issues such as Worker Power, Student Power, or Black Power will be viewed differently under the assumption of a fixed total amount of power as opposed to a variable one. An understanding of the variable pie of power, therefore, can help improve industrial organizations and other social institutions just as the widely held assumption about the variable economic pie helps make economic policy more realistic than it would be under the fixed pie assumption.

Although it may seem paradoxical, *managers can enhance their control through increasing the control exercised by others.* This is by no means a simple formula in action. The participative model cannot be fully realized simply by *giving* subordinates control, or by telling them that they have authority.

Participation is not simply delegation, and certainly not shibboleths about teamwork and cooperation. If the goal of participation is to be achieved, the organization must have a corresponding structure.

The participative organization is a complex social system requiring high levels of understanding. The social-psychological aspects of organization are as important to the manager as the technological, administrative, and economic factors making up his organigram.

Because it is a more complex system than the conventional organization, the participative organization requires a special commitment on the part of leading personnel. They must sincerely adhere to the principles of participative management, including the notion that power in a system may expand.

THE LESSON FOR EUROPE

Strong, not weak, leadership is needed for the participative system. Management's control is more pervasive and more effective than its counterparts in less participative organizations. It is a power maximized system, valid in Yugoslavia, in the United States, in Europe. For large or small firms trying to update their management the lesson is clear.

FOOTNOTES

1. One study, involving four organizations, suggests support for the theory. See Kavcic, B., Rus, V., and Tannenbaum, A., "Control, Participation and Effectiveness in Four Yugoslav Industrial Organizations," *Administrative Science Quarterly* (in press). A second study involving six organizations provided support for some aspects of the theory, but not for others. Kavcic, B. *Razvitost Samoupravnih Odnosov* ("Degree of Realization of Self-Management Relations"), Center of Public Opinion Research, Republican Council of Slovenian Trade Unions, Ljubljana, December 1968, p. 44.

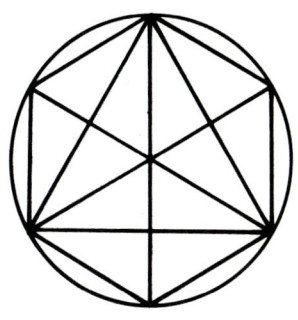

Part II
Research Studies
in
Participative Management

Karlene Roberts is at the University of California, Berkeley. Raymond E. Miles is at the University of California, Berkeley. L. Vaughn Blankenship is at State University of New York at Buffalo.

This article is reprinted with permission from the Academy of Management Journal, *December 1968, pp. 401-414.*

Support for the research upon which this paper is based was received from the Center for Research in Management Science and the Institute of Industrial Relations, University of California, Berkeley. The authors wish to acknowledge the unusually high order of cooperation and support provided by the corporate executives and division managers who participated in this study. The authors also wish to acknowledge the assistance of Allen Gulezian in the preparation of materials for this article.

Organizational Leadership Satisfaction and Productivity: A Comparative Analysis

KARLENE ROBERTS, RAYMOND E. MILES,

and L. VAUGHN BLANKENSHIP

Over the past two decades, a number of management scholars have offered theories which describe a more or less similar pattern of linkages among the set of four variables examined in this study: leadership attitudes, leadership behavior, satisfaction, and performance.

Among the more prominent statements, the late Douglas McGregor's discussion of classical (Theory X) and modern (Theory Y) leadership models suggests the nature of this relationship.[1] According to McGregor, classical leadership theory (Theory X) rests on a set of leadership attitudes or assumptions which hold that man is basically indolent, self-centered, gullible, and resistant to change. Given these attitudes or assumptions, Theory X prescribes autocratic leadership practices, emphasizing tight, unilateral control. On the other hand, McGregor suggests, more modern leadership concepts (Theory Y) rest on a set of underlying attitudes or assumptions which hold that people learn to seek responsibility and that the capacity to exercise creativity, self-direction, and self-control is widely distributed in the population. Logically linked with these attitudes are leadership practices or behavior which focus attention on the development and utilization of human resources, encouraging broad participation in decision making, emphasize joint goal setting between managers and their subordinates, and provide for the design of challenging, rewarding, self-directed, and controlled tasks. McGregor's discussions suggest that managers who hold and follow Theory Y will obtain higher over-all levels of performance and satisfaction than their Theory X counterparts.

More recently, Rensis Likert has described a broad theoretical framework which links attitudes of support and confidence in subordinates with participative leadership practices and views these as partial determinants of subordinate satisfaction and organizational performance.[2] Expanding on McGregor's formulation, Likert describes four systems of management ranging along a continuum from Theory X (System I) to Theory Y (System IV), or more specifically, from a highly authoritarian total system of leadership, communications, and control to a system emphasizing participative, self-controlled groups operating in an atmosphere of reciprocal trust and open communication.

Despite the widespread interest generated by the theories of McGregor, Likert, and others, the full set of relationships among leadership attitudes, leadership behavior, satisfaction, and performance suggested in their writings has not been subjected to systematic analysis across organizations. While a thorough review of the relevant research literature is beyond the scope of this paper, the lack of comprehensive, comparative analysis of the full set of relationships discussed here is apparent in a brief examination of three of the most prominent collections of leadership researches.

The early Ohio State studies, for example, utilized the Leadership Behavior Description Questionnaire in their attempts to relate subordinate reports of supervisory *behavior* to measures of *performance* and *satisfaction*.[3] The later Ohio State studies employed the Leadership Opinion Questionnaire to obtain measures of supervisors' *attitudes* toward leadership practices and related these scores to employee turnover and *satisfaction*.[4] Paper and pencil instruments were also used in the Illinois studies[5] to measure the leader variable called Assumed Similarity of Opposites (ASO). Leaders' scores on this attitude variable were then related to measures of group *performance*.[6] As described, the typical study in these two sets of researches has tended to focus on only two or three of the variables in the leadership attitude, leadership behavior, satisfaction, and performance set, and few if any of these studies have attempted to characterize total organizations or even major organizational units with respect to the full set of variables discussed here.

The Michigan studies have perhaps come closest to covering the full set of relationships suggested in the McGregor-Likert theories.[7] Much of the early Michigan work attempted to relate observer and subordinate reports of the leadership *behavior* of superiors to subordinate *satisfaction* and work group *performance*. These studies did not, however, regularly attempt to link basic leadership attitudes or assumptions about people to leadership behavior and in turn to satisfaction and performance.[8] Further, while the most recent Michigan researches have characterized organizational units and total organizations in terms of subordinate described leadership behavior, satisfaction, and performance, they, too, have not included measures of managers' leadership attitudes as such—their basic attitudes and assumptions about their subordinates.[9]

The present study is designed to extend previous researches by attempting to measure explicitly leadership attitudes, leadership behavior, satisfaction, and performance and by attempting to relate aggregate scores on each of these variables across six sizeable organizational units. The basic hypothesis under examination here reflects the central theme of the McGregor-Likert theories: that basic attitudes of trust and confidence in subordinates will be associated with democratic-participative leadership behavior and that these variables will in turn be positively related to satisfaction and performance.

THE SAMPLE

The participants in this study were managers from five levels in six operating divisions of a West Coast firm. As shown in Table 1, our sample included all managers at the top two levels in each of the six divisions—the six division managers and their 42 immediate subordinates. The 42 managers at level two represent the heads of the major functional areas, e.g., production, marketing, engineering, in each division. The managers at level three are generally heads of major departments in each of these functional areas. Managers at levels four and five are heads of smaller components within the various functional areas. The response rate, as indicated in Table 1, was extremely high at all levels.

Although, as shown in Table 1, nearly 400 managers participated in this study, our units of analysis are the six operating divisions of the corporation. As indicated earlier, the questionnaire responses of managers in each division are combined to provide aggregate measures of leadership attitude, leadership behavior, and satisfaction, and company data are employed to rank each division in terms of performance.

MEASURES

The data presented here on managers' leadership attitudes and behavior and on their general job satisfaction were collected from a "Management Decision-Making, Attitude, and Job Satisfaction" questionnaire. Respondents' self-reports on attitude items described below were used to compute their leadership attitude and satisfaction scores. Leadership behavior scores were computed from managers' ratings of the behavior of their superiors.

Leadership Attitude Measure

The leadership attitude measure employed in this study is taken from a portion of the questionnaire which attempts to tap managers' basic

TABLE 1
Distribution of Participating Managers by Division and by Level

Number of questionnaires distributed and number of respondents by level*

Level	Division A No. Dist.	No. Resp.	% Resp.	Division B No. Dist.	No. Resp.	% Resp.	Division C No. Dist.	No. Resp.	% Resp.	Division D No. Dist.	No. Resp.	% Resp.	Division E No. Dist.	No. Resp.	% Resp.	Division F No. Dist.	No. Resp.	% Resp.
1	1	1	100	1	1	100	1	1	100	1	1	100	1	1	100	1	1	100
2	9	9	100	6	6	100	6	6	100	8	8	100	7	7	100	6	6	100
3	28	25	89	24	24	100	16	15	94	22	21	95	25	22	88	29	25	86
4	21	20	95	38	37	97	16	13	81	14	13	93	17	15	88	12	12	100
5	9	9	100	11	10	91				40	38	95	24	21	88	13	13	100
Overall by Division	68	64	94	80	78	98	39	35	90	85	81	95	74	66	89	61	57	93

Total Distributed = 407   Total Returned = 381   Response Rate Overall = 94%

*Level 1 is top level, i.e., division manager. Responses were sought from all managers at Levels 1, 2, and 3. At Levels 4 and 5 only managers with supervisory responsibilities were included in our sample.

assumptions about the values and abilities of themselves and those above and below them in their organizations. In this section, participants were asked to indicate the relative degree to which ten traits and abilities (i.e., Judgment, Creativity, Alertness, Dependability, Responsibility, Pride in Performance, Initiative, Self-Confidence, Long Range Perspective, and Willingness to Change) were possessed by the typical member of each of four groups: (1) their superiors, (2) persons at their own levels, (3) their own immediate subordinates, and (4) low-level employees. With respect to each of the ten traits, participants distributed the four groups along a seven-point scale ranging from a minimum amount of a particular trait to a maximum amount, using a convenient set of abbreviations. For example, with respect to the traits Judgment and Responsibility, a participant might have placed the groups as shown in Figure 1.

For each trait, the point at which the respondent placed his own immediate subordinates was subtracted from the point at which he placed himself (persons at his own level). Referring again to Figure 1, with respect to the trait Judgment, the number four (the point at which subordinates are placed) would be subtracted from six (the point at which the respondent placed persons at his own level). With respect to the trait Responsibility in Figure 1, the own minus subordinate difference would be zero, since both groups are placed at the same point on the scale.[10]

Each respondent's own minus subordinate difference score was computed for each of the ten traits; an average difference score was then obtained for each respondent across all ten traits. This score is taken as a measure of the degree to which managers have trust in their subordinates and confidence in their abilities—the closer they place their subordinates

---

FIGURE 1

Judgment

(min) 1	Emp 2	3	Sub 4	5	Own 6	Boss 7 (max)

Responsibility

(min) 1	2	Emp 3	4	Own Sub 5	Boss 6	7 (max)

Key: Emp = Rank-and-file employees
    Sub = Individuals at the level of participant's immediate subordinates
    Own = Individuals at participant's own level
    Boss = Individuals at the level of participant's own superior

to themselves (the smaller the difference score), the greater their trust and confidence in their subordinates.

After each manager's leadership attitude score was obtained in the manner described above, an aggregate leadership attitude score was calculated for each of the six divisions. In all but one division (Division C), the aggregate score was obtained by computing the average for all respondents at the upper four levels in that division. Respondents from the lowest level in each division were excluded from this calculation since none of their subordinates were included in the sample and thus no evaluation of their actual leadership behavior could be obtained. In Division C, only four levels of managers were included in our sample and thus the leadership attitude aggregate score was obtained by averaging the scores of respondents from the top three levels.

Leadership Behavior Measure

The leadership behavior scores employed here were aggregated from individual responses of subordinates about their superiors on five items drawn from Likert.[11] As shown in Appendix A, respondents checked each of the items on a twenty-point scale, where the lower scores reflect autocratic behavior, the middle scores reflect pseudo-participative behavior, and the upper scores indicate a high level of democratic-participative behavior. Respondents rated: (a) the extent of their superiors' awareness of problems, (b) the amount of trust and confidence which their superiors show in their subordinates, (c) the extent to which their superiors obtained and made use of their subordinates' ideas, (d) the manner in which goal setting is carried out by their superiors, and (e) how control data are employed by their superiors, e.g., for punishment or for self-evaluation. Each respondent's mean response to the combined five items constitutes his estimate of his superiors' behavior and is employed as the leadership behavior measure in this study.

As before, each division's leadership behavior score was computed by averaging the individual scores of managers in that division. In this instance, however, the leadership behavior scores of the respondents from the top level in each division were excluded from the calculation, since the leadership behavior descriptions they gave referred to corporate officials outside their division.

Satisfaction Measure

A satisfaction score for each participant was obtained by averaging his responses (on five-point scales from very satisfied to very dissatisfied) to statements concerning: (a) his future in his organization, (b) the extent to which his job utilizes his abilities, (c) his immediate superiors, (d) high-level management in his organization, and (e) his job in general (see

Appendix B). An aggregate satisfaction score was obtained for each division by averaging the responses of all participants from that division.

Performance Measure

Objective performance data for the preceding fiscal period were available for each of the six divisions. The performance data were based on the following criteria: (a) per cent growth in shipments, (b) operating profit as a per cent of sales, (c) warranty expense, (d) return on assets. Rank order standings on each of these dimensions were combined to provide a single, overall performance measure for each division. As can be seen in the list of specific criteria, the overall performance rank for each division reflects several of the most important measures of organizational success, i.e., quantity of output, quality, growth, and profitability.

RESULTS

Attitude and Behavior Data

Table 2 presents the attitude and behavior data for each division in the sample, along with a measure of dispersion and the number of respondents contributing to each measure. These measures, as indicated above, were obtained by averaging the scores of individual managers in each division. The leadership attitude aggregate score for each division was obtained by

TABLE 2

Organization Mean Scores on Managers' (Claimed)
Leadership Attitudes and their Perceptions
of the Leadership Behavior of their Superiors

	Claimed Leadership Attitudes			Perceived Leadership Behavior		
Division	Attitude Score*	Standard Deviation	Subjects Contributing	Behavior Score**	Standard Deviation	Subjects Contributing
A	.77	.39	53	14.78	2.46	59
B	.79	.43	67	14.31	2.45	75
C	1.00	.49	31	13.32	2.88	34
D	.66	.50	40	15.06	2.19	79
E	.97	.53	43	14.71	2.87	58
F	.76	.49	40	12.95	2.38	54

*Low scores equal attitudes of support, trust, and confidence in subordinates.
**High scores equal democratic-participative behavior.

combining the scores of managers at the top four levels in that division, levels one through four. The division scores for leadership behavior were computed by combining the scores of managers at levels two through five in that division.

As will be noted, neither the leadership attitude scores nor the leadership behavior scores differ greatly from division to division—the process of averaging of course obscures the precise pattern of responses in each division. Nevertheless, while the absolute differences in scores between divisions are not large, the top scores do tend to be statistically different from the bottom scores. For example, with respect to the leadership attitude measure, the lowest score, .66 (Division D), is significantly lower than the highest score, 1.00 (Division C), at the .01 level (two-tailed test). Similarly, the next to the lowest score, .76 (Division E), is significantly lower than the next to the highest score, .97 (Division E), at the .10 level (two-tailed test). Further, the two highest scores on leadership behavior, Division D and Division A, are significantly larger than the two lowest scores, Division C and Division F, at the .01 level of confidence (two-tailed).

Satisfaction and Performance Figures

Table 3 shows the overall mean satisfaction scores for each division, along with each division's combined ranking in terms of four objective performance measures. Once again differences among divisions, with respect to their mean satisfaction scores, are not large in absolute terms,

TABLE 3
Mean Satisfaction Scores and Performance Rankings for Each Division

Division	General Satisfaction Score*	Standard Deviation	Subjects Contributing	Combined Ranking on Four Performance Variables**
A	1.72	.53	63	1
B	1.99	.64	78	3
C	1.96	.53	35	4
D	1.76	.54	80	2
E	2.04	.65	66	6
F	2.27	.73	57	5

*Low scores equal high satisfaction.
**Rank 1 equals best performance.

yet the two lowest scores, Divisions A and D, are significantly lower than the two highest scores, Divisions E and F, at the .01 level of confidence (two-tailed).

Ranking and Classification of Measures

To facilitate analyses, the data presented in Tables 2 and 3 are summarized in Table 4 and presented in a form which allows easy comparison. As our data on the performance variable were already in rank order form, we felt that comparisons could most easily be made if the divisions were also ranked according to their scores on the remaining three variables. Thus, scores on attitude and behavior were used to rank the divisions from one to six (from high to low), with rank one, maintaining the McGregor-Likert logic, indicating the highest degree of trust and confidence in subordinates and the highest degree of democratic-participative behavior, and rank six indicating the lowest degree of supportive attitudes and participative behavior. For the attitude variables, as indicated earlier, the *lower* a division's average score, the *greater* the degree to which the average manager indicates trust and confidence in his subordinates. Therefore, on the attitude variable, the division with the lowest score, Division D, was ranked number 1, and the Division with the highest score, Division C, was ranked number 6.

For the leadership behavior variable, as explained earlier, the higher scores indicated higher degrees of democratic participative behavior. Thus, on the behavior variable, Division D, which had the highest score, received the number 1 rank and Division F, which had the lowest score, received the number 6 rank.

TABLE 4

Ranks and Classifications of Divisions on Leadership Attitudes, Leadership Behavior, Satisfaction, and Performance

	Classification (ranks given in parentheses) on:			
Division	Performance	General Satisfaction	Leadership Behavior*	Leadership Attitudes**
A	High (1)	High (1)	High (2)	Medium (3)
B	Medium (3)	Medium (4)	Medium (4)	Medium (4)
C	Medium (4)	Medium (3)	Low (5)	Low (6)
D	High (2)	High (2)	High (1)	High (1)
E	Low (6)	Low (5)	Medium (3)	Low (5)
F	Low (5)	Low (6)	Low (6)	High (2)

*High ratings (ranks 1 and 2) equal more participative behavior.
**High ratings (ranks 1 and 2) equal more democratic attitudes.

As was true with the attitude variable, scores on the satisfaction variable run counter to the usual form, with the *lowest* scores indicating the *highest* degree of satisfaction. Division A, therefore, which had the lowest average score on this variable, was ranked number 1 in terms of satisfaction; Division F, which had the highest average score on this variable, was ranked number 6.

To further ease comparison across the six divisions on the full set of four variables, each division was also classified as high, medium, or low with regard to leadership attitudes, leadership behavior, satisfaction, and performance. For this purpose, ranks one and two are classified as high, ranks three and four as medium, and ranks five and six as low. Thus a high ranking on all four variables would demonstrate a relationship among attitudes of support and confidence in subordinates, democratic-participative behavior, high satisfaction, and high performance. The reader should recognize that these classifications are rather arbitrary, since the differences in actual scores in the middle ranks are frequently quite small.

Comparison Across Divisions

Perhaps the most striking feature of the results shown in Table 4 is the extremely close relationship between satisfaction and performance. Using our high, medium, and low classifications, these variables are perfectly related. Comparing the ranks on these two variables, the Spearman rank correlation coefficient, r_s, is .89 which is significant beyond the .05 level.[12]

Although not as striking as the relationship between satisfaction and performance, the pattern of relationships across the three variables, leadership behavior, satisfaction, and performance, is worth noting. For four of the divisions, the high, medium, and low classifications are consistent across all three variables, and for the other two divisions only a one-degree shift occurs. Turning attention to the actual ranks, the Kendall Coefficient of Concordance, W, for the three variables is .82 indicating a relationship which is significant at the .01 level of confidence.[13] Again, it should be pointed out that while we are presenting measures of significance, the fact that only six divisions are included in our sample and the fact that rankings are based on scores whose absolute differences are quite small prescribes caution in interpreting these results.

Finally, when the relationships among the full set of four variables are examined across the six divisions a still less striking but nevertheless relatively consistent pattern emerges. Leadership attitudes are clearly not as closely related to leadership behavior, satisfaction, and performance as these three variables are to each other. The classifications across all four variables remain consistent for Divisions D and B, shift only one degree on one variable for Divisions A and E, and shift more than one degree or on more than one of the variables for Divisions C and F. Examining the relationship among the ranks for all four variables, the Kendall Coefficient of Concordance, W, is .64 and the relationship is significant at the .01 level. The caveat stated above applies of course to the interpretation of these findings.

DISCUSSION

We have purposely taken a venturesome but, we believe, useful direction in these analyses. The decision to compute and compare aggregate division scores not only restricts our sample size and limits the use of complex analytical techniques, but it also very likely tends to obscure some of the relationships which may exist among our set of four variables, leadership attitudes, leadership behavior, satisfaction, and performance. We have lumped together the responses from managers at various levels and areas in each division, thus ignoring the impact of structure and technology, and have made no effort to examine the relationships among our variables where they are most likely to be strongest—in the actual work teams composed of the manager and his immediate subordinates.[14] Nevertheless, we feel that processing our data in this form for this study is worthwhile, in part for the simple reason that studies employing aggregate data for comparative analyses across organizations or major organizational units are rare. The fact that a pattern of relationships of any sort did emerge from this admittedly crude approach suggests (1) that the actual relationships among these variables may be quite strong indeed, and (2) that comparative research using aggregate measures across organizations is not only possible, but is perhaps more profitable than some have believed.

We interpret our results here as providing support for three links in the McGregor-Likert *et al.* logic—that democratic-participative leadership behavior is related to satisfaction and to performance—and some suggestion of support for the fourth link in the chain, that attitudes of support and confidence in subordinates are related to the other three variables. The linkage between leadership attitudes and the other three variables is, we feel, likely to be the most difficult to demonstrate, since attitudes may be expressed in a variety of behaviors or may not be expressed in behavior at all.

Causality, of course, is not suggested by the relationships found here. It may well be that performance causes satisfaction, rather than the reverse.[15] Further, good performance may not only produce satisfaction, it may also provide managers with the opportunity to behave in a more democratic-participative fashion and reinforce their attitudes of support and confidence in their subordinates. Finally, we have taken all of our measures from these organizational units at one point in time. It may well be that the leadership attitudes and behaviors reported here are more accurately reflected in subsequent measurements of the performance and satisfaction variables. Our best guess is that these relationships, if they exist, are quite circular, and that in an ongoing organization no truly sound technique presently exists for determining cause and effect.[16]

It is important at this point to repeat and add to our earlier caveat. The relationships found here are not extremely strong, and our sample is quite small. Moreover, our organizations are all divisions of a single firm, and must operate, even though geographically separated and possessing considerable autonomy, under a common corporate atmosphere.[17] The findings reported here must therefore clearly be treated with caution, particularly with regard to generalization beyond our sample. This limitation can, of course, be alleviated by replicating this study across a broader sample of organizations and including repeated measurements over time, a step which we must strongly recommend.

APPENDIX A

Items Used for Leadership Behavior Measure

Place one check mark at the appropriate place on the scale beneath each of the following questions to indicate how you believe your superiors behave in your organization.

1. To what extent are your superiors aware of problems, particularly those at lower levels in the organization?

Often are unaware or only partially aware	Aware of some, unaware of others	Moderately aware of problems	Generally quite well aware of problems

2. To what extent do your superiors have trust and confidence in their subordinates?

Have no confidence and trust in subordinates	Have condescending confidence and trust, such as master to servant	Substantial but not complete confidence and trust. Still wish to control decisions	Complete confidence and trust in all matters

3. To what extent do your superiors generally try to get their subordinates' ideas and opinions and make constructive use of them in solving job problems?

Seldom get ideas and opinions of subordinates in solving job problems	Sometimes get ideas and opinions of subordinates solving job problems	Usually get ideas and opinions and usually try to make constructive use of them	Always get ideas and opinions and always try to make constructive use of them

4. In what manner is goal setting or ordering carried out by your superiors?

Orders issued	Orders issued, opportunity to comment may or may not exist	Goals are set or orders issued after discussion with subordinate(s) of problems and planned action	Except in emergencies, goals are usually established by means of group participation

5. How do your superiors use control data (e.g., accounting, productivity, cost figures, etc.)? Do they use it for group problem solving with their subordinates? Do they allow their subordinates to use these data for self-guidance? Is this information used by your superiors in a punitive, policing manner?

Used for policing and in punitive manner	Used for policing coupled with reward and punishment, some times punitively. Used somewhat for guidance, but in accord with orders	Largely used for policing with emphasis usually on reward but with some punishment. Used for guidance in accord with orders. Some use also for self-guidance	Used for self-guidance and for coordinated problem solving and guidance. Not used punitively

Adapted from R. Likert, *The Human Organization* (New York: McGraw Hill, 1967). Used by permission.

APPENDIX B

Items Used for Satisfaction Measure

V. In this section we are asking some general questions about job satisfaction. Read each of the statements and then select the response which best reflects your general feelings most of the time.

1. All things considered, how do you feel about your future in this division? (check one)

a. _____ Very enthusiastic   d. _____ Not so good
b. _____ Fine   e. _____ Not good at all
c. _____ All right

2. In your opinion, how well does your present position match your personal abilities? (check one)

a. _____ Very well   d. _____ Only partly
b. _____ Fairly well   e. _____ Not well at all
c. _____ Don't know; undecided

3. How satisfied are you with your immediate supervision? (check one)

a. _____ Very satisfied   d. _____ Dissatisfied
b. _____ Satisfied   e. _____ Very dissatisfied
c. _____ Somewhat satisfied, somewhat dissatisfied

4. How satisfied are you with *high-level management* in the division? (check one)

a. _____ Very satisfied   d. _____ Dissatisfied
b. _____ Satisfied   e. _____ Very dissatisfied
c. _____ Somewhat satisfied, somewhat dissatisfied

5. Taking everything into account, how satisfied are you *with your job in general* in this division? (check one)

a. _____ Completely satisfied   d. _____ Dissatisfied
b. _____ Satisfied   e. _____ Very dissatisfied
c. _____ Somewhat satisfied, somewhat dissatisfied

FOOTNOTES

1. D. McGregor, *The Human Side of Enterprise* (New York: McGraw Hill, 1960).

2. R. Likert, *The Human Organization: Its Management and Value* (New York: McGraw Hill, 1967).

3. E.A. Fleishman, E.F. Harris, and H.E. Burtt, *Leadership and Supervision in Industry* (Columbus: Ohio State University, Bureau of Educational Research, 1955); R. Stogdill and A. Coons (eds.), *Leader Behavior: Its Description and Measurement* (Columbus: Ohio State University, Bureau of Business Research, Research Monograph No. 88, 1957).

4. E.A. Fleishman and E.F. Harris, "Patterns of Leadership Behavior Related to Employee Grievances and Turnover," *Personnel Psychology*, XV (1962), 43-56.

5. F.E. Fiedler, *Leader Attitudes and Group Effectiveness* (Urbana: University of Illinois Press, 1958).

6. In later studies, F.E. Fiedler, "The Contingency Model: A Theory of Leadership Effectiveness," *Problems in Social Psychology*, ed. C. Backman and P. Secord (New York: McGraw-Hill, 1966), looks simultaneously at the relationships among power held by the leader, degree of task structure, and the leader's relations with members of his work group.

7. R.L. Kahn, D. Katz, "Leadership Practices in Relation to Productivity and Morale," *Group Dynamics: Research and Theory*, ed. D. Cartwright and A. Zander (2nd ed.; Evanston, Ill.: Harper and Row, 1960); R. Likert, *New Patterns of Management* (New York: McGraw Hill, 1961).

8. Likert, 1961, reports at least one Michigan study in which leaders' "attitudes toward men" scores were measured by questionnaire methods and related to subordinate attitudes and performance, and V. Vroom and F. Mann, "Leader Authoritarianism and Employee Attitudes," *Personnel Psychology*, XIII (1960), 115-141, related leader authoritarianism to subordinate attitudes.

9. R. Likert, 1967.

10. For a detailed description of this section of the questionnaire and its use in other research, see R.E. Miles, "Conflicting Elements In Managerial Ideologies," *Industrial Relations*, IV (1964), 77-91, and R.E. Miles, L.W. Porter, J.E. Craft, "Leadership Attitudes Among Public Health Officials," *American Journal of Public Health*, LVI (1962), 1990-2005.

11. R. Likert, 1967.

12. S. Siegel, *Non parametric Statistics* (New York: McGraw Hill, 1956).

13. S. Siegel, 1956.

14. Later analysis of our data examining the relationships among attitudes, behavior, satisfaction, performance, and other variables within work teams and across the entire sample have been and are being completed. For the most part, these findings indicate relationships among these variables stronger than those reported here. These analyses are also taking into account structural and personality variables.

15. For a discussion of this interpretation, see R. Miles, "Human Relations or Human Resources," *Harvard Business Review*, XLIII (1965), 148-163; L. Porter and E. Lawler, *Managerial Attitudes and Performance* (Homewood, Illinois: Irwin Dorsey, 1968).

16. The most recent Michigan research is providing some beginning evidence that improvements in performance and satisfaction do flow from changes in managerial behavior, which is in turn believed to be in part the result of changes in managerial attitudes. The Michigan work is taking time into account specifically, comparing leader behavior in one period with work team satisfaction and performance in following periods. See R. Likert, 1967.

17. The argument can of course be reversed. For units operating in common environment, variations in attitude behavior, satisfaction, etc. might logically be expected to be minimized and thus relationships more difficult to discover.

Victor Vroom is Professor of Administrative Science and Psychology at the School of Organization and Management, Yale University, New Haven, Connecticut.

This paper is based on a dissertation submitted to the Department of Psychology, University of Michigan, in partial fulfillment of the requirement for the degree of doctor of philosophy. The writer is indebted to J. Atkinson, J.R.P. French, Jr., and F. Mann for their helpful comments and criticisms, and to the United Parcel Service for their financial support of this research.

Some Personality Determinants of the Effects of Participation

VICTOR H. VROOM

Psychologists have long realized the importance of both environmental and personality variables in the explanation of behavior. Theorists have employed a variety of terms to describe the necessity of using both sets of concepts. Lewin (1951), for example, illustrates this dual focus in his statement that "behavior (B) is a function (F) of the person (P) and of his environment (E), B = F(P,E)" (p. 239).

There has, however, been a tendency for investigators in social psychology to concentrate on one or the other of these sets of variables in their explanation of social phenomena. Some emphasize personality, conceived as the relatively enduring psychological properties of an individual, as the locus of the basic causes of behavior, while others look to environmental variables such as group structure, communication, and role. Few have investigated environmental and personality determinants of behavior simultaneously.

The implications of this point of view for problems of leadership have been described by a number of writers (Gibb, 1954). The general conclusion is that leadership cannot be regarded as a unitary trait and must be evaluated in terms of a number of other variables including the attitudes, needs, and expectations of the followers. The most effective behavior in dealing with individuals with certain personality characteristics may be ineffective in dealing with persons differently predisposed.

A similar point is made by those who argue for the adaptive nature of leadership. After reviewing research on the effectiveness of different methods of supervision in industry, Likert (1958) reaches the following conclusion:

> Supervision is, therefore, always an adaptive process. A leader, to be effective, must always adapt his behavior to fit the expectations, values, and interpersonal skills of those with whom he is interacting (p. 327).

The "authoritarian-democratic" continuum represents one aspect of leadership that has received much attention. In discussing studies dealing with this dimension Krech and Crutchfield (1948) suggest that its effects may vary from culture to culture:

> All the experimental evidence to be reported has been obtained by the study of so-called "authoritarian" and "democratic" leadership situations in our democratic culture. It is entirely possible that similar studies in other cultures might yield different results. The advantages for morale, the experiments find, seem to be with the democratically led group, but in an autocratic culture the reverse might possibly hold true (p. 423).

Despite frequent speculations that the superior effects of democratic leadership are specific to certain personality types or cultures, relatively little research has been done on this problem. The few studies which have been carried out (French, Israel, & As, in press; Sanford, 1950; Tannenbaum & Allport, 1956) have produced positive results. The task remains to determine the nature of the personality variables and their manner of interaction with democratic leadership.

The major purpose of the present study is to determine whether the effects of one aspect of the democratic leadership process—participation in decision-making—vary with the personality structure of the follower. Previous research has demonstrated that participation, or conceptually similar variables, has positive effects on the attitudes and performance of the participants. The general hypothesis of this study is that participation interacts with certain personality characteristics of the participant in determining both attitudes and performance.

The personality variables thought to be relevant in determining an individual's response to participation are (a) need for independence and (b) authoritarianism. Participation is hypothesized to have more positive effect on the attitudes and performance of persons with strong than weak independence needs and to have less positive effect on authoritarians than equalitarians. The relevance of need for independence in determining a person's reactions to participation was suggested by McGregor (1944), while Sanford (1950) has shown that authoritarians say they prefer more strongly directive kinds of leadership.

Participation, the independent variable in this study, has been used in a number of ways and has seldom been clearly defined. The present investigation employs the definition put forth by French, Israel, and As (in press): a process of joint decision-making by two or more parties in which the decisions have future effects on those making them. The amount of participation by any individual is the amount of influence he has on the decisions and plans agreed upon.

It is important to distinguish between psychological participation, or the amount of influence he perceives he has on decision-making and objective participation, or the amount of influence he actually does have on decision-making. If perception is veridical, the amount of psychological participation equals the amount of objective participation. Frequently, however, they differ as a result of the influence of processes such as the effects of needs on perception. Concern here is limited to psychological participation and, unless otherwise noted, the term "participation" is used to designate this variable.

METHOD

This study was carried out in a large company whose basic function is the delivery of small parcels and packages from department and other retail stores to private residents. The Ss were 108 first, second, and third line supervisors in the company's two largest plants.

Measures were obtained on each of the following variables:

1. *Psychological participation.* This index is derived by summing the responses of each supervisor to the following questions:

   (a) In general, how much say or influence do you have on what goes on in your station? (b) Do you feel you can influence the decisions of your immediate superior regarding things about which you are concerned? (c) Does your immediate superior ask your opinion when a problem comes up which involves your work? (d) If you have a suggestion for improving the job or changing the setup in some way, how easy is it for you to get your ideas across to your immediate superior?

Each of these questions was answered by checking the most applicable alternative on a five-point scale. Scores ranging from 1, representing low participation, to 5, representing high participation, were assigned to each question and total scores were obtained for each person by summing his scores for the four items.

The test-retest reliability of this index over a seven-month period is .61 for 91 supervisors. When 14 supervisors who changed either their position or their superior during this period were removed from this group, the reliability coefficient increased to .63. The correlation for the transferees is .44.

2. *Attitude toward the job.* The measure of attitude toward the job

consists of the following items:

> (a) How well do you like supervisory work? (b) How much of a chance does your job give you to do the things that you are best at? (c) How good is your immediate superior in dealing with people?

Each of the questions calls for the respondent to check the most appropriate answer on a five-point scale. Scores of 1 to 5 were assigned to each question and a total score obtained by adding over the three questions.

The test-retest reliability of this index over a seven-month period was computed for 91 supervisors and found to be .66. When 14 supervisors who had changed their superior or their position within the organization during this period were removed, the reliability coefficient was increased to .75. The reliability for the transferees was .06.

3. *Need for independence.* The measure of need for independence used in this study consists of 16 questionnaire items.[1] Some of these items refer to the frequency with which the S regularly engages in independent behavior (e.g., "How often do you find that you can carry out other people's suggestions without changing them any?"), while others deal with the satisfaction that he gets from this behavior (e.g., "When you have a problem, how much do you like to think it through yourself without help from others?"). The items are adapted from a larger number employed by Tannenbaum and Allport (1956). Each item required the S to check one of five alternatives.

No data were available concerning the reliability of this measure. However, the test-retest reliability over a seven-month period of a short form, made up of eight items selected on the basis of item analysis from the original items, was found to be .61 for 90 supervisors.

4. *Authoritarianism.* The degree of authoritarianism of the Ss[2] is measured by responses to 25 items from Forms 40 and 45 of the F scale developed by Adorno, Frenkel-Brunswick, Levinson, and Sanford (1950). In keeping with the rest of the questionnaire, Ss were asked to check their degree of agreement with each of the statements on a five-point scale, unlike the six-point scale usually used.

5. *Job performance.* Ratings of the job performance of 96 of the supervisors in the sample were completed by the immediate superior of the man being rated and reviewed by one other person who was acquainted with his work. These ratings consisted of two scores—over-all performance and summary appraisal. The over-all performance rating was obtained from a modification of the forced-choice merit rating technique. It consisted of ten sets of five statements, each describing some aspect of job behavior. The rater is asked to rank order the statements within each group in terms of the degree to which they describe accurately the man whose performance they are rating. The rankings on the ten sets of statements are scored to yield a single over-all performance score. The summary appraisal rating was of the graphic type. The rater is asked to check on a five-point scale his general evaluation of the degree to which the individual meets the demands of his job.

The hypothesis that participation has different effects on persons with different personality characteristics was tested in the following manner: The sample was divided into three approximately equal groups on the basis of their scores on each of the personality variables. Pearson product-moment correlation coefficients were then computed between participation and both attitude toward the job and job performance for the entire sample and for each of the subgroups.

RESULTS

The findings presented first deal with the effects of participation in decision-making on the attitudes toward the job of persons with different personality characteristics. More positive relationships between participation and attitude toward the job are predicted for persons who received relatively high scores on the need for independence measure and low scores on the authoritarianism measure than for persons at the opposite ends of these two scales.

The data in Table 1 support this prediction. The correlation between the measure of participation and attitude toward the job is significantly positive, confirming past findings. Significant differences are found, however, between the magnitude of the correlations for the different personality groups. As predicted, the most positive relationships between psychological participation and attitude toward the job are found for persons high in need for independence and low in authoritarianism. Both correlations are significant at the .01 level of confidence. The least positive relationships are found for persons low in need for independence and high in authoritarianism. Neither of these correlations is significantly different from zero. The differences between correlations for high and low groups on both personality variables are statistically significant.

The data are interpreted as meaning that the attitudes toward the job of low authoritarian persons and of persons with high independence needs are favorably affected by opportunities to participate in making decisions in their jobs. On the other hand, the attitudes of highly authoritarian individuals and of individuals with low independence needs are relatively unaffected by this experience.

The correspondence between the findings for need for independence and authoritarianism suggests the possibility that the measures of these two variables have a high negative relationship with one another. This possibility was tested by intercorrelating the two measures. The Pearson product-moment correlation coefficient between authoritarianism and need for independence is $-.11$ for 107 Ss. When age, occupational level, and education are partialled out from this relationship, the correlation is changed to .02, indicating that the two measures are independent.

Table 2 shows the intercorrelations between the measure of participation and the two measures of job performance for the entire sample and for the six subgroups. The significant correlations for the entire sample support previous findings that participating in making decisions in a job generally has positive effects on the job performance of the participant. In addition, some support is provided the hypothesis that the effects of participation on performance are a function of the need for independence and authoritarianism of the participant. Although none of the differences between correlations is significant, all of the high-low differences and most of the other differences are in the predicted directions.

The use of the correlational methods of field studies instead of the more precise techniques of laboratory experimentation increases the possibility that the results may be attributable to failure to control for

TABLE 1

Relationship Between Psychological Participation and Attitude Toward the Job for Persons With Different Personality Characteristics

	Number of Cases	
Total Group	108	.36***
1. High Need Independence	38	.55***
2. Moderate Need Independence	32	.31**
3. Low Need Independence	38	.13
diff (1, 3) t = 2.04[a]		
P = .02		
diff (1, 2) t = 1.20[a]		
P = .12		
diff (2, 3) t = ——[a]		
P = ——		
4. High Authoritarian	34	.03
5. Moderate Authoritarian	34	.35**
6. Low Authoritarian	39	.53***
diff (4, 6) t = 2.33[a]		
P = .01		
diff (4, 5) t = 1.36[a]		
P = .09		
diff (5, 6) t = ——[a]		
P = ——		

** $P < .05$.
*** $P < .01$.
[a] Indicates that the difference between correlations is in the predicted direction; t ratios over 1.00 are shown. Inasmuch as the direction of results has been specified in our hypotheses, one-tailed tests of significance have been performed.

TABLE 2

Relationship Between Psychological Participation and
Ratings of Job Performance for Total Group and for Persons
With Different Personality Characteristics

	N	Over-all Perfor- mance	Summary Appraisal
		Pearson r's Between Participation and Supervisors' Rating on:	
Total Group	96	.20**	.20**
1. High Need Independence	33	.33**	.25*
2. Moderate Need Independence	28	.19	.33**
3. Low Need Independence	35	.06	−.01
diff (1, 3) t =		1.12a	1.08a
P =		.13	.14
diff (1, 2) t =		——a	——
P =		——	——
diff (2, 3) t =		——a	1.30a
P =		——	.10
4. High Authoritarian	30	−.08	−.06
5. Moderate Authoritarian	33	.28*	.23*
6. Low Authoritarian	32	.28*	.27*
diff (1, 3) t =		1.37a	1.26a
P =		.08	.10
diff (1, 2) t =		1.42a	1.12a
P =		.08	.13
diff (2, 3) t =		——	——a
P =		——	——

* $P < .10$.   ** $P < .05$.   a In the predicted direction.

relevant variables. The effects of age, education, and occupational level of the Ss in the present sample were determined by partialling out these variables from the relationships between participation and the three dependent variables for the entire sample and for each of the six personality classifications. Table 3 shows the third-order partial correlation for each of these relationships.

TABLE 3
Relationship Between Psychological Participation and Attitude Toward the Job and Ratings of Job Performance for Persons With Different Personality Characteristics With Age, Education, and Occupational Level Held Constant

	Pearson r's Between Participation and:		
	Attitude toward the Job	Over-all Performance	Summary Appraisal
Total Group	.27*** (108)	.21** (96)	.20** (96)
1. High Need Independence	.51*** (38)	.51*** (33)	.42** (33)
2. Moderate Need Independence	.25* (32)	.18 (28)	.33** (28)
3. Low Need Independence	−.04 (38)	.04 (35)	.00 (35)
diff (1, 3)	t = 2.40[a]	1.93[a]	1.61
	$P <$ .01	.03	.05
diff (1, 2)	t = 1.15[a]	1.31[a]	——[a]
	P = .12	.10	——
diff (2, 3)	t = 1.15[a]	——[a]	1.26[a]
	P = .12	——	.10
4. High Authoritarian	.09 (34)	−.13 (30)	.14 (30)
5. Moderate Authoritarian	.35** (34)	.24* (33)	.18 (33)
6. Low Authoritarian	.50*** (39)	.33** (32)	.26* (32)
diff (4, 6)	t = 1.77[a]	1.68[a]	——[a]
	P = .04	.05	——
diff (4, 5)	t = 1.04[a]	1.32[a]	——[a]
	P = .15	.09	——
diff (5, 6)	t = ——[a]	——[a]	——[a]
	P = ——	——	——

* $P < .10$.
** $P < .05$.
*** $P < .01$.
[a] Indicates that the difference between correlations is in the predicted direction.

A comparison of Table 3 with Tables 1 and 2 shows that partialling out the effects of background variables generally increases the magnitude of the differences between correlations and provides increased support for the hypothesis of interaction between participation and personality. All of the differences in correlations are in the predicted direction, and five of the six high-low differences are significant at the .05 level.

DISCUSSION

The present study corroborates previous findings that participation in decision-making has positive effects on attitudes and job performance. It further demonstrates that the magnitude of these effects is a function of certain personality characteristics of the participants. Authoritarians and persons with weak independence needs are apparently unaffected by the opportunity to participate in making decisions. On the other hand, equalitarians and those who have strong independence needs develop more positive attitudes toward their job and greater motivation for effective performance through participation.

There is no evidence of any unfavorable effects of participation either on attitudes or on performance. It should be noted, however, that the sample of supervisors used in this study is not representative of workers in general. It is possible that nonsupervisory employees might be more authoritarian and have weaker independence needs which might lead, in the extreme, to negative consequences of participation.

These results suggest the inadequacy of generalizations concerning the effects of participation. Studies that ignore the interaction of participation and personality yield relationships that are nothing more than average effects of participation for all the persons in the group. The statistic used to estimate the degree of relationship underestimates the effects of participation on some persons and overestimates the effects on others.

A word of caution should be injected here. The measure of participation used in this study was based on Ss' reports and conforms with what we have defined as psychological participation. Enough is known about distorting influences in complex perceptions of this sort to make it impossible to infer that our measure of psychological participation corresponds with objective participation. Since no data are available on objective participation, extension of the present findings to cover the latter variable will require further research.

The results suggest that an adequate theoretical explanation of the effects of participation in decision-making should include a consideration of the influence of personality variables that interact with participation. The present study also gives general support to a situational theory of leadership and indicates the possible value in simultaneous examination of environmental and personality variables.

SUMMARY

The primary purpose of this study was to determine the effects of participation in decision-making on persons with different personality characteristics. It was hypothesized that equalitarians and individuals with strong independence needs would be more positively affected by the opportunity to participate in making decisions than authoritarians and persons with weaker independence needs.

The findings corroborated previous evidence that participation generally has positive effects on both attitudes and job performance. Hypotheses were also confirmed that the magnitude of these effects is a function of certain personality characteristics of the participant. Authoritarians and persons with weak independence needs are apparently unaffected by the opportunity to participate in making decisions. On the other hand, equalitarians and those who have strong independence needs develop more positive attitudes toward their jobs and increase in performance through participation.

This study suggests that an adequate theoretical explanation of the effects of participation in decision-making should include a consideration of the influence of personality variables. It also indicates the possible value of investigating the joint effects of leader and follower characteristics.

FOOTNOTES

1. Tables showing the items, scoring keys, means, and standard deviations for the need for independence, authoritarianism and job performance measures have been deposited with the American Documentation Institute. Order Document No. 5965 from ADI Auxiliary Publications Project, Photoduplication Service, Library of Congress, Washington 25, D.C., remitting in advance $1.25 for microfilm or $1.25 for photocopies. Make checks payable to Chief, Photoduplication Service, Library of Congress.

2. One S declined to complete the F scale, limiting the sample on this variable to 107 persons.

REFERENCES

Adorno, T., Frenkel-Brunswick, Else, Levinson, D.J., & Sanford, N. *The authoritarian personality.* New York: Harper, 1950.

French, J.R.P., Jr., Israel, J., & As, D. An experiment on participation in a Norwegian factory. *Hum. Relat.*, in press.

Gibb, C.A. Leadership. In G. Lindzey (Ed.), *Handbook of social psychology.* Cambridge: Addison-Wesley, 1954. Pp. 877-920.

Krech, D., & Crutchfield, R.S. *Theory and problems in social psychology.* New York: McGraw-Hill, 1948.

Lewin, K. Behavior and development as a function of the total situation. In D. Cartwright (Ed.), *Field theory in social science.* New York: Harper, 1951. Pp. 238-303.

Likert, R. Effective supervision: An adaptive and relative process. *Personnel Psychol.*, 1958, *11*: 317-332.

McGregor, D. Getting effective leadership in an industrial organization. *J. consult. Psychol.*, 1944, *8*, 55-63.

Sanford, F.H. *Authoritarianism and leadership.* Philadelphia: Institute for Research in Human Relations, 1950.

Tannenbaum, A., & Allport, F.H. Personality structure and group structure: An interpretative study of their relationship through an event-structure hypothesis. *J. abnorm. soc. Psychol.*, 1956, *53*, 272-280.

Robert J. House is the Shell Professor of Organization Behavior at the University of Toronto, Ontario, Canada. Alan C. Filley is a Professor of Business at the University of Wisconsin; and Steven Kerr is an Assistant Professor of Management Sciences at the Ohio State University. This article is reprinted with permission from Administrative Science Quarterly, *March 1971, pp. 19-30.*

Relation of Leader Consideration and Initiating Structure to R and D Subordinates' Satisfaction

ROBERT J. HOUSE, ALAN C. FILLEY, and STEVEN KERR

The purpose of this paper is to report tests of hypotheses about the relationship between consideration and initiating structure of superiors and the satisfaction of subordinates in research and development installations. The hypotheses were derived from previous research on the relationship between leader behavior and subordinate satisfaction in other occupations.

PREVIOUS RESEARCH

Initiating Structure

Initiating structure deals with the instrumental behavior of leaders. According to Parsons (1951), instrumental activities, which are highly directive and task oriented, are necessary for an organization as a social system to solve the basic functional problems of adaptation to its environment and of goal attainment by allocation and mobilization of resources.

Instrumental activities relate to the input of means and their distribution within the organization, whereas expressive activities involve the interrelations and integration of the units of the system. Bales (1953), in a series of small-group experiments, showed that these two sets of activities tend to become segregated into instrumental roles and expressive roles.

The initiating structure scale used in this study to measure instrumental behavior was factor analytically developed by members of the Ohio State University leadership group (Stogdill and Coons, 1957). Eleven of the items describe the degree to which the leader makes specific work assignments, emphasizes deadlines, evaluates quality of work, and establishes well-defined work patterns and procedures. The remaining four items describe leadership behavior which is authoritarian and arbitrary: for example, ruling with an iron hand, speaking in a manner not to be questioned, refusing to explain actions, and acting without consulting the group.

Leaders high on initiating structure have repeatedly been found by the Ohio State University researchers to be highly rated by their superiors and to have high scores on such objective measures of leader performance as productivity, scrap, and cost (Harris, 1952; Halpin and Winer, 1957). Findings from field studies (Stouffer, 1949; Moore and Smith, 1952; Moore, 1953) and small-group laboratory experiments (Bales, 1953) using similar measures were highly consistent with the findings of the Ohio State University group.

Researchers at the University of Southern California developed three measures of leader behavior very similar to many of the items contained in the Ohio State University initiating-structure factor: advanced planning, organizing, and formalization. Leaders scoring high on advanced planning and organizing were described by their subordinates as men who anticipated future problems of scheduling, organized the work group, and clearly defined authority and responsibilities. Formalization was related to the degree to which the organization operated according to written specifications such as schedules, organization charts, job descriptions, procedures, and instructions. Forest rangers, aircraft supervisors, and government administrators described by subordinates as high in advanced planning, organizing, and formalization were also given high performance ratings by their superiors or had high productivity, as measured by units of production or scrap (Comrey et al., 1954).

Studies at the University of Michigan (Katz et al., 1950; Katz and Kahn, 1953) showed that managers judged to be effective by their superiors spent more time planning and organizing activities than did less effective managers. These and other studies (Bass and Dunteman, 1963; Bass et al., 1963; Dunteman and Bass, 1963) showed that leaders who ranked high on measures of instrumental or structuring leadership also ranked high on measures of effectiveness as viewed by superiors and had more productive work groups. However, findings on the effects of high task orientation are not always positive. For example, Fleishman and

Harris (1962) found that production supervisors scoring high in initiating structure also had higher rates of grievances and employee turnover than did low-scoring supervisors. Korman (1966) revealed several studies showing no relationship between initiating structure and performance or subordinate satisfaction.

Consideration

The consideration dimension of leader behavior is similar to that frequently described as supportive, socioemotional, or expressive (Parsons, 1951; Etzioni, 1961). According to these authors, expressive activities serve the function of social and normative integration of group members. The consideration scale used to measure expressive behavior in this study was also developed by the Ohio State leadership group. Responses to the items on this scale describe a leader who is seen by subordinates as considerate of subordinate needs, willing to explain his actions, and warm, supportive, and friendly. In studies where this scale has been used, a positive relationship was frequently found between consideration and measures of subordinate satisfaction (Halpin, 1954; Halpin and Winer, 1957). High consideration leaders also have work groups which display more intragroup harmony and member cooperation (Oaklander and Fleishman, 1964), as well as low turnover and grievance rates (Fleishman and Harris, 1962). In the summary of research conducted by the Institute of Social Research at the University of Michigan, Likert (1961) reported that in the majority of studies, supervisors of departments with high productivity showed more supportive leadership than did those with low productivity.

Positive effects of supportive leadership on attitudes and satisfaction of subordinates have been reported in industrial plants (Comrey *et al.*, 1954; Indik *et al.*, 1960; Patchen, 1960; Danielson and Maier, 1957; Argyle *et al.*, 1958), in military settings (Moore, 1953; Moore and Smith, 1952; Spector *et al.*, 1960), in research laboratories (Baumgartel, 1956; 1957), among forest workers (Comrey *et al.*, 1954), in educational institutions (Hemphill, 1957; Seeman, 1960), and in government organizations (Comrey *et al.*, 1954). Supportive leadership has also frequently been found to have a positive relationship to departmental and individual productivity (Likert, 1961; Argyle *et al.*, 1958; Blau and Scott, 1962; Katz and Kahn, 1953; Katz *et al.*, 1950; Indik *et al.*, 1960).

Initiating Structure and Consideration

Several studies, including some of the above, have dealt with both supportive and instrumental leadership, constructs similar to consideration and initiating structure. Borgatta *et al.* (1954) selected 11 men from 126 experimental subjects on the basis of high task ability, individual assertiveness, and social acceptability. They designated these as great men and assigned them as leaders to problem-solving groups. The great men retained their ratings throughout a series of difficult problem-solving sessions, and the groups they led achieved higher ratings of suggestion and agreement, lower ratings of showing tension, and higher ratings of showing solidarity and tension release than comparable groups without great men.

From several studies concerned with both instrumental and expressive behavior or leaders, it is clear that superiors and subordinates view leaders from fundamentally different perspectives and evaluate them in terms of fundamentally different criteria. For example, Moore and Smith (1952), interviewing 301 officers, airmen, and noncommissioned officers, found that subordinates judged the noncommissioned officer a good leader if he was considerate, whereas superiors judged him a good leader if they saw him as exhibiting high instrumental behavior. These findings were confirmed in a subsequent factor analysis of 280 ratings of noncommissioned officers in supervisory jobs in which more vigorous statistical tests were used (Moore, 1953). The Ohio State studies (Stogdill and Coons, 1957) and a study by Stouffer (1949) have yielded essentially the same results. Thus, as Berelson and Steiner (1964: 372) stated, "the leader is subject to conflicting demands from above and below. This is a classic situation for foremen and middle managers, chief nurses, committee chairmen, deans, school superintendents, noncommissioned officers and people in similar positions." Leaders' superiors tend to evaluate highly leaders who are task-oriented, exercise close rather than general supervision, and are decisive in their relationships with their subordinates. In contrast, most subordinates tend to evaluate highly those leaders who are considerate, provide general supervision, and are permissive or democratic in their decision making.

Studies using the Ohio State leadership scales suggest that more precise measuring instruments may help to determine the kind of behavior necessary for effective leadership. Studies such as those of Halpin (1954), Halpin and Winer (1957), and especially those of Fleishman and Harris (1962) and Oaklander and Fleishman (1964), showed that while scores on initiating structure and consideration are often independent of each other, leaders rated high on both initiating structure and consideration were more likely to be judged effective by their superiors and to have desirable effects on productivity and group morale.

Oaklander and Fleishman (1964) found that consideration by supervisors served to harmonize internal working relationships within a group and minimized intragroup tension, hostility, and noncooperative relationships, while initiating structure prevented tension and conflict between groups. Thus, initiating structure can be interpreted not only as a means of encouraging production and directing subordinates in their work activities, but also as a means of protecting them from outsider interference, political influence, and arbitrary rule of higher authority. Fleishman and Harris (1962) found that for production supervisors scoring high on both dimensions, the negative effects of initiating structure were minimal, and they concluded that high consideration foremen could increase instrumental behavior with very little increase in grievances and no increase in turnover.

METHOD

Although there has been much research conducted with the Ohio State University scales, few studies have dealt with research, engineering, or development personnel.

Sample

The data for the study were collected from the research, development, and design departments of three large organizations: a petroleum refinery, a business machine manufacturer, and an air-frame manufacturer. Samples in the first two organizations were selected randomly and stratified by organizational level, and questionnaires were administered in groups; in the third organization, questionnaires were mailed to all employees in the department. Respondents were requested, in a letter from the head of the research and engineering divisions in each organization, to participate in the study: 118 completed questionnaires from the first company, 234 from the second, and 104 from the third. All respondents were assured of anonymity.

Hypotheses

Two hypotheses were tested:
Hypothesis 1. The satisfaction of subordinates will be positively related to leader consideration.
Hypothesis 2. With low consideration, satisfaction will be negatively related to initiating structure; with high consideration, satisfaction will not be related to initiating structure.
In general, then, an inverse relationship was expected between initiating structure and a subordinate's satisfaction with role expectations, with consideration acting as a moderating variable (Figure 1).
The basis for the first hypothesis is the previous investigations on the effect of supportive leadership. The basis for the second hypothesis is the research reviewed concerned with both dimensions. The specific form of the second hypothesis is derived from the research of Fleishman and Harris (1962), whose findings showed consideration to moderate the relationship between leader structure and employee turnover and grievances. Although the measures of dependent variables are not the same, and the statistical

FIGURE 1
Hypothesized Moderating Effect of Consideration on the Relationship Between Structure and Satisfaction

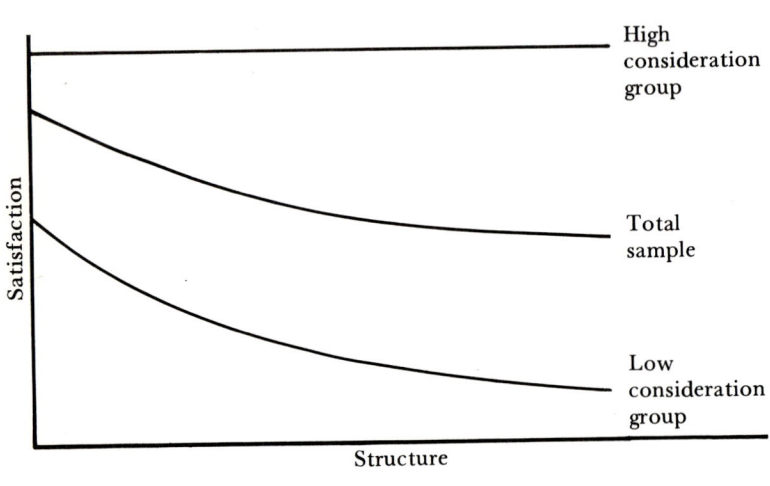

method of analysis is somewhat different from theirs, this hypothesis is closely related to theirs and could be considered a constructural, as opposed to operational, replication.

Measures Employed

Three measures were used to test the hypotheses:

1. Satisfaction of subordinate role expectations. Two questionnaires, both developed by the Personnel Research Board of the Ohio State University, were used. The first was the job description questionnaire, with 12 questions scaled 1-5, measuring the employee's attitude toward the organization and its management. Sample items included:

Management's interest in welfare of employees
Credit given by my supervisor for doing a good job
My pride in working for this company
Credit given by the company for good work

The response choices were—very poor, poor, fair, good, and very good.

The seven other measures of satisfaction with role expectations are contained in a job expectation questionnaire. Employee satisfaction was measured with respect to the following classes of role expectations: work; advancement; the respondent's job as compared with jobs of others; pay; freedom; family attitudes toward the respondent's job; and job security. Respondents were asked to indicate the degree to which each characteristic of the job satisfied their expectations. Each class of expectation was measured by summing the score of the seven questions. An item representative of each class of expectations follows:

Liking for the work I am doing here
My chances of getting ahead in this company
My job compared with my friends' jobs
The amount of money I am paid
Freedom to make decisions about my work
My family's pride in my job
Chances of keeping this job as long as I want it

The response choices were—much poorer than expected, poorer than expected, same as expected, better than expected, and much better than expected. The job description and job expectation scales are considered sufficiently reliable for research purposes, although validity data are not available (Stogdill, 1960).

2. Leadership consideration. Consideration scores were obtained from 15 scored questions in the 40-item leader behavior description questionnaire (Stogdill and Shartle, 1955; Stogdill and Coons, 1957). Subordinates were asked to describe the behavior of their superior by responding to 15 items similar to the following:

He does personal favors for group members.
He looks out for the personal welfare of individual group members.
He finds time to listen to group members.
He is friendly and approachable.
He keeps the group working together as a team.

The response choices included always, often, occasionally, seldom, and never. The sum of the consideration scale scores described the degree to which the respondent perceived his superior as warm and friendly with group members, considerate, concerned with group welfare, respectful with member integrity, helpful, and approachable.

3. Initiating structure of leader. Initiating structure scores were also obtained from 15 questions in the leader behavior description questionnaire. Sample questions included:

He makes his attitudes clear to the group.
He assigns members to particular tasks.
He schedules the work to be done.
He speaks in a manner not to be questioned.
He refuses to explain his actions.

The response choices were the same as for consideration. This scale measures the degree to which the leader was perceived as (1) structuring the work environment, and (2) authoritarian or arbitrary in his interactions with subordinates.

Method of Analysis

To test hypothesis 1, which dealt with the relationship between leader consideration and subordinate role satisfaction, product-moment correlations were computed for each of the three companies for structure, consideration, and eight measures of satisfaction.

To test hypothesis 2, which had to do with the effect of structure on subordinate role satisfaction under different conditions of perceived leader consideration, the data from each company were first subdivided into equal groups of low, medium, and high consideration. The groups were then examined to ensure that the last respondent in the low consideration subdivision did not have the same score as the first respondent in the medium group, nor the last respondent in the medium group the same score as the first in the high category. For ties, a respondent in the medium group was moved to the appropriate extreme group. Then the medium consideration group in each of the companies was removed from the sample and the remaining low and high groups in each firm were further subdivided into five equal groups, according to the position on the structure scale. The same approach was taken to ensure that no two respondents with the same structure score would be placed in different structure categories. All tied respondents were placed in categories in such a way that the number of respondents in each structure subdivision would remain as similar to the number in the other subdivisions as possible. The number of respondents in each consideration-structure category is shown in Table 1.

Finally, the categorized data were used as inputs to 24 two-way analyses of variance, consisting of one for each of the eight measures of subordinate role satisfactions, for each of the three companies.

RESULTS

Hypothesis 1

The zero order correlations between consideration and satisfaction in Table 2 show that all satisfaction scores for all three companies were

---

TABLE 1
Numbers of Respondents in Each
Consideration-Structure Category

Company	Consideration category	Structure category				
		A	B	C	D	E
Refining	Low	7	7	9	10	10
	High	9	8	9	8	10
Business	Low	16	18	16	16	15
machine	High	16	16	16	15	17
Air frame	Low	7	7	6	8	7
	High	7	7	7	6	7

TABLE 2
Zero-Order Correlations Among Consideration, Structure, and Satisfaction Measures

Company	Consideration			Structure		
	Refining	Business machine	Air frame	Refining	Business machine	Air frame
Structure	.16	.43**	.38**			
Satisfaction measures						
Company	.40**	.37**	.42**	.36**	.46**	.38**
Job	.39**	.33**	.14	.32**	.11	.03
Advancement	.44**	.35**	.16	.15	.12	.16
Friends' attitudes	.24**	.33**	.04	.20*	.15*	.04
Pay	.14	.28**	.12	−.02	.15*	.03
Job freedom	.46**	.40**	.40**	.04	.08	.10
Family attitudes	.23*	.17**	.01	.26**	.17*	−.03
Job security	.10	.02	.16	.15	.00	−.02

* Significant at the .05 level.
** Significant at the .01 level.

positively related to perceived leader consideration. Of the 24 correlations, 14 are significant at the .01 level, and one at the .05 level. The strongest correlations at the .01 level between consideration and satisfaction were concerned with satisfaction with company and satisfaction with job freedom. The weakest relationship appeared to be satisfaction with job security; although positively correlated with consideration in all firms, it did not approach significance.

In general, then, hypothesis 1 may be said to be confirmed, in that a positive relationship between perceived leader consideration and subordinate role satisfactions was found in all three companies studied, although the magnitudes of the correlations varied widely. Specifically, the correlations for the air frame company were rather consistently lower than the other two companies. This finding will be discussed in more detail below.

Hypothesis 2

Table 3 summarizes the interactions between structure and consideration for the eight satisfaction measures in each company. Significant F values were obtained in only five cases. Since hypothesis 2 specified that there would be a significant interaction between the two independent variables, the findings fail to support the hypothesis. Because all five of the significant interactions were obtained from the same firm, the possibility remained that hypothesis 2 might be supported for that organization.

To learn the nature of these interactions the ANOVA cell means for the satisfaction scores were examined, and graphs of these are presented in Figure 2. These graphs show that the mean satisfaction scores increased as structure increased in all five cases of high consideration, but no clear pattern of relationships between satisfaction and structure is apparent with low consideration.

To determine whether the curves for the high consideration groups in Figure 2 were significant, eta coefficients were computed for each, and the following results were obtained:

Measure of satisfaction with	Eta coefficient
Company	.430
Advancement	.504
Job freedom	.386
Family attitudes	.475
Job security	.390
$N = 43$	

It is clear that with high consideration condition there is a significant and positive curvilinear relationship between structure and satisfaction, in all five cases.

Table 2 shows that structure was also found to have a significant positive linear relationship to four of the eight satisfaction scores for the total sample of the refining company. After computing eta correlations for the high consideration group, three of the four relationships between structure and satisfaction scores that were not linearly correlated for the

TABLE 3
ANOVA Interactions Between Structure and Consideration—
4 Degrees of Freedom

	F values		
Satisfaction measures	Refining company	Business machine company	Air frame company
Company	2.5*	1.6	0.1
Job	1.5	1.5	1.6
Advancement	3.6**	1.7	0.9
Friends' attitudes	1.4	1.0	0.7
Pay	1.5	1.4	1.1
Job freedom	4.3**	0.5	0.7
Family attitudes	3.4*	2.2	0.9
Job security	3.3*	1.0	0.2

* Significant at the .05 level.
** Significant at the .01 level.

Significant Interactions Between Consideration and Structure
for Refining Company

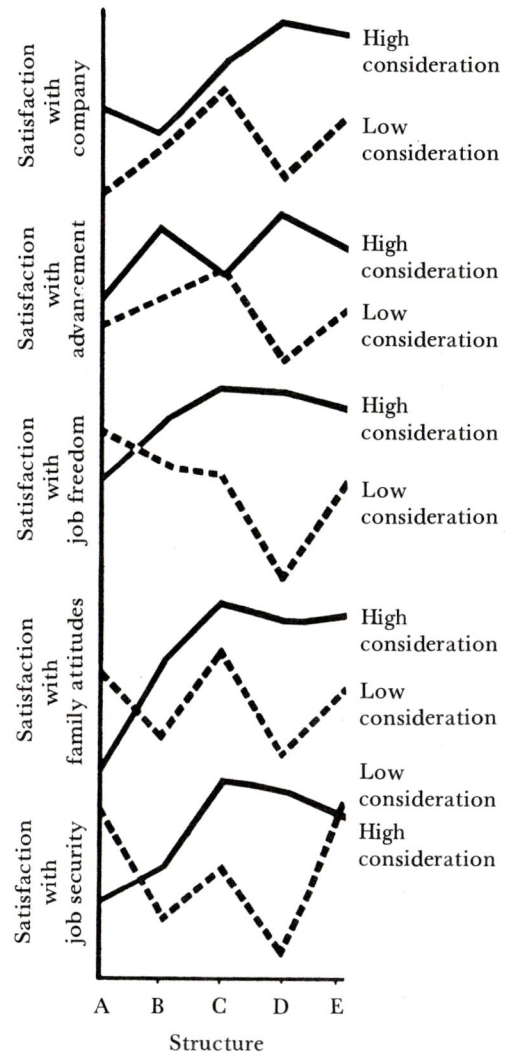

refining company—advancement, job freedom, job security—were curvi-linearly related in the high consideration group. In this company, there-fore, contrary to the hypothesis suggested by Fleishman and Harris (1962), when the entire sample was treated, structure was significantly related to four of the eight satisfaction scores. Furthermore, under conditions of high consideration structure also showed a positive curvilinear relationship to three of the other four satisfaction scores.

In the total samples of the other two companies—business machine and air frame—structure had a significant linear relationship to only four of the eight satisfaction scores in the business machine company, and to only one of the eight satisfaction scores in the air frame company (Table 2). Furthermore, since none of the F values for the interaction between structure and consideration in the ANOVAs were significant in these two companies, no definitive relationship emerged under conditions of either high or low consideration.

The data not only fail to support hypothesis 2 in all three companies, but suggest its opposite in one company; that is, structure is not found to have a significant negative relationship to any satisfaction score, and is found to have positive significant relationships to some satisfaction scores in either total sample, or with high consideration.

DISCUSSION

Although the perceived consideration of the leader is related to satisfaction of role expectations of subordinates, the present study showed rather wide differences in the magnitude of the relationships from company to company and between classes of role satisfactions. That is, this study supports the position that leadership behavior has differential effects of different classes of role satisfactions, and under different organizational climates.

Although there is no empirical basis for determining why the relationships between consideration and role satisfaction were generally low in the air frame company, some speculation is possible. First, the possibility was considered that the distribution of the scores was restricted, reducing the chances of obtaining significant relationships. However, a comparison of the means and the standard deviations of the scores for all the variables (Table 4) indicated no significant differences among the three companies. Because the air frame company was a defense contractor, the task assignments and the satisfactions associated with work might have been more determined by specific contractual arrangements than by the behavior of immediate superiors. Government contracts specified not only the performance requirements of the end product, but also many of the management practices and control techniques that the company must follow in carrying out the contract. For example, the government contract required critical path methods of scheduling and control, which clearly resulted in increased formalization of task assignments and limited the supervisor's ability to make demands on subordinates that were not consistent with task requirements. Such formalization may have negated the effects of varying amounts of consideration by preventing superiors from exercising arbitrary authority, or by increasing acceptance by subordinates of unreasonable or illegitimate demands.

A second unexpected finding was the generally positive relationships between initiating structure and role satisfaction, which was most evident in the business machine company, and least evident in the air frame company. If indeed the formalization resulting from the government contract served to structure the environment of the respondents, then it is not surprising that the amount of initiating structure exhibited by superiors in the air frame company would bear little relationship to the satisfactions of subordinates, for initiating structure could well have been viewed as redundant with the existing formalization resulting from the government contract, or merely as unnecessary to clarify the requirements that subordinates were expected to meet.

In the other two companies the finding might be explained by the differences in this study's population as compared with the previous populations studied with the initiating structure measure. Fleishman and Harris (1962) worked with low-skilled blue-collar workers in an industrial plant, while this study's populations were predominantly made up of engineers and technicians. Perhaps highly technically trained personnel prefer leadership which provides for clear definition of role relationships and clear specification of work methodology.

Physical science training emphasizes the need for careful methodological specifications before engaging in engineering or research activities. Consequently, it is plausible that as a result of their previous training, the respondents in the business machine company and the refining company preferred orderly, systematic leadership behavior that provided for clear definition of policies and ground rules in the work environment to one of relative ambiguity.

This conclusion is consistent with Baumgartel's (1957) finding that employees in research and development laboratories preferred democratic leadership to laissez faire styles, and with the studies by Filley and Grimes

TABLE 4
Means and Standard Deviations of Structure, Consideration, and Satisfaction Measures for Three Companies

	Air frame company		Refining company		Business machine company	
	Mean	Standard deviation	Mean	Standard deviation	Mean	Standard deviation
Structure	37.59	8.20	37.67	7.44	38.87	8.51
Consideration	39.25	9.71	40.75	8.17	40.53	8.30
Satisfaction measures						
Company	47.25	6.16	46.53	5.59	47.01	7.42
Job	14.18	2.86	13.80	2.61	13.10	5.20
Advancement	12.75	2.89	12.02	2.74	11.97	5.48
Friends' attitudes	13.51	2.00	12.57	2.37	13.15	3.02
Pay	12.77	2.32	11.41	2.24	11.61	2.56
Job freedom	13.69	2.63	14.09	2.59	13.97	3.38
Family attitudes	13.72	2.35	13.42	2.04	13.65	2.47
Job security	13.59	1.97	13.64	2.10	14.44	2.68

(1967) and Vollmer (1960) which showed that skilled workers and organizational cosmopolitans sought greater clarification of policies and rules than less skilled workers or organization locals. It is also consistent with Pelz's (1967) conclusion that highly autonomous scientists and engineers in development laboratories experienced less stimulation and became less interested in their work when their efforts were loosely coordinated with others than when they were moderately coordinated, and that productivity was higher when goals were set in conjunction with their colleagues and superiors (Pelz and Andrews, 1966; Pelz, 1967). Furthermore, Engel (1969) found that physicians experienced more autonomy in a moderately bureaucratic setting than in a nonbureaucratic or highly bureaucratic one. Finally, Wigdor (1969) found that boss structure, consideration, technical competence, and influence were positively related to both satisfaction and performance of cosmopolitans, but not related to satisfaction or performance of locals.

Initiating structure was not linearly related to satisfaction with freedom in any of the three companies (Table 1). Thus, while structure may not enhance or restrict freedom, it can be expected to make the environment less ambiguous, and appears to be more satisfying to higher occupational status employees.

In addition to differences in occupational status, the population studied differed from that of Fleishman and Harris (1962) in that the intrinsic aspects of their work were probably more interesting and enjoyable. Perhaps initiating structure reduced role ambiguity generally, but under conditions of unpleasant work, role ambiguity permits subordinates to exert less effort and not be held accountable for low levels of performance. When work is not intrinsically satisfying, one would expect increased resentment and dissatisfaction as the imposition of deadlines and structure increases. Employees of high occupational levels are less likely to have highly programmed, routine, repetitive tasks than semiskilled or skilled laborers; therefore it is not surprising that they would respond more favorably to initiating structure than do employees in lower level occupations.

One might speculate about the relationships between the dimensions of leader behavior and satisfaction under various conditions of organizationl formalization and occupational level or intrinsic job interest. The above interpretations of the findings suggest a two-by-two matrix which yields four combinations of formalization and occupational level. This matrix is presented in Figure 3.

If the degree of formalization serves as a constraint on the magnitude of the relationship between leader behavior and role satisfaction, and if the occupational level or intrinsic satisfaction associated with the job determine the sign of the relationship between structure and role satisfaction, then one could predict differential relationships between the two dimensions of leader behavior and role satisfaction, depending on the cell in which the respondent is located. Specifically, it is predicted that in cell number one there would be low positive relationships between the two dimensions of leader behavior and role satisfaction. Here initiating structure would serve to reduce role ambiguity, and consideration would serve to increase the pleasantness of the environment of the respondent. However, the effect of both leader dimensions would be limited by the high degree of formalization.

FIGURE 3
Combinations of Formalization and Occupational Level

	High formalization	Low formalization
High occupational level	1	2
Low occupational level	3	4

Under conditions of low formalization and high occupational level, cell two, positive relationships between both dimensions of leader behavior and role satisfaction are predicted, and the magnitudes of these relationships would be higher than those of cell number one, where formalization is high. Under conditions of cell three, high formalization–low occupational level, a low negative relationship between structure and role satisfaction and a low positive relationship between consideration and role satisfaction is predicted. That is, at low occupational levels, structure would be perceived as a form of external control, and consideration would be seen as a form of supportive supervision. However, since in cell three organizational formalization is high, the effects of leader behavior would be restricted, and therefore the magnitude of relationships between the dimensions of leader behavior and role satisfaction would be low. Under conditions of low formalization and low occupational level, cell four, the same relationships as predicted for cell three are predicted, but with higher magnitudes. The higher magnitudes would be a function of the low amount of formalization which permits the leader to have more discretionary control and greater effect on the behavior and role satisfactions of his subordinates.

Clearly the above predictions are speculative, resulting from post hoc interpretations of findings. However, they are believed to be sufficiently important to warrant the extra effort required to collect data on occupational level and organization formalization when studying leadership behavior in future investigations.

REFERENCES

Argyle, Michael, G. Gardner, and F. Cioffi. 1958. "Supervisory methods related to productivity, absenteeism and labor turnover." *Human Relations*, 11: 23-40.

Bales, Robert F. 1953. "The equilibrium problem in small groups." In Talcott Parsons, Robert F. Bales, and Edward A. Shils (eds.), Working Papers in the Theory of Action: 111-161. Glencoe, Ill.: Free Press.

Bass, Bernard M., and Edward A. Dunteman. 1963. "Behavior in groups as a function of self-interaction, and task orientation." *Journal of Abnormal and Social Psychology*, 66: 419-428.

Bass, Bernard M., Edward A. Dunteman, R. Frye, R. Vidulich, and H. Wambach. 1963. "Staff interaction and task orientation inventory scores associated with overt behavior and personality factors." *Educational Psychology Measurements*, 23: 101-106.

Baumgartel, Howard. 1956. "Leadership, motivations, and attitudes in research laboratories." *Journal of Social Issues*, 12: 24-31.

———. 1957. "Leadership style as a variable in research administration." *Administrative Science Quarterly*, 2: 344-360.

Berelson, B., and Gary Steiner. 1964. *Human Behavior*. New York: Harcourt, Brace, and World.

Blau, Peter M., and W. Richard Scott. 1962. *Formal Organizations*. San Francisco: Chandler.

Borgatta, Edgar F., Robert F. Bales, and Arthur S. Couch. 1954. "Some findings relevant to the great man theory of leadership." *American Sociological Review*, 19: 755-759.

Comrey, Andrew L., J. Pfiffner, and Wallace S. High. 1954. *Factors Influencing Organizational Effectiveness*. Los Angeles: University of Southern California.

Danielson, L.E., and Norman R.F. Maier. 1957. "Supervisory problems in decision making." *Personnel Psychology*, 10: 169-180.

Dunteman, Edward A., and Bernard M. Bass. 1963. "Supervisory and engineering success associated with self, interaction, and task orientation scores." *Personnel Psychology*, 16: 13-21.

Engel, Gloria V. 1969. "The effect of bureaucracy on the professional autonomy of the physician." *Journal of Health and Social Behavior*, 10: 30-41.

Etzioni, Amitai. 1961. *A Comparative Analysis of Complex Organizations*. Glencoe, Ill.: Free Press.

Filley, Alan C., and Andrew J. Grimes. 1967. *The Bases of Power in Decision Processes*. Working paper, University of Wisconsin.

Fleishman, Edwin A., and Edwin F. Harris. 1962. "Patterns of leadership behavior related to employee grievances and turnover." *Personnel Psychology*, 15: 43-56.

Halpin, Andrew W. 1954. "The leadership behavior and combat performance of aircraft commanders." *Journal of Abnormal and Social Psychology*, 49: 19-22.

Halpin, Andrew W., and B. James Winer. 1957. "A factorial study of the leader behavior descriptions." In Ralph M. Stogdill and Alvin E. Coons (eds.), *Leader Behavior: Its Description and Measurement*:

39-51. Columbus: Bureau of Business Research Monograph 88, Ohio State University.

Harris, Edwin F. 1952. *Measuring Industrial Leadership and Its Implications for Training Supervisors*. Doctoral dissertation, Ohio State University.

Hemphill, John K. 1957. "Leader behavior associated with the administrative reputations of college departments." In Ralph M. Stogdill and Alvin E. Coons (eds.), *Leader Behavior: Its Description and Measurement*: 74-85. Columbus: Bureau of Business Research Monograph 88, Ohio State University.

Indik, B.P., Stanley E. Seashore, and Basil S. Georgopoulos. 1960. "Relationships among criteria of job performance." *Journal of Applied Psychology*, 44: 195-202.

Katz, Daniel, and Robert L. Kahn. 1953. "Leadership practices in relation to productivity and morale." In D. Cartwright and A. Zander (eds.), *Group Dynamics: Research and Theory*: 612-628. Evanston, Ill.: Row and Peterson.

Katz, Daniel, Nathan M. Maccoby, and Nancy C. Morse. 1950. *Productivity, Supervision and Morale in an Office Situation*. Ann Arbor: Survey Research Center, University of Michigan.

Korman, Abraham K. 1966. "Consideration, initiating structure, and organizational criteria—a review." *Personnel Psychology*, 19: 349-361.

Likert, Rensis. 1961. *New Patterns of Management*. New York: McGraw-Hill.

Moore, J.V. 1953. Factor Analytic Comparisons of Superior and Subordinate Ratings of Same NCO Supervisors. Working paper, U.S. Air Force Human Resources Research Center, Technical Report.

Moore, J.V., and R.G. Smith, Jr. 1952. Aspects of Non-Commissioned Officer Leadership. Working paper, U.S. Air Force Human Resources Research Center, Technical Report No. 52-53.

Oaklander, Harold, and Edwin A. Fleishman. 1964. "Patterns of leadership related to organizational stress in hospital settings." *Administrative Science Quarterly*, 8: 520-532.

Parsons, Talcott. 1951. *The Social System*. Glencoe, Ill.: Free Press.

Patchen, Martin. 1960. "Absence and employee feeling about fair treatment." *Personnel Psychology*, 13: 349-360.

Pelz, Donald A. 1967. "Creative tensions in the research and development climate." *Science*, 157: 160-165.

Pelz, Donald A., and Frank M. Andrews. 1966. *Scientists in Organizations*. New York: Wiley.

Seeman, Melvin. 1960. *Social Status and Leadership: The Case of the School Executive*. Columbus: Bureau of Education Research, Ohio State University.

Spector, A.J., R.A. Clark, and A.S. Glickman. 1960. "Supervisory characteristics and attitudes of subordinates." *Personnel Psychology*, 13: 301-316.

Stogdill, Ralph M. 1960. *Manual for Job Description and Job Expectation Questionnaire*. Columbus: Bureau of Business Research, Ohio State University.

Stogdill, Ralph M., and Alvin E. Coons (eds.). 1957. *Leader Behavior: Its*

Description and Measurement. Columbus: Bureau of Education Research Monograph 88, Ohio State University.

Stogdill, Ralph M., and Caroll L. Shartle. 1955. *Methods in the Study of Administrative Leadership.* Columbus: Bureau of Business Research, Ohio State University.

Stouffer, Samuel A. 1949. *The American Soldier, I.* Princeton, N.J.: Princeton University Press.

Vollmer, H.M. 1960. *Employee Rights and the Employment Relationship.* Berkeley: University of California Press.

Wigdor, Lawrence A. 1969. *Effectiveness of Various Management and Organizational Characteristics on Employee Satisfaction and Performance as a Function of the Employee's Need for Independence.* Doctoral dissertation, City University of New York.

Edward E. Lawler III and J. Richard Hackman are in the Department of Administrative Sciences, Yale University. The authors would like to thank H. Elston, M. Nunes, and R. Breck for their cooperation with the study. Wendy Silin deserves special mention for her help with the data analysis. This article appeared in the Journal of Applied Psychology, *1969, Vol. 53, No. 6, pp. 467-471. Copyright © 1969 by the American Psychological Association. Reprinted by permission.*

Impact of Employee Participation in the Development of Pay Incentive Plans: A Field Experiment

EDWARD E. LAWLER III and J. RICHARD HACKMAN

Literally thousands of different pay incentive plans have been developed and used in an effort to increase the motivation of employees in work organizations. These plans have tried to motivate a number of different behaviors: productivity, sales, cost reduction, job attendance, etc. They also have differed widely in form: some have used individual incentives, others have provided rewards on a group or organization-wide basis; some have been based on small units of behavior while others have been based on relatively long-term performance.

A good deal of research has attempted to determine the relative effectiveness of different kinds of incentive plans. For example, group plans have been compared with individual plans and bonus plans have been compared with salary increase plans. The results suggest that these characteristics of plans do affect their success (see, e.g., Opshal & Dunnette, 1966; Rothe, 1960; Viteles, 1953). Nevertheless, it is striking to note the number of instances in which an identical plan is successful in one situation but unsuccessful in another (e.g., Whyte, 1955). Apparently the success of pay incentive plans is determined by more than just the operating mechanics of the plans themselves.

Virtually no research has been done to identify the nonmechanistic factors that are important in determining the success of pay plans. The present study attempts to determine the impact of one such nonmechanistic factor on the success of a pay plan. Specifically, this study examines how the way a pay plan is developed and implemented influences its effectiveness.

Previous research (e.g., Coch & French, 1948) suggests several reasons why the way a plan is developed and introduced may be crucial in determining how successful it is.

If a pay plan is to be successful it is important that all the participants understand it, be committed to it, and believe that it will be administered fairly. Clearly, all of these factors can be influenced strongly by the way the plan is developed and introduced. A pay plan that is developed by a mistrusted management and imposed upon workers is not likely to be understood by employees, nor are the workers likely to be committed to its success. On the other hand, a plan that is participatively developed by workers is very likely to be understood by them and they are more likely to be committed to its success. The plan also is likely to be appropriate to the situation in which the workers find themselves. The basic hypothesis of the study therefore is: pay incentive programs will be more effective if they are participatively developed than if they are imposed upon a group of employees by management. It should be noted here that there is no intention to indicate that just because a pay plan is participatively developed it will be successful. It seems unlikely that any plan will work if it is not set up properly and administered well, even if it is participatively developed.

METHOD

Research Strategy

The basic hypothesis of the study was tested in a field experiment. The experimental approach was chosen because it allows the causal impact of the experimental factor (in this case, participative development of the pay plan) to be assessed with relatively little ambiguity. The study was done in a field setting to ensure that the manipulation would be realistic and important to Ss and to increase the likelihood that the results would be generalizable to other field settings.

Research Site and Subjects

The research was conducted in a small company that provides building maintenance services on a contract basis. The Ss were part-time employees of the company, who clean buildings during the evening. Most Ss worked 4 hours a night. Prior to the study, the company had experienced extremely high rates of absenteeism and turnover among these employees.

The Ss worked in groups ranging in size from 2 to 25. There were about 15 such groups in the company at the time of the study. Each group was responsible for doing all the cleaning work in one building. Although the groups did similar work, they were highly autonomous. The employees always reported for work at the building they were to clean and never came to the company offices. Because of this there was virtually no contact between employees in different work groups.

The Ss tended to have very low educational levels, and most were members of minority groups. A number of them were illiterate. Approximately half the Ss were women, many of whom were housewives during the day. For most of the male Ss, the maintenance work was a second job. The Ss ranged in age from 16 to over 70.

Procedure

Nine work groups were involved in the experiment. Three designed their own incentive plans (the participative groups), two had incentive plans imposed on them (the imposed groups), two talked with the researchers but their pay plans were not changed, and two received no treatment at all (the control groups). There were no apparent differences among the groups assigned to the different treatment conditions. The groups all worked in comparable buildings, and the members of the different groups were similar demographically (e.g., age, education, experience, and social class).

Participative groups

Three groups (of 10, 9, and 8 members) were selected as participative experimental groups. Both of the authors met with one of the groups to help the employees develop an incentive plan, and each of the authors met separately with one of the other two groups. Both researchers worked with one of the groups, so that they would be able to behave in similar ways with the groups they were handling on an individual basis.

In all cases the researchers were introduced to the employees during regular working hours by a member of top management. The manager told the employees that the company was concerned about high rates of absenteeism, and expressed his hope that the employees would work with the researchers in developing an appropriate plan for rewarding good attendance.

The manager then left and the researcher opened the discussion by emphasizing that it was his objective to help the employees develop a plan and not to tell them what kind of plan they should develop. In all three groups an extensive discussion followed this introduction. During the initial phases of the discussion the workers expressed a great deal of mistrust of the researcher and they displayed considerable hostility toward both the researcher and the company. They continually demanded to know what kind of plan the company wanted them to develop, and they asked why the researcher was interested in working with them. The researcher allowed the initial discussion to continue for about 45 minutes, at which point he asked the employees to talk things over among themselves and said that he would be back the next night to continue the discussion. The employees then returned to their work and the researcher left.

For all three groups the second meeting resulted in much more progress than did the first. Although still suspicious of the motives of the company and the researcher, the employees began to discuss what might constitute an acceptable plan. Much of this discussion focused on how large the bonus should be. During the discussion the researcher took on the role of a resource person for the group. At no time did he suggest a plan, although if he was asked about a specific idea he did react to it by stating a few general principles about what makes for successful pay incentive plans (e.g., it is important to relate pay to behavior). One group decided to ask for a very large amount ("since the company will cut whatever we ask for in half anyway"); the other two groups seemed more responsible and settled on dollar amounts that were less than the company had originally anticipated offering.

By the third meeting in one group and the fourth in the others, a plan had been developed and agreed to by all group members. The three plans that were developed by the groups did show some important differences. Two groups wanted their bonus to be computed on a weekly basis, while the other group wanted a monthly bonus. There were also differences in the size of bonuses requested and in the number of days of sick leave that should be allowed. The researchers presented the plans to management, and they all were quickly accepted with minor alterations. The alterations involved adjustment of the amount of the bonuses so that they would be equivalent for all three groups and specification of what would constitute an "excused" absence from work.

As finally instituted, all plans offered cash bonuses of about $2.50 per week for perfect attendance. In one plan the bonuses were to be computed and paid at the end of each month, while the other two plans were on a weekly basis. When the plans were instituted, a manager of the company returned to each group to answer any final questions and to explain why the changes had been made in the original proposals of the work groups. He did not ask them to approve the changes formally.

Imposed groups

Plans identical to those developed by the employees in the participative condition were imposed by the company on two other groups ($N = 13$; $N = 26$). One group received the weekly plan and the other received the monthly plan.

The same manager who had worked with the researchers in the participative condition instituted the plans in these groups. Accompanied by one of the researchers, he met with the groups and explained why a bonus plan was being instituted and how it was to operate. He spent considerable time with each of the groups, and appeared to do an adequate job explaining the plans and showing the employees how they personally would benefit if they came to work more regularly.

Control groups

The researchers visited two other groups ($N = 9$; $N = 8$) and talked with these employees at length about incentive plans and about problems of absenteeism and turnover. It was stressed in these meetings that the researchers were interested in studying how people react to wages and that the company was concerned about the current high rates of absenteeism. No changes were made in the pay plans of these two groups. In two other groups ($N = 26$; $N = 8$) no changes in the pay plans took place and the researchers did not meet with the employees, but the attendance of the groups was monitored.

RESULTS

Results are presented in Figures 1 and 2. The data are expressed in terms of the percentage of an employee's scheduled work week that he actually worked. For most employees the work week was 20 hours long. Thus, if an employee worked 10 hours, he was scored as working 50% of his scheduled hours; if he worked 15 hours, he was scored as 75%. Figure 1 shows the mean percentage of scheduled hours actually worked for Ss in the three participative groups. Figure 2 shows analogous data for Ss in the two groups that had incentive plans imposed on them. In both figures, data are presented for 12 weeks before the plans were instituted and for the first 16 weeks after the plans went into effect.

Before the incentive plans were introduced, the average employee in the participative groups worked 88% of his scheduled hours; after the plan went into effect, the average employee worked 94% of his scheduled hours. This before-after difference was tested for statistical significance by a median test yielding a chi-square of 9.35 ($p < .001$).

As is shown in Figure 2, there was no improvement in attendance for groups in which the identical incentive plans were imposed by management. Before the imposed plans were instituted, the average employee worked 83% of his scheduled hours; in the 16 weeks after the plans were put into effect, the figure remained at 83%.

Data gathered from the control groups (whose pay plans were unchanged) showed no significant changes during the period of the study.

Thus, the data show that employee attendance improved only in those

FIGURE 1

Mean attendance of the participative groups for the 12 weeks
before the incentive plan and the 16 weeks after the plan
(Attendance is expressed in terms of the percentage of hours
scheduled to be worked that were actually worked.)

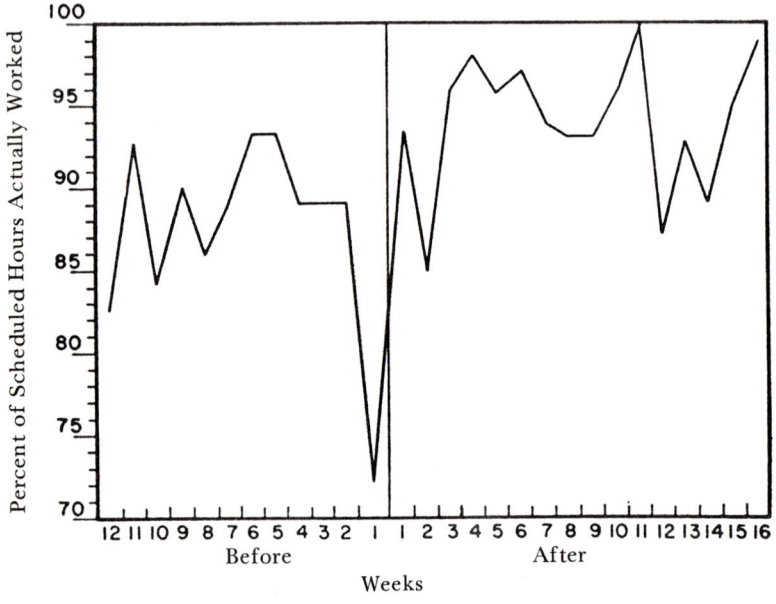

groups that participatively developed their own incentive plans. Neither
the incentive plan alone nor participation and discussion alone yielded any
changes in attendance.

DISCUSSION

The results of this study strongly support the notion that attention to
the technical characteristics of a pay plan alone (i.e., the mechanics of its
design and administration) may be insufficient to ensure the success of the
plan. Indeed, the data suggest that participation in the development and
implementation of a plan may have more of an impact on the effectiveness
of a plan than the mechanics of the plan itself.

Why should participation be so important to the success of a pay
incentive plan? One possibility is that participation can improve the
quality of decisions that are made (Vroom, 1964). Thus, it could be
argued that the participatively developed plans in this study were uniquely
suited to the groups that developed them—but somehow inappropriate for
the other groups on which the plans were imposed. This explanation seems

FIGURE 2

Mean attendance of the imposed groups for the 12 weeks
before the incentive plan and the 16 weeks after the plan
(Attendance is expressed in terms of the percentage of
the hours scheduled to be worked that were actually worked.)

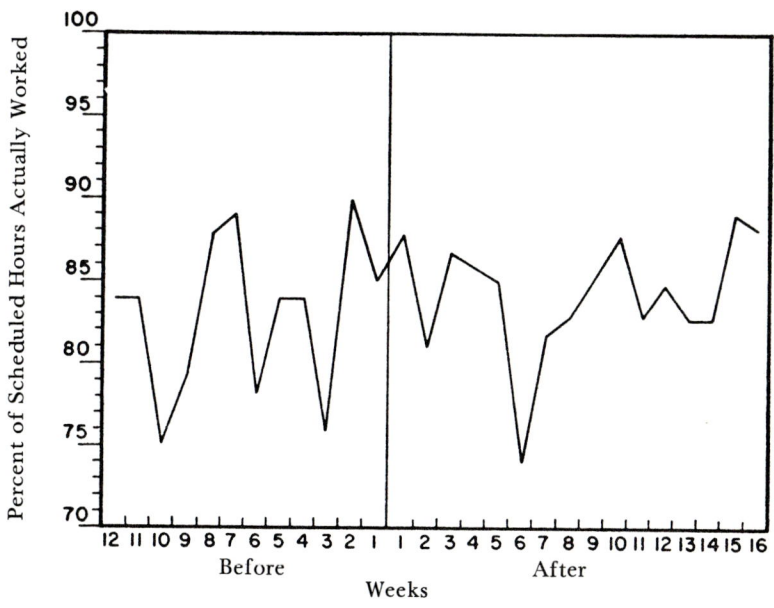

unlikely in the present study, however, since all the work groups in the
company were highly similar and there was nothing especially unique
about the plans developed by the three participative groups.

It did seem that members of the participative groups more fully understood the plans than did members of the imposed groups. Despite a
carefully rehearsed introductory talk given by the company manager, the
imposed groups did not receive as much information about the plan as did
the participative groups. They did not feel as free to ask questions about
the plan as did the participative groups, and they did not have as much
time to think about questions or to ask them as did the participative
groups. The imposed groups received all their information about the plan
in one session, whereas members of each participative group talked
together about the plan for several hours over a week or two—possibly
increasing their understanding of the plan and its implications.

It also appeared that the participative groups were more committed to
the success of the plans than were the imposed groups. There was evidence
that the plans were viewed as "just another attempt by management to
exploit us" by some members of the imposed groups. By participating in
the development of the plans, many members of the participative groups

appeared to become more trusting of management's intentions to administer the plans fairly. Their pride in "owning" the plans, coupled with the increased trust of management, may have enhanced considerably the desire of the participative employees to cooperate in making the plans a success.

A final comment may be in order about the characteristics of the *S* population studied. The employees were, almost without exception, of a low socioeconomic class, and all were working at low-level jobs. Thus, it is perhaps surprising that they responded to the opportunity for participation as well as they did. For most of them it was the first time they had ever had an opportunity to contribute meaningfully to any decision making about their jobs. There was hostility and suspicion at the outset of the experiment. Yet, after the initial discussion with the researchers, a substantial number of the employees began to respond to the challenge of developing a viable incentive plan—and they ultimately came up with plans that would have to be considered technically adequate. Thus it appears that—if a researcher or a manager is willing to deal with some initial hostility and suspicion—it should be possible to involve most employees in meaningful decision making about their jobs. And, if the results of this study have generalizability, the payoff for both the employees and the organization should make the effort well worthwhile.

FOOTNOTES

1. This before-and-after comparison essentially uses each participative group as its own control group. This was done because the initial differences between the attendance levels of the imposed and the participative groups make post-comparisons between these groups artificial.

REFERENCES

Coch, L., & French, J.R.P., Jr. Overcoming resistance to change. *Human Relations*, 1948, 1, 512-532.

Opshal, R.L., & Dunnette, M.D. The role of financial compensation in industrial motivation. *Psychological Bulletin*, 1966, 66, 94-118.

Rothe, H.F. Does higher pay bring higher production? *Personnel*, 1960, 37, 20-27.

Viteles, M.S. *Motivation and morale in industry*. New York: Norton, 1953.

Vroom, V.H. *Work and motivation*. New York: Wiley, 1964.

Whyte, W.F. *Money and motivation: An analysis of incentives in industry*. New York: Harper, 1955.

Lynn R. Anderson is at the University of Illinois and Fred E. Fiedler is Professor of Psychology at the University of Washington. This article appeared in the Journal of Applied Psychology, *1964, Vol. 48, No. 4, pp. 227-236. Copyright © 1964 by the American Psychological Association. Reprinted by permission.*

This work was supported by Contract NR 177-472, Nonr 1834(36), "Group and organizational factors influencing group creativity," between the Office of Naval Research (Group Psychology Branch) and the University of Illinois (Fred E. Fiedler, Lawrence M. Stolurow, and Harry C. Triandis, Co-Investigators). It represents Technical Report No. 7. The authors are grateful for the assistance of Doyle W. Bishop, William Higgs, Lorand Szalay, Lewis Rambo, Nancy K. Barron, Patricia Chesebro, L.C. Anderson, Joseph E. McGrath, James W. Julian, and Willem A.T. Meuwese, as well as the staff of the Naval Science Department, University of Illinois.

The Effect of Participatory and Supervisory Leadership on Group Creativity

LYNN R. ANDERSON and FRED E. FIEDLER

The present study compares two types of leadership conditions; namely, the more usual "participatory" situation in which the chairman of the group contributes freely to the group discussion, and a "supervisory" condition in which the leader acts as the coordinator and evaluator of the group's problem solving attempts.

The supervisory condition of leadership, although here artificially created, is not at all uncommon in real life. A director of a research program, or the supervisor of a project, frequently assigns problem solving and development tasks to a group of subordinates who then report back to him at appropriate intervals to obtain further guidance and critique. This latter experimental condition is, thus, also related to some extent to the studies by Parnes and Meadow (1959) and Meadow, Parnes, and Reese (1959) which have shown that the creative process in groups is enhanced if the phases of idea generation and idea evaluation are separated in time. We have sought here to separate these two aspects of the creative process in the supervisory leadership condition by assigning them to different members of the group, i.e., the leader's responsibility. was mainly one of evaluation, while only the members were responsible for the generation of creative ideas.

There has been very little research on participatory and supervisory leadership. Most notable is a study of small group discussion by Hare (1953) which showed that participatory leaders had more influence than supervisory leaders, and that they were also more effective in increasing intragroup agreement.

As suggested by Parnes' work (1959) as well as by Hare's study (1953), the quality of group performance was expected to be higher under supervisory leadership. On the other hand, groups in the participatory leadership condition were expected to generate a higher quantitative performance score due to having an additional group member contributing ideas.

The present study sought to extend these findings by comparing two types of leader-member interactions and by investigating performance on a wider range of creative tasks. The study was also designed to explore further the conditions in group processes under which leader or member abilities contribute optimally to group performance (Fiedler and Meuwese, 1963).

METHOD

Subjects

A total of 120 men, enrolled in the Naval Reserve Officers Training Corps (NROTC) program at the University of Illinois, participated in this study. Men in this program are selected on the basis of intelligence and aptitude tests, and they tend to be above the average college student in intelligence and academic performance.

The study was based on 30 four-man groups. The leaders were senior midshipmen enrolled in a Naval Leadership Course. The group members were freshmen and sophomores in the NROTC program. Leaders as well as group members were given to understand that the study constituted part of their regular training and that their performance would be evaluated and made part of their record.

Pretests

Intelligence tests. A short 15-item vocabulary test and a 15-item information test were administered and scored before the study. These tests, published by the Psychological Corporation,[1] are timed subtests of a larger general intelligence scale (*The Multi-Aptitude Test*) and are considered adequate indices of intellectual functioning for the purposes of this study.

Navy ROTC ratings. Regular assessments of senior midshipmen by their Navy instructors as well as by their peers were available. These consisted of the usual effectiveness ratings which asked each of the 30 seniors to judge each other senior on leadership ability and potential ability to perform a variety of leadership tasks. These ratings also contained friendship choices, e.g., "If you wanted to talk to someone about an important personal problem, which of your classmates would you prefer to consult?"

Pretest of creativity. All leaders were given individual tests parallel to those which the groups were to receive later on. These tests consisted of (a) writing three stories from a Thematic Apperception Test (TAT) card projected on a screen, (b) listing unusual uses for some common household objects (see Guilford, 1954), (c) listing creative solutions to a problem dealing with a summer recreation project (see Triandis, Bass, Ewen, and Mikesell, 1962), and (d) listing arguments (both pro and con) concerning a controversial military leadership award to be given to decisive war-time leadership successes achieved by commanders acting against the order of their superiors.[2]

Experimental Manipulation

Immediately prior to the experiment the leaders of the groups in the participatory and supervisory condition were called aside and given separate instructions.

The 15 leaders in the *participatory condition* were told that they were to be chairmen of their groups, and that it was their responsibility to obtain maximum task performance. They might do this in any way they wished, including, of course, active participation in the group discussion.

The 15 leaders in the *supervisory condition* were instructed to "take a role" which they would frequently have to assume later as Navy officers, i.e., they would supervise the work of others, but they would not actually do the work itself: they could encourage their group members, they could make procedural suggestions, and they could praise or reject ideas which were proposed by their group members, but *under no circumstances* were they to contribute ideas of their own to the solutions of the problems.

Since the group sessions were part of the NROTC course, Navy officers were present in uniform throughout the testing sessions. The presence of these officers plus the fact that the leaders knew they would be evaluated on their performance served to increase the leaders' motivation to have their groups perform well.

Postsession Measures

Immediately following the group sessions, all subjects (*S*s) were given individual questionnaires. These were designed to assess the success of the experimental manipulation and to indicate the reaction of the members to the group tasks and to each other. The *S*s were assured that these data were to be treated confidentially.

Group session evaluations. These were obtained by means of an eight-question, five-point scale asking *S* how he liked his own group and how well he enjoyed the task. For example, the first two items read, "How much did you enjoy being a member of this group?" and "How much did you influence your group's product?"

Group atmosphere scale. All *S*s completed a 17-item bipolar rating scale describing the climate of their group. The items contained such polar adjectives as "friendly-unfriendly," "pleasant-unpleasant" and was scored on an 8-step scale of the semantic differential form (see Fiedler, 1962).

Effectiveness of Experimental Manipulation

Two items were included in the postmeeting questionnaire to determine the extent to which leaders had followed the experimental instructions regarding their role as participatory or supervisory leaders. These two items read: "Did your leader participate in the solution of the problems?" and "Did your leader add ideas to the stories, arguments, and problem solutions?" A comparison of responses of group members showed highly significant differences between the two conditions, and practically no overlap between the two groups ($p < .001$). These results, as well as post-session questionnaire responses obtained from leaders, indicate quite clearly that the experimental manipulation was successful.

CREATIVITY TASKS

Four different types of tasks were utilized to determine the generality of previously obtained findings. Each of these tasks was timed, and all groups worked on them in the same order.

TAT stories. This task consisted of writing two short stories based on TAT Card No. 11. Groups were given 15 minutes in which to complete this assignment. The stories were to be written out, and handed in at the end of the allotted time. This task had been used in previous studies of group creativity and it was here included, in part, as a marker variable, which would provide comparisons with these previous results.

Evaluation of the stories was based on a manual by which four independent judges rated five different categories on a six-point scale (Fiedler, Meuwese and Oonk, 1961). Categories to be rated were (a) originality of title, (b) originality of plot, (c) plot elaboration, (d) expressiveness of language, and (e) suspense and humor. The average intercorrelation among judges was .72. The total qualitative score represents the sum of the ratings of the five categories given to the two stories by the four judges. The correlation of ratings on the two stories for the 30 groups was .43 ($p < .05$). A simple quantitative score was based on the total number of words produced by the group on the two stories. This quantitative score was not, however, independent of the qualitative score as shown by the high correlation ($r = .65$, $p < .01$) between the two scores.

Unusual Uses test. A modification of Guilford's Test (1954) was given with instructions that the groups were to think of unusual uses for two common objects, viz., a wire clothes hanger and a ruler. Ten minutes were allowed for this task.

This task was scored on the basis of how frequently a given "use" or response occurred in any of the 30 groups. Each response was scored from one point (frequent response) to five points (unusual, off-beat or infrequent response) based on a frequency distribution of the occurrence of all of the responses produced by the 30 groups. A repetition of the same response in the same group was scored zero. The total group score represents the sum of the points given to each of the 10 uses which the group listed for each of the two items. The correlation of the two items over the 30 groups was .60 ($p < .01$). Since all but two of the groups completed the answer sheet by providing 10 uses for each item, a quantitative score could not be computed for this task. The obtained score is probably best seen as a qualitative score in that it indicates the degree to which the group was able to produce unusual responses in comparison with the other groups in the experiment.

Argument construction. A third task required the Ss to develop arguments for, as well as against, a controversial military issue. The problem involved the use of a military training program of a very rigorous and dangerous nature which could be expected to result in a relatively high rate of casualties during the training phase, but which would pay off by leading to a relatively low death rate during actual battle conditions.

After a 5-minute period in which the group members worked individually on the problem, group members were given another 5 minutes to develop additional arguments jointly, i.e., arguments which differed from those produced by the members individually. The task score was computed by rating the quality of each argument produced by the group and by the individual members on a scale from zero to three points and then summing the ratings. A quantitative score was based on the total number of arguments produced by the group and by the individual members.

Fame and immortality task. The last task was somewhat similar to the third in that the members first worked alone for 5 minutes and then as a group for the remaining 5 minutes. The problem of the task was, "how can a person of average ability achieve fame and immortality even though he does not possess any particular talents?" This task was developed by Triandis, et al., (1962) and was scored by means of Triandis' manual. The qualitative score was the average evaluation of each of the suggested answers while the quantitative score was a tally of solutions produced. The split-half correlation of the qualitative score for the 30 groups was .89 ($p < .001$).

As shown by Table 1, the scores from different tasks are essentially uncorrelated. The relations between the Fame quality scores and TAT quantity and Fame quantity scores in the supervisory condition, and the negative relations between the Fame quantity and the Unusual Uses (quality) scores seem to reflect condition as well as task differences.

RESULTS

Supervisory versus Participatory Leadership

One of the most important questions asked by this study concerns the comparative effectiveness of the two types of leadership. The results related to this question are presented in Table 2.

As can be seen, the differences on the TAT task were nonsignificant for

TABLE 1
Intercorrelation of Criterion Scores

	1	2	3	4	5	6	7
Supervisory condition[a]							
1. TAT quantitative	65*	−16	33	24	56*	−11	
2. TAT qualitative		−40	46	08	58*	−35	
3. Unusual uses qualitative			−06	26	−41	35	
4. Argument construction quantitative				−26	60*	−17	
5. Argument construction qualitative					−07	23	
6. Fame quantitative						21	
7. Fame qualitative							
Participatory condition[a]							
1. TAT quantitative	64*	09	28	10	11	−25	
2. TAT qualitative		02	12	−04	23	15	
3. Unusual uses qualitative			19	−46	−66*	−06	
4. Argument construction quantitative				−49	−12	15	
5. Argument construction qualitative					24	−03	
6. Fame quantitative						05	
7. Fame qualitative							

[a]$N = 15$.
*$p \leqslant .05$.

both the qualitative and the quantitative scores. On the other hand, the groups working under supervisory leadership yielded significantly better qualitative scores on the Unusual Uses and the Fame and Immortality tasks. The participatory leadership condition led to better quantitative scores on the Argument Construction task.

These results are generally in line with the theoretical expectations based on the work of Parnes (1959) and others. The participatory leader was an extra source of ideas in his group and he was therefore likely to increase the quantitative output of his team. The supervisory leader, on the other hand, could devote his attention to guiding the group and to screening out ideas of low quality.

Leaders' Reactions to the Experimental Conditions

The mean scores of the leaders on the postmeeting questionnaire are presented in Table 3. The three items which discriminated between the two leadership conditions indicated that the participating leader felt he had more influence in the group (Item No. 2), was more relaxed (Item No. 3), and was more satisfied with his own *individual* performance (Item No. 4). However, there were no significant differences between the participating and supervising leaders regarding their satisfaction with the *group product* (Item No. 6). These differences on Items 2, 3, and 4 are probably not a result of motivational differences between the two conditions

TABLE 2
Mean Group Performance Scores for Groups in
Participatory and Supervisory Leadership Conditions

| | Leadership condition | | |
Task	Participatory	Supervisory	p
TAT stories			
Quantitative	11.60	11.00	ns
Qualitative	100.67	95.80	ns
Unusual uses			
Quantitative	—	—	
Qualitative	44.00	49.60	$<.05$
Argument construction			
Quantitative	29.87	27.20	$<.01$
Qualitative	35.20	34.00	ns
Fame problem			
Quantitative	4.73	4.00	ns
Qualitative	2.68	3.91	$<.05$

since leaders in both conditions were equally interested in the tasks (Item No. 5) and they also equally enjoyed being a member of their group (Item No. 1). The fact that the supervising leaders tended to perceive their role as less influential than did leaders who participated directly in the solution of the problems may also explain why these supervisory leaders felt less relaxed in their role than the participating leaders.

A similar analysis of the eight postmeeting questionnaire items for the group members showed no significant differences between conditions on any of the eight items. This negative result is interesting inasmuch as it indicates that the experimental manipulations and the structuring of the groups had very little or no effect on members' satisfaction, tenseness, influence, or enjoyment. Similarly, no differences were found between conditions on the members' rating of the group atmosphere or the members' evaluation of their leader. Although major differences were found between the creativity of groups under the two leadership styles, the morale and satisfaction of the members were apparently not affected by the experimental manipulations.

The Contribution of the Leader to Group Performance

Verbal intelligence. A recent report by Fiedler and Meuwese (1963) showed that the leader's intelligence contributed to group task performance only in groups in which he was accepted by his members or where the

TABLE 3
Mean Score on the Various Postmeeting Instruments

| | Leadership condition | | |
Task	Participatory	Supervisory	p
Postmeeting questionnaire (leaders only)			
1. How much did you enjoy being a member of this group?	3.60	3.80	ns
2. How much did you influence your group's product?	3.67	3.00	$<.05$
3. How relaxed and comfortable did you feel in this group?	4.33	3.53	$<.01$
4. How satisfied are you with your individual contribution?	3.40	2.73	$<.05$
5. Did you find these tasks interesting?	3.20	3.06	ns
6. How satisfied are you, personally, with your group's products?	3.93	3.60	ns
7. Did you feel anxious or tense in this group?	1.53	1.53	ns
8. How well did group members seem to communicate with each other, to understand each other's points?	3.93	3.80	ns
Evaluation of the "group atmosphere"			
By the leader	110.60	107.53	ns
By the members	108.31	107.62	ns
Esteem given to the leader by the group members	110.44	108.67	ns

Note.—A high score indicates high agreement with the item, high evaluation of group atmosphere and high esteem of leader.

group was cohesive. The present study provided an opportunity to explore how the contribution of the leader was affected by our experimentally introduced leader-follower interactions.

Table 4 presents the correlation between the leader's verbal intelligence and the qualitative score on each of the four tasks.[3] It is apparent that the leader's contribution, or his ability to contribute to the task, depends in a large measure on the task itself. Thus, leader intelligence correlated with TAT performance in the participatory condition, but it was uncorrelated, if not indeed negatively related, to group productivity on the Unusual Uses test.

We must here take note of the fact that the TAT story development required a high degree of verbal facility. The participatory leader apparently was able to integrate the flow of *his own* ideas and the ideas contributed by the group members into a consistent and unified plot. The Unusual Uses test, on the other hand, required discreet or isolated responses of high quality. On this task the verbally facile leader was likely to make many suggestions which, in the absence of adequate screening, tended to be of lower quality.

TABLE 4
Correlation of Group Creativity With the Leader's Verbal Intelligence Score and With the Mean of the Group Members' Verbal Intelligence Scores

| | Leadership condition | | | |
| | Participatory[a] | | Supervisory[a] | |
Task	Leader's IQ	Mean of members' IQ	Leader's IQ	Mean of members' IQ
TAT stories	.61**	−.48	−.01	−.59*
Unusual uses	−.40	.14	−.16	.65**
Argument construction	−.19	−.04	.65**	−.18
Fame problem	.25	.22	.03	.36

[a]$N = 15$.
*$p \leqslant .05$.
**$p \leqslant .01$.

In the supervisory condition the leader's verbal intelligence is significantly related to performance only on the Argument Construction task. This task required highly logical and practical solutions rather than extremely unusual or imaginative responses from the group members. Assuming that the intelligent leader is also somewhat more "practical minded," this task then provided an opportunity for him to assess and screen the members' contributions on a more familiar criterion.

Correlations of the sum of the members' verbal intelligence scores and group performance are also presented in Table 4. It should be noted that the significant correlations with the TAT task and the Unusual Uses task were both found in the supervisory condition. This is to be expected since the members' individual abilities should be more important when the leader cannot contribute directly to the solution of the problem. This effect is especially emphasized on these first two tasks when we consider the zero-order correlations of the supervising leader's verbal intelligence and group performance on the same tasks. The negative correlations obtained on the TAT task are of particular interest. They suggest that group members who were especially high in verbal ability produced too many unusual ideas which could not effectively be integrated into one story plot by the leader. Hence, confusion resulted with a correspondingly low group product. However, when these many unusual ideas of the members could be individually utilized without having to be integrated into an overall plot, the highly verbal members produced a better group product. This is seen most clearly on the Unusual Uses task.

A further comparison was made of the group performance under the two conditions when the verbal intelligence of the leader exceeded (or was less than) the intelligence of his group members. For each leader a difference score was computed between his own verbal score and that of his group member with the highest verbal intelligence score. Thus, a high positive "D-score" indicates that the leader was quite high in verbal intelligence when compared to his most intelligent group member, while a negative D-score indicates that the leader was actually less intelligent than his brightest group member. Since a correlation of his D-score and group performance would not account for differences in the absolute level of intelligence of the group or leader, a partial correlation was computed with the level of group intelligence (based on the highest member's score) held constant. These partial correlations are presented in Table 5. The significant positive correlations in the participatory conditions indicate that higher group creativity resulted on two of the four tasks when the leader was relatively brighter than his group members. There was no relationship of the leader's D-score and group performance in the supervisory condition except on the Unusual Uses task. On this particular task the leader who was more intelligent than his group members was actually detrimental to group creativity ($p < .01$).

The overall results from this analysis suggest some interesting differences in abilities which are desirable for effective performance as a participating and supervising leader. It would appear that the participating leader was generally more effective when he was more intelligent than his group members. The supervising leader, however, was apparently less effective on some tasks when he was more intelligent than his group members. This was particularly true on the Unusual Uses task. Here the supervisory leader's relatively greater intelligence might have hindered group creativity because

TABLE 5

Partial Correlations of "D-Score" of Leaders' Intelligence
(Leader IQ Minus Highest Members' IQ) and Group
Performance, With Level of Group IQ Held Constant

	Leadership condition	
Task	Participatory	Supervisory
TAT stories	.73**	.16
Unusual uses	−.28	−.89**
Argument construction	.56*	.11
Fame problem	.32	−.32

*$p \leqslant .05$.
**$p \leqslant .01$

the leader was too practical or critical in accepting wildly unusual and unique uses which received a higher number of points.

Individual creativity tests and group performance. Since each of the 30 leaders had been pretested on tasks which were basically identical or parallel to the four group creativity tasks it seemed reasonable to expect that the scores of the leaders should correlate even more highly with group performance than the more general verbal intelligence measures. This, however, was not the case (Table 6). While the relations under the participatory leadership condition tended to be slightly higher, none of the correlations was significant, and the difference between the two conditions was very slight as far as these relations are concerned. Whether or not these lower relations merely reflect lower reliability of the individual creativity tests is a possibility which needs to be considered in interpreting these results.

Navy ROTC ratings. Table 7 shows the correlations of group performance and the sum of the "buddy ratings" choices received by the leader from each of the other senior midshipmen. Table 7 also shows the correlation of group performance and the evaluations of the 30 leaders made by their NROTC instructors (Military Aptitude Score). Although there was a high correlation of the buddy ratings and the instructor's rating ($r = .65$, $p < .05$) it appears that neither of these scores was an adequate predictor of leadership effectiveness on the creative tasks.

Additional data were also available for the 30 leaders from their aptitude testing in the Naval ROTC program. Included in Table 7 are the correlations of the various aptitude scores and group performance. Here again there appears to be very little relation of the individual aptitude of the leader and group performance. Approximately half of the correlations presented in this table are negative, while about half are positive, and only two correlations were significant. This overall lack of relationship between

---

TABLE 6
Correlation of the Leader's Individual Pretest Score on Each Task and His Group's Performance on That Task

| | Leadership condition | |
Task	Participatory	Supervisory
TAT stories	.35	−.38
Unusual uses	.43	.05
Argument construction	−.39	.11
Fame problem	.10	.08

Note.—No correlation was significant.

TABLE 7
Correlation of the Leader's Aptitude Scores,
Ability Score, Peer Ratings, and Group
Performance

	Leadership condition	
Aptitude	Partici-patory	Super-visory
Leader's Military Aptitude Ratings (by NROTC instructors)		
TAT stories	.19	.13
Unusual uses	.24	−.12
Argument construction	−.08	.09
Fame problem	−.37	.26
Leader's NROTC "Buddy Ratings" (by NROTC classmates)		
TAT stories	−.17	.01
Unusual uses	.40	−.43
Argument construction	−.37	.03
Fame problem	−.48	.34
Mechanical Aptitude (NROTC battery)		
TAT stories	−.25	.26
Unusual uses	.21	−.60*
Argument construction	−.34	−.26
Fame problem	−.17	−.45
Mathematical Aptitude (NROTC battery)		
TAT stories	−.09	.32
Unusual uses	.15	−.38
Argument construction	−.13	−.04
Fame problem	−.02	−.32
Verbal Aptitude (NROTC battery)		
TAT stories	.15	.13
Unusual uses	.01	−.38
Argument construction	−.61*	.57*
Fame problem	.16	−.10

*$p \leq .05$.

the leader's military ability and aptitude and the creative performance of his group points once again to the dangers in generalizing leadership results across situations and task conditions.

DISCUSSION

The results of the present study indicate the very complex relationship between type of leadership and group effectiveness. An understanding of these complexities is central not only to further theoretical development in the study of social relations, but it is also crucial to effective construction of work groups and the identification and training of successful group leaders. More and more the individual finds his occupational as well as his leisure time activities to be part of a team or group effort. His own contributions are measured by his advancement of group goals and, consequently, his personal satisfactions and rewards are distributed according to group accomplishments. The role of the leader thus becomes important in relation to both the final group achievement and the satisfaction and morale of the individual members. Indeed, these two separate leadership functions may represent our best criteria to assess the relative effectiveness of the leader's performance.

The two "styles" of leadership which were selected for study probably represent extremes on one important dimension of leader behavior, viz., the leader's contribution to the group task. General conceptions of leadership are most likely to denote the leader as the most influential member working on the group task. This corresponds to our participatory condition where the leader was allowed to offer his own ideas in the solution of the creative tasks. The polar opposite of this type of leadership is represented by the leader whose responsibilities are solely those of coordination and supervision of subordinate's activities. Such situations are encountered in research, military and industrial settings in which a supervisory or administrative director assigns topics or problems to various task units and coordinates activity among these units but does not himself directly engage in the problem solving efforts of any one unit. Our supervisory leadership condition would seem to parallel this type of organizational structure.

Although most of the results were specific to the creative task, some tentative conclusions can be drawn regarding differences in group performance under participating and supervising leaders. Participatory groups seemed to produce a high quantity of solutions (Argument Construction task) probably because they had one more man who contributed ideas. The supervisory groups, on the other hand, seemed to produce a high quality of group solutions (Unusual Uses task and Fame and Immortality task) possibly as a result of the screening or censoring function of the supervising leader role.

The relation of the leader's individual attributes (i.e., intelligence, attitudes, and special creative aptitudes) to effective group performance was again specific to the group task as well as to the experimental condition. In general, it would appear that these personality characteristics of the leader were more highly relevant to group achievement in the participatory condition. The leader-member interaction here was apparently less formal and perhaps based more on personal relationships. The personality traits of the supervisory leader, on the other hand, seemed to be somewhat less decisive to group creativity than the prescribed demands of his more formal and structured supervisory role.

The study also points to the importance of more carefully identifying the nature of the group task itself. Too little attention and research effort has been given to the structure and organization which the task imposes upon the group. Conversely, it becomes imperative to know those leadership styles and group structures which are most conducive to the solution of a specific task. Such an analysis has been proposed by Fiedler (1963) in a recent paper. Further research exploring the dimension of task structure is now in progress. The four group creativity tasks included in the present experiment exemplify the problems encountered in trying to generalize specific effects of leadership and group structural variables to a wide range of tasks. The results of the present study only confirm the belief that the task domain obviously remains one of the most basic of areas to be methodologically explored and systematized.

An adequate formulation of leadership behavior would, of necessity then, include a statement identifying leader abilities requisite for effective performance in a close and personal participatory role as distinguished from those abilities which bolster an individual's effectiveness in the more formal structure of the supervisory role. Our data show the danger of oversimplifying the leadership problem when these differences in group structure are ignored.

FOOTNOTES

1. Copyright by the Psychological Corporation, New York 17, New York, 1955.

2. This task and the parallel group task were developed by Dr. Lorand Szalay for this study.

3. The performance scores presented in the remaining sections of the paper are the *qualitative* scores derived for each of the four creativity tasks. This score was adopted as the single criterion score because of its closer approximation to current definitions of "creativity," while the quantitative score seems to correspond to what has been called "originality" (Maltzman, 1960).

REFERENCES

Fiedler, F.E. Leader attitudes, group climate, and group creativity. *J. abnorm. soc. Psychol.*, 1962, 65, 308-318.

Fiedler, F.E. A contingency model for the prediction of leadership effectiveness. Technical Report No. 10, 1963, University of Illinois, Group Effectiveness Research Laboratory.

Fiedler, F.E., Bass, A.R., and Fiedler, Judith M. The leader's perception of co-workers, group climate, and group creativity: A cross-validation. Technical Report No. 1, 1961, University of Illinois, Group Effectiveness Research Laboratory.

Fiedler, F.E., London, P., and Nemo, R.S. Hypnotically induced leader attitudes and group creativity. Technical Report No. 11, 1961, University of Illinois, Group Effectiveness Research Laboratory.

Fiedler, F.E., and Meuwese, W.A.T. Leader's contribution to task performance in cohesive and uncohesive groups. *J. abnorm. soc. Psychol.*, 1963, 67, 83-87.

Fiedler, F.E., Meuwese, W.A.T., and Oonk, Sophie. An exploratory study of group creativity in laboratory tasks. *Acta psychol.*, Amsterdam, 1961, 18, 100-119.

Golb, Eileen F., and Fiedler, F.E. A note on psychological attributes related to the score assumed similarity between opposites (ASo). Technical Report No. 12, 1955, University of Illinois, Group Effectiveness Research Laboratory.

Guilford, J.P. Factors in problem-solving. *ARTC Instructors J.*, 1954, 4, 197-204.

Hare, A.P. Small group discussions with participatory and supervisory leadership. *J. abnorm. soc. Psychol.*, 1953, 48, 273-275.

Maltzman, I. On the training of originality. *Psych. Rev.*, 1960, 67, 229-242.

Meadow, A., Parnes, S.J., and Reese, H. Influence of instructions and problem sequence on a creative problem solving test. *J. appl. Psychol.*, 1959, 43, 413-416.

Parnes, S.J., and Meadow, A. Effects of "brainstorming" instructions on creative problem solving on trained and untrained subjects. *J. educ. Psychol.*, 1959, 50, 171-176.

Triandis, H.C., Bass, A.R., Ewen, R.B., and Mikesell, Eleanor H. Team creativity as a function of the creativity of the members. Technical Report No. 6, 1962, University of Illinois, Group Effectiveness Research Laboratory.

Martin Patchen is Professor of Sociology, Purdue University, West LaFayette, Indiana. This article is reprinted with permission from Administrative Science Quarterly, *September 1965, pp. 149-174.*

Labor-Management Consultation at TVA: Its Impact on Employees

MARTIN PATCHEN

In most American industries today, formal conferences between labor and management are limited to discussion of the conditions of work— wages, hours, benefits, seniority, layoffs, and so on. There has long been, however, an interest both by industry and by social scientists in the possible advantages of giving employees a role in decisions concerning the actual operation of the enterprise, including the planning and execution of work. Practical experiments to give employees a voice in work decisions have been particularly prominent in Europe in recent years, under such names as "joint consultation" in England, "worker councils" in Yugo- slavia, and "codetermination" in Germany.[1] In the United States, a system of employee representation called "works councils" became fairly wide- spread in the first two decades of this century,[2] and a system of labor- management committees functioned in some industries during World War II.[3] Although these various programs of employee-management co- operation have differed in a variety of ways, their common denominator has been the attempt to introduce greater "democracy" in industry.

A number of possible advantages have been suggested for programs of employee representation in decision making, including better union- management relations, greater protection of employee interests, greater efficiency of operation, and the creation of a more truly democratic society. In addition to these important possible institutional effects of employee representation programs, it has been suggested that such programs may improve employee attitudes toward their jobs and toward their work organization. In particular, there has been the hope that such programs would create a sense of common interest and common purpose at all levels of the work organization.[4] There is little systematic evidence available, however, either to support or to refute this expectation.[5] A major purpose of this paper is, therefore, to present some evidence relevant to this expectation.

Probably the outstanding example of an employee representation program in the U.S. today is the program of co-operative conferences and committees of the Tennessee Valley Authority (TVA). The Survey Research Center of the University of Michigan has recently conducted a study at TVA of employee involvement in their jobs. As a part of this study, some information is available about the impact of TVA's co-operative program on how employees look at their jobs and at the organization for which they work.[6]

This paper reports some of these findings. It considers the relation between extent of participation in the TVA co-operative program and (a) job motivation, (b) general interest in innovation on the job, (c) attitudes toward the organization and toward management, and (d) acceptance of work changes introduced by management. The paper also considers the relative importance of employee influence in the immediate job situation, as compared to influence through the division or branch-wide co-operative program.

DESCRIPTION OF THE CO-OPERATIVE PROGRAM

The co-operative program at TVA is composed of co-operative conferences or committees. A co-operative conference or committee is a continuing series of meetings between representatives of management and of the unions that represent TVA employees.[7] The unit covered by a conference or committee is usually a fairly large one—like an engineering division or a power plant—although smaller units sometimes have their own conferences. The top executives of the unit concerned represent management, while employees are represented by about eight to ten employees chosen by the men in various parts of the unit. The employee representatives are union members, but usually do not hold official union positions. Meetings are generally held once a month for several hours. The agendas are usually heavily concerned with improvements in working methods, but also cover many other topics of mutual interest, such as hospitalization plans, training, and community fund drives. Decisions are usually made by consensus rather than by voting, and management retains final responsibility for accepting and executing decisions. Information about conference activities is supposed to be given to other employees by their representatives and through printed summaries. During the period between conference meetings, various committees work on projects initiated by the conference and report their progress back to the conference.

The vigor of the co-operative program differs from one unit to another. Some conferences have the full support of local management; some have only half-hearted backing. In some units, employees are kept fully informed about what is happening and even instruct their representatives; in other units rank-and-file employees are less informed about conference activities. Conferences may be typically routine sessions where technical suggestions are processed, or they may be true forums where broader problems of labor-management co-operation are discussed.

From one perspective, the beneficial results are both concrete and obvious. In all of these units—but especially in the power plants—a large number of suggestions for work improvement are processed by the co-operative committees and put into effect. For example, an agenda of one power plant co-operative committee, gave the following suggestions, which were being implemented through the co-operative program: "provisions for hanging hoist or chain-fall on soot-blower steam-regulating valves"; "completion of catwalk on units 1 and 2 coal transport gates"; "hanger rods be put up over pulverizer exhaustors on units 1 and 2." There were fourteen other work improvements which were being implemented on this one meeting's agenda. Work improvements of this kind save TVA a great deal of money and often make the work safer or easier for employees. (Employees do not get cash awards when their suggestions are adopted, though their accomplishment is usually publicized within the unit and sometimes more widely.)

But are these work improvements—as well as the other concrete accomplishments—of the co-operative program its total result? If so, there are those, within TVA as well as elsewhere, who would argue that there might be more efficient mechanisms for achieving these results. Why spend so much top management as well as employee time in these meetings? Perhaps the same suggestions could be elicited through a more usual suggestion system and judged by some competent management group, probably with cash awards for money-saving suggestions.

To this kind of argument, the supporters of the co-operative program would answer that the program is more than just a glorified suggestion system. In 1956, Harry Case, the Director of Personnel at TVA, said:

> The co-operative program sees the employees in their organized capacity as among the groups which have a vital interest in the TVA program. Indeed, what group conceivably might have the same intensity of interest—if that interest is properly motivated?[8]

There has been, in short, the hope that the co-operative program, as a mechanism for employee participation in job decisions, can increase employees' enthusiasm for their work and dedication to the larger purposes of TVA. This is, perhaps, a great deal to expect from a program whose formal meetings usually occur only about once a month. What do the research data show?

UNITS COVERED BY STUDY

Data are available from TVA employees in eight administratively separate co-operative programs, in five geographically separate units. Two of these programs cover engineering divisions, one in Knoxville, Tennessee, the other in Chattanooga, Tennessee. Most employees are mechanical, civil, or electrical engineers, with draftsmen and some other supporting personnel (e.g., architects) also represented. One engineering division plans major installations, like power plants and dams. The other designs facilities that carry the power, including transmission lines and substations. In general, the type of work and the type of personnel in the two engineering divisions are very similar.

Three other co-operative programs (*A* programs) cover most employees in each of three power plants, located in different sections of Tennessee. The three power plants are almost identical in technology and in administrative organization. Employees in the main co-operative programs fall into two major groupings: (a) maintenance craftsmen, such as machinists, boilermakers, steam fitters, and electricians; and (b) operating personnel, who are responsible for checking and guiding the operation of a largely automated complex of equipment. These operating employees are trained technicians with at least a high school education.

Three additional co-operative programs (*B* programs) are found in the same three power plants. Most employees covered by the *B* programs are found in the laboratory section of each power plant. The men working in each laboratory section include material testers (who weigh, sample, and test coal) and chemical laboratory analysts. These jobs are skilled jobs, but most are subprofessional. The *B* programs cover a smaller number of employees (approximately 50) than do the *A* programs (about 150) in each power plant.

A representative sample of nonsupervisory employees in most units of the engineering division and power plants was chosen to complete a questionnaire about their jobs.[9] The percentage of the sample filling out the questionnaire was 95 percent and 98 percent in the two engineering units; and 84 percent, 87 percent, and 88 percent in the three power plants. The lower percentage of response in the power plants was due primarily to problems of scheduling caused by a three-shift operation. In all, 377 employees in the two engineering divisions and 457 employees in the three power plants completed the questionnaire.[10]

DATA ON THE CO-OPERATIVE PROGRAM

Questions asked concerning the co-operative program were the following:

1. Have you ever served as a representative to the co-operative conference or committee in this unit?

2. Have you ever served on any committees which report to the co-operative conference or committee?

3. How many suggestions have you submitted to the co-operative conference or committee during the past three years?

4. How much do you usually hear about what goes on in the meetings of the co-operative conference or committee of your unit? (Five alternatives from "A full account of what goes on" to "Nothing of what goes on.")

5. How interested are the people you work with in the work of the co-operative conference or committee? (Four alternatives from "They pay little attention to it" to "They pay very close attention to it and are very interested in its work.")

6. How much interest in the work of the conference or committee do you think the *management* of your division takes? (Four alternatives from "They pay very little attention to it" to "They pay very close attention to it and are very interested in its work.")

7. How much do you feel the work of the co-operative conference or committee in your unit helps to make TVA a better place to work? (Five alternatives from "Helps a great deal" to "Doesn't help at all.")

8. If you were to submit a good suggestion to the co-operative conference or committee in your unit, how seriously do you think it would be considered? (Three alternatives from "Very serious consideration" to "Little serious consideration; ideas are given only a quick look.")

Each employee was given a score (arbitrary) on each question, depending on the response he chose. Mean scores on each question were computed for employees covered by each of the eight co-operative programs.[11] Mean scores were also computed for each work group consisting of employees who reported to the same immediate supervisor. There are ninety such work groups in the sample, counting groups in all eight co-operative programs.

Each co-operative program (and each smaller group) was also scored on an index of participation through the co-operative program, based on average responses to four of the above questions (Questions 1, 2, 3, and 8). This index is intended to indicate the extent to which the co-operative program represents a channel for active participation in work decisions.

Finally, data were obtained from TVA records showing the number of suggestions submitted to the co-operative program in each unit during the year preceding the administration of the questionnaire.

Motivation and Interest in Innovation

To what extent is a high level of participation in the co-operative program and favorable attitudes toward that program associated with high job motivation? And how much does the innovative spirit encouraged by the co-operative program carry over into the everyday work situation?

To assess general job motivation, we used an index based on these questions:

1. On most days on your job, how often does time seem to drag for you? (Five alternatives from "About half the day or more" to "Time never seems to drag.")

2. Some people are completely involved in their job—they are absorbed in it night and day. For other people, their job is simply one of several interests. How involved do you feel in your job? (Five alternatives from "Very little involved; my other interests are more absorbing" to "Very strongly involved; my work is the most absorbing interest in my life.")

This short index has some validity as a measure of job motivation, as indicated by the positive associations of this measure with attendance and with supervisors' ratings of each employee's "concern for doing a good job."[1][2]

To assess general employee interest in innovation, three questions were used:

1. In your kind of work, if a person tries to change his usual way of doing things, how does it generally turn out? (Three alternatives from "Usually turns out worse; the tried and true methods work best in my work" to "Usually turns out better; our methods need improvement.")

2. In my kind of job, it's usually better to let your supervisor worry about new or better ways of doing things. (Four alternatives from "Strongly agree" to "Strongly disagree.")

3. How many times in the past year have you suggested to your supervisor a different or better way of doing something on the job? (Six alternatives from "Never had occasion to do this during the past year" to "More than ten times had occasion to do this during the past year.")

The validity of this index measure is indicated by its positive associations with supervisors' ratings of each employee on the extent to which he is "on the lookout for new ideas."[1][3]

For employees in each of the eight co-operative programs, mean scores of job motivation and of interest in innovation were computed. These scores were then correlated with measures indicating the extent of participation by employees in each of the co-operative programs. These results are shown in Table 1. Table 1 shows, first, that the vigor of each co-operative program has only a small and nonsignificant association with the motivation to do a good job shown by employees in that program. Examination of the scatter plots from which these correlations are derived indicates that even this small positive association is due primarily to the effect of one co-operative program. Evidently job motivation is affected mainly by factors other than participation in the co-operative program.[1][4]

Also, Table 1 does not show a positive association between vigor of the co-operative program and general interest in innovation. There is, in fact, a negative association between interest in innovation and several indicators, especially perceived group interest in the program, general evaluation of

TABLE 1

Vigor of the co-operative program as related to job
motivation and to interest in innovation on the job.*

Vigor of co-op program	Job motivation · index	General interest in innovation index
1. Amount of information	.44	−.12
2. Perceived group interest in co-op program	.35	−.46
3. Perceived interest of management	.38	.16
4. Perceived attention given suggestions	.41	.05
5. General evaluation of program	.04	−.55
6. Percentage who served on co-op committee	.21	−.47
7. Suggestions: no. reported, 3 yrs.	.24	−.48
8. Suggestions: no. recorded, 1 yr.†	.04	.20
9. Index of program as channel for active participation (based on 4, 6, 7 above)	.31	−.27

*Pearson product-moment correlations; N = 8 co-operative programs.
†N = 7 for this line of the table.

the program, percentage serving on a program committee, and number of
suggestions reported. These negative associations may reflect a tendency of
employees in units with vigorous co-operative programs to rely on these
programs as the source of new ideas at the expense of continual personal
attention to better ways of doing things. However, the differences in
interest in innovation among co-operative programs are small and far from
statistically significant, when units of comparable technology are
compared: i.e., the two engineering divisions, the three main power plants,
and the three power-plant laboratories. This, together with the correlations
not being statistically significant, suggests that the negative association
found may be due to chance. On the other hand, there is clearly no
evidence that, besides eliciting many formal suggestions, a vigorous
co-operative program also promotes a general increase in interest in
innovation on the job.

Identification with Work Organization

What is the association between the vigor of the co-operative program
in a unit and the feeling of employees in that unit toward the larger work
organization? Do employees who participate more actively in the program
have a greater feeling of belonging to, of "oneness," with TVA? For
measuring "identification with TVA," responses to the following questions
were used:

1. If someone asked you to describe yourself, and you could tell only
one thing about yourself, which of the following answers would you be
most likely to give? (Five choices including "I work for TVA." Each
employee was also asked to indicate second and third choices.)

2. How do you feel when you hear (or read about) someone criticizing the TVA method of public power or comparing it unfavorably to private power? (Four alternatives from "I mostly agree with the criticism" to "It gets me quite mad.")

3. Following are two somewhat different statements about the relations between management and employees at TVA:

A. The relations between management and employees at TVA are much different than in private industry, because in TVA both are working together toward the same goal of building the Valley.

B. Relations between management and employees at TVA are not really very different than in private industry; management is looking out for the organization's interests, and employees have to look out for their own interests.

Which of the two statements above comes closer to *your* own opinion? (Four alternatives from "Agree completely with A" to "Agree completely with B.")[15]

4. If you could begin working over again, but in the same occupation as you're in now, how likely would you be to choose TVA as a place to work? (Five alternatives from "Definitely would choose another place over TVA" to "Definitely would choose TVA over another place for my occupation.")

Again, there is some evidence that responses to questions are related to the actual behavior of employees. The principal evidence is a marked association between scores on the identification index and (a) turnover rates and (b) reporting the display of TVA auto stickers.[16]

For employees in each of the eight co-operative programs and each of ninety smaller work groups, a mean score on the index of identification with TVA was computed. The first column of Table 2 shows the associations between scores on identification with TVA and aspects of participation in the co-operative program, for the eight co-operative programs. There is generally a strong positive association between the vigor of a co-operative program and identification with TVA. The strongest association is between identification and perception of the extent to which suggestions to the co-operative program are seriously considered ($r = .94$). Employee identification with TVA is also strongly related to the amount of information employees receive about the co-operative program, over-all employee evaluation of the co-operative program, the percentage of employees who have served on a program committee, and the index of participation through the co-operative program.

Examination of the scatter plots on which the correlations are based shows that the associations tend to hold for each sub-set of the co-operative programs compared: i.e., for the two engineering programs, for the *A* programs, and for the *B* programs at the three power plants. The scatter plot for the strongest association—that between identification and perceived attention given to suggestions submitted to the co-operative program—is shown in Figure 1.

TABLE 2

Vigor of the co-operative program as related to attitudes
toward the organization and toward management, and to
acceptance of changes introduced on the job.[a]

Vigor of co-op program	Over-all identification with TVA	Feelings of common purpose with management[b]	Acceptance of change
1. Amount of information	.80[c]	.86[d]	.95[e]
2. Perceived group interest in co-op program	.67	.52	.70
3. Perceived interest of management	.64	.54	.61
4. Perceived attention given suggestions	.94[e]	.87[d]	.85[d]
5. General evaluation of program	.73[c]	.55	.79[c]
6. Percentage who served on co-op committee	.75[c]	.71[c]	.90[d]
7. Suggestions: no. reported, 3 yrs.	.38	.28	.51
8. Suggestions: no. recorded, 1 yr.[f]	.04	−.22	−.28
9. Index of program as channel for active participation (based on 4, 6, 7 above)	.83[c]	.77[c]	.90[d]

[a]Pearson product-moment correlations; $N = 8$ co-operative programs.
[b]The question indicating feelings of common purpose with management is one of those composing the index of identification with TVA.
[c]$p < .05$, 2-tailed test.
[d]$p < .01$, 2-tailed test.
[e]$p < .001$, 2-tailed test.
[f]$N = 7$ for this line of the table.

The second column of Table 2 shows the correlations between participation in the co-operative program and the item of the identification index that is of greatest interest in this context—that concerning feelings of common purpose between employees and management. The vigor of the co-operative program, and especially the perceived attention given to suggestions and the amount of information employees receive about the program, has a marked positive correlation with employees' feelings of common purpose with management.

How should the positive association between reactions to the co-operative program and favorable attitudes toward the organization (and especially toward management) be interpreted? First we may consider the possibility that this association is a spurious one and that both reactions to the co-operative program and identification with TVA are the results of some third variable. It is possible to suppose, for example, that both reactions to the co-operative program and positive feelings toward the organization are the results of general satisfaction on the job. To check on this possibility, we examined responses by employees in each co-operative program to the question:

How satisfied are you with the following things on your job: chances for promotion; immediate supervisor; present salary; co-workers? (A five-point scale from "Not at all satisfied" to "Completely satisfied" was provided for each aspect of satisfaction.)

An over-all index of satisfaction shows no association with organizational identification ($r = .03$ for the eight co-operative programs). Several specific aspects of satisfaction also have little or no positive associations with organizational identification. Moreover, neither the over-all index of satisfaction nor specific aspects of satisfaction are positively associated with participation in and attitudes toward the co-operative program. In fact, the associations tend to be negative. Thus, the association found between identification with TVA and an active co-operative program cannot be a spurious one caused by the effect of general satisfaction. Of course the possibility remains that some other third variable is producing a spurious association between identification and reactions to the co-operative program; but we have found no evidence of this. However, it may be that the vigor of the co-operative program is just one major indi-

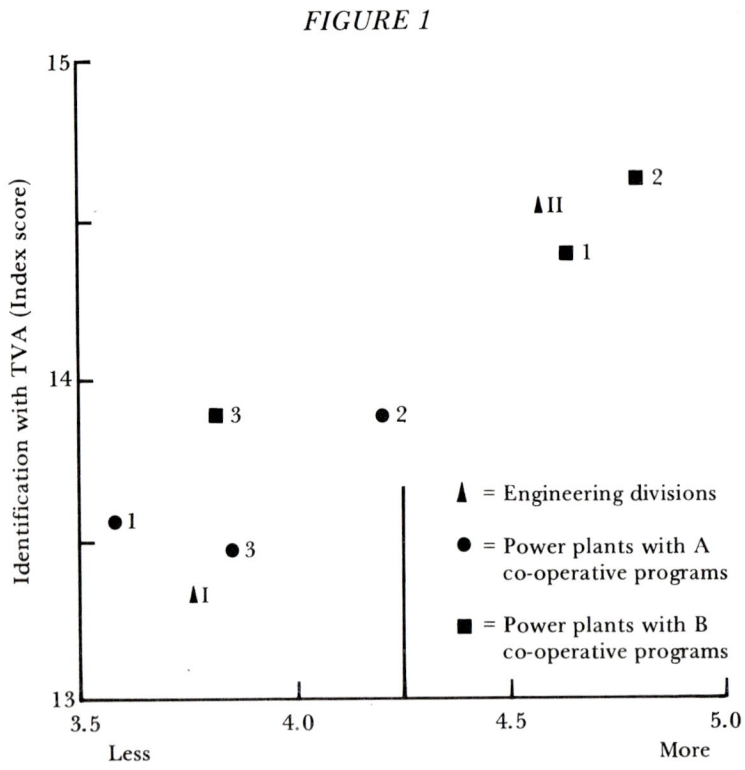

FIGURE 1

Perceived seriousness of consideration
given to suggestions by co-operative program

cator of a general pattern of management-employee consultation and co-operation and that it is the total pattern which determines attitudes toward the organization.

Another question may be raised about the direction of clusation. Does a positive reaction to the co-operative program bring greater identification with the organization; does causation work the other way; or does it work both ways? It is not possible to answer this question with any certainty from the data at hand. There are, however, some data about the conditions under which the relation holds most strongly, which may help to clarify the meaning of the results. In the next section these data will be examined.

Participation in Co-operative Program, Influence in Immediate Job Situation, and Identification with TVA

Participation through the co-operative program is one channel, reaching right up to division management, through which employees can have an influence on decisions. But there is, of course, a more immediate arena in which employees may have some influence—the work group under the first-level supervisor. To what extent is the relation between identification with TVA affected by the amount of control and influence which employees can exert within their own immediate group?

Employees were asked the following question:

In general, how much say or influence do you think each of the following persons actually has on what goes on in your present immediate work group? (Five hierarchical levels were listed in engineering divisions and four in power plants, including the first-line supervisor and "the nonsupervisory employees as a group." Employees were asked to rate the degree of influence exerted by each level on a five-point scale ranging from "almost no influence" to "great influence.")

Among the measures derived from these data was the average discrepancy in influence between first-line supervisor and nonsupervisory employees for each work group.

Work groups were divided into high, medium, and low with respect to discrepancy of influence between the immediate supervisor and his subordinates. They were further subdivided into high, medium, and low with respect to the index of employee participation in the co-operative program. For each of the resulting nine sets of groups, the mean group score on identification with TVA was computed.

Table 3, which shows these data, reveals that both high participation in the co-operative program and high employee influence in the immediate work group have an independent association with high identification with TVA. Moreover, the impact of high influence in each sphere appears to be greatest when influence in the other respect is also high. It is the combination of high influence both in the immediate work group and in the larger organization that brings a sharp rise in identification with TVA.

Two other measures of employee influence in the immediate work group are also available. One is an index of employee "control over means" based on four questions covering such matters as the extent to which work methods are covered by formal rules and the likelihood that the immediate supervisor will go along with the suggestions of subordinates. The final influence measure is an index of "control over goals" based on seven questions concerning such subjects as how much influence employees have over setting of time schedules, and the extent to which employees have a say about what things they will work on next. A mean score on "control over means" and on "control over goals" was computed for each immediate work group.

When work groups are sorted according to the index of control over

TABLE 3

Mean scores of identification with TVA, for work groups*
differing in degree of participation in co-operative program
and in perceived discrepancy of influence between
themselves and supervisor.

Participation of work group in co-operative program (index)	Discrepancy in influence between employees and their immediate supervisor			
	High discrepancy	Medium discrepancy	Low discrepancy	Total
Low participation	A† 12.53 (8)††	B 13.02 (12)	C 13.87 (8)	J 13.12 (28)
Medium participation	D 13.34 (14)	E 14.17 (6)	F 13.66 (8)	K 13.61 (28)
High participation	G 13.44 (10)	H 13.44 (8)	I 15.97 (12)	L 14.45 (30)
Total	M 13.17 (32)	N 13.41 (26)	O 14.71 (28)	P 13.74 (86)

*Groups in engineering divisions and power plants were combined for this analysis.
†Significance of difference between cells: A X C, $p = .10$ (1-tail); A X D, $p = $ NS; A X G, $p = $ NS; A X I, $p < .001$; B X E, $p < .10$ (1-tail); C X I, $p < .01$; F X I, $p < .001$; G X I, $p < .01$; H X I, $p < .001$; J X L, $p < .01$; K X L, $p < .05$ (1-tail); M X O, $p < .01$; N X O, $p < .001$.
††Numerals in parentheses indicate number in groups; four small groups are omitted from the table because the number of persons answering one or more of indices was too small to compute a mean for the group.

means or on the index of control over goals, the results shown in Table 3 are essentially duplicated. In other words, whatever measure of influence on the immediate job is used, the data indicate that both influence in the immediate group and through the co-operative program are associated with organizational identification, and also that the impact of each type of influence is greatest when the other is also high.

Differences Between
Professional and Nonprofessional Employees

Although employee influence is associated with organizational identification for all the units studied, there is evidence that this association is stronger among professionals than among nonprofessionals. For 38 work groups in the engineering divisions, composed primarily of professional engineers, there are significant positive correlations (in the .30's, .40's, and .50's) between various measures of employee influence in the immediate work group and the level of identification with TVA. The parallel correlations for 35 work groups in the power plants and 17 for nonprofessional groups (like drafting units) in the engineering divisions are close to zero. For work groups in both the engineering divisions and power plants the correlation ($r = .34$) between the index of participation through the co-operative program and identification with TVA is the same; however, there are much stronger associations among engineering work groups (especially professional groups) between identification and most aspects of interest and participation in the co-operative program. In general, then, the association between participation in work decisions and favorable attitudes toward the organization appears more clearly and consistently among professional than among nonprofessional groups.

This finding of a difference in the degree of association between employee influence and feelings toward the organization within subgroups of the same larger organization has its parallel in results from a comparative study of organizations. Smith and Brown[17] have summarized results from several studies in which the "slope"[18] of organizational control has been related to some measure of member loyalty. Greater relative influence at the bottom of the organization is associated with high member loyalty in a set of voluntary organizations and in a union but not in a set of sales organizations.

In trying to explain the differential association of employee influence with organizational identification among professionals and nonprofessionals at TVA, the measure of commitment to one's occupation was used. This measure is an index based on responses to seven questions about how the person would feel about going into the same type of work again and how he would feel about his son entering the same occupation. As might be expected, professional engineers generally scored higher on organizational commitment than did nonprofessionals in the engineering divisions or power plant employees. However, even among a subgroup of power plant groups which have occupational commitment at about the same high level as professional engineers, there was no consistent strong association between influence on work decisions and organizational identification Thus, it appears to be something beyond devotion to one's occupation which makes influence in work decisions an important determinant of organizational identification. It seems likely that professionals like engineers have an image of their ideal work roles which includes an active role in planning of projects and selection among alternative methods. It seems likely also that professionals are more apt than skilled workers to view such participation as legitimate and for such participation to be important to their self-images as first-rate members of their occupations. If this is so, then the extent to which professionals (and those with similar work needs) value their organizational roles would be expected to depend fairly strongly on the extent to which the organization gives them the chance to participate in work decisions.

Acceptance of Change

At TVA, as in most enterprises today, there are many work changes introduced by management. These include changes in the equipment men work with, work procedures, job standards and requirements, and the kind of records to be kept.

A major concern of the co-operative program is with the improvement of work facilities and methods to make them more efficient, and also with making work safer and more convenient. To what extent is high participation and interest in the co-operative program related to acceptance of changes introduced by management?[19]

To assess employee resistance to change, an index was constructed based on the following four questions:

1. Sometimes changes in the way a job is done are more trouble than they are worth because they create a lot of problems and confusion. How often do you feel that changes which have affected you and your job at TVA have been like this? (Five alternatives from "Fifty percent or more of the changes have been more trouble than they're worth" to "Only five percent or fewer of the changes have been more trouble than they're worth.")

2. From time to time changes in policies, procedures, and equipment are introduced by the management. How often do these changes lead to better ways of doing things? (Five alternatives from "Changes of this kind never improve things" to "Changes of this kind are always an improvement.")

3. How well do the various people in the plant or offices who are affected by these changes accept them? (Five alternatives from "Very few of the people involved accept the changes" to "Practically all of the people involved accept the changes.")

4. In general, how do you *now* feel about changes during the past year

that affected the way your job is done? (Five alternatives from "Made things somewhat worse" to "Been a big improvement.")

Again there is evidence that responses to these questions are related to the actual behavior of employees on the job. In nine out of ten units where scores for acceptance of change were related to supervisors' ratings of willingness "to go along with changes management has made," there was a positive, though low, correlation between individual scores and supervisor ratings of the same individuals.[20]

A mean score on acceptance of change was computed for employees in each of the eight co-operative programs (and also in each of the ninety immediate work groups). These scores on acceptance of change were then correlated with scores indicating the vigor of the co-operative program. The data, presented in the third column of Table 2, show a strong association between the vigor of a co-operative program and acceptance of change in that program. The association is strongest ($r = .95$) between the amount of information employees get about the co-operative program and acceptance of change. Acceptance of change is also strongly related to the percentage of employees who served on any committee of the co-operative program ($r = .90$), to perceptions of the consideration given to suggestions ($r = .85$), and to the index of participation through the co-operative program ($r = .90$).

Figure 2 shows the scatter plot of the relation between participation in the co-operative program (index scores) and acceptance of change. This plot shows that the association holds separately for each of the three types of work units as well as for all eight co-operative programs combined. It should be noted, however, that the differences between acceptance of change scores are generally greater among power plant units than between engineering divisions. Also differences in acceptance of change among immediate work groups are more strongly related to participation in the co-operative program within power plants than within engineering divisions. It may be that engineering employees are more likely to judge proposed changes by objective professional standards, while the reaction to change of power plant employees is more affected by their participation in the change process.

The over-all results are consistent with findings from earlier studies which have found employee participation in decisions affecting their job to lead to greater acceptance of necessary job changes. The most notable of the previous studies is the now classic work of Coch and French.[21] Participation in the pajama factory studied by Coch and French was much more direct, however, than in the TVA sites. In the "representation" condition at the pajama factory, all of the operators were present at a meeting at which management explained the need for and nature of changes. Then several operators out of the total of thirteen participated in working out details of the change. Finally, another meeting was held with all operators to present details of the new job. In the TVA co-operative program, there is little direct participation by most employees. Moreover, the proportion of employees serving as representatives at any one time is much lower than in the pajama factory.[22] That a less direct program, covering a large organizational unit, can have effects similar to the more intensive program in the pajama factory is especially noteworthy.

Influence Through the Co-operative Program and On the Job

If participation through the co-operative program is generally related to acceptance of change, is this relationship affected by influence in the immediate job situation? And does influence on the immediate job, like influence through the co-operative program, increase acceptance of

FIGURE 2

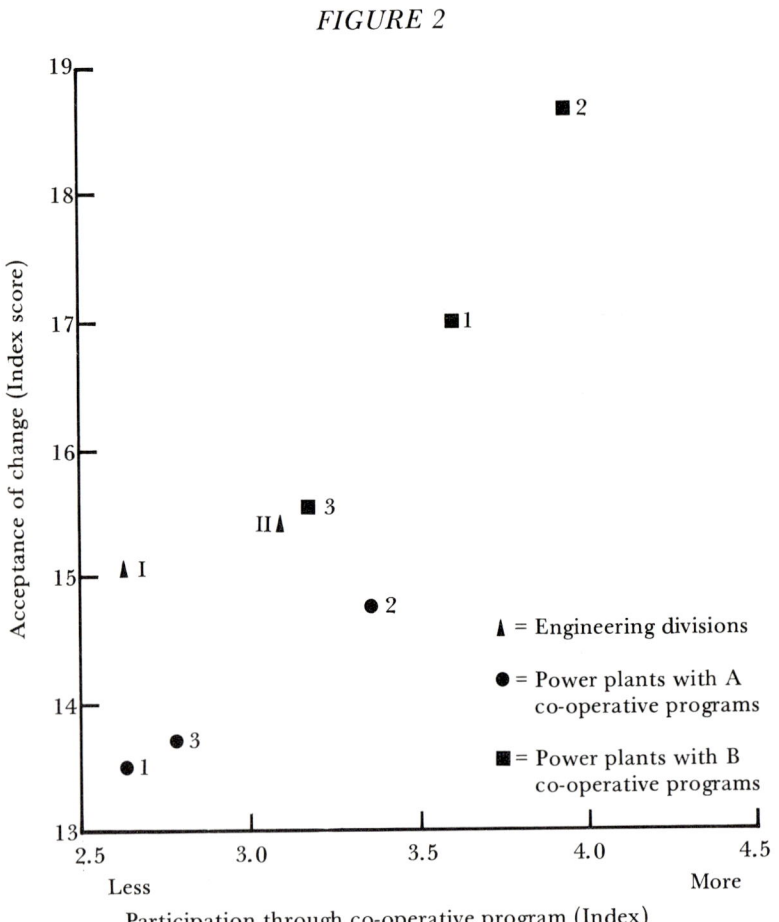

Participation through co-operative program (Index)

TABLE 4
Mean scores of acceptance of change, for work groups*
differing in degree of participation in co-operative program
and in perceived discrepancy of influence between
themselves and supervisor.

Participation of work group in co-operative program (index)	Discrepancy in influence between employees and their immediate supervisor			
	High discrepancy	Medium discrepancy	Low discrepancy	Total
Low participation	A† 14.58 (8)††	B 14.92 (10)	C 14.74 (8)	J 14.76 (26)
Medium participation	D 14.55 (14)	E 14.74 (6)	F 14.20 (8)	K 14.49 (28)
High participation	G 15.14 (10)	H 15.13 (9)	I 16.24 (12)	L 15.56 (31)
Total	M 14.74 (32)	N 14.95 (25)	O 15.23 (28)	P 14.96 (85)

*Groups in engineering divisions and power plants were combined for this analysis.
†Significance of difference between cells: A × G, p = NS; A × I, $p <.01$ (1-tail); G × I, $p <.05$ (1-tail); C × I, $p <.05$; F × I, $p <.01$; K × L, $p <.01$; J × L, $p <.05$; M × O, $p <.10$ (1-tail).
††Numerals in parentheses indicate number in groups; five small groups were omitted from this analysis because number of persons answering relevant questions was not sufficient to compute mean.

change? To help answer these questions, we again classified all immediate work groups according to their standing on two aspects of influence: participation through the co-operative program and discrepancy in influence between nonsupervisory employees and their immediate supervisor.

Table 4 shows the mean scores for acceptance of change for groups in various influence categories. These data show that participation through the co-operative program tends to affect acceptance of change, regardless of influence in the immediate work group; however, the co-operative program appears to have its greatest impact when influence in the immediate work group is also high. Conversely, influence in the immediate work group also tends to be related to acceptance of change, but only when participation through the co-operative program is also high. The work groups which stand out as high in acceptance of change are those in which employees enjoy high influence in both spheres. Similar results are found when influence in the immediate work group is measured either by the index of control over means or by the index of control over goals. These data indicate again that influence at both organizational levels—through the co-operative program covering the larger unit and in the immediate work group—contributes to employee acceptance of change.

Attitude toward Management and Acceptance of Change

Why should high employee influence, especially through participation in the co-operative program, be related to increased acceptance of change? We can again rule out the possible explanation that general job satisfaction may be behind both greater participation in the co-operative program and more favorable attitudes. As noted above, there is no association between various aspects of job satisfaction (e.g., with wages, with promotion chances) and participation through the co-operative program. Nor is there any positive association between over-all job satisfaction and acceptance of change ($r = -.17$) for the eight co-operative programs.

Another possible explanation is that attitudes toward management may play a key role, perhaps as an intervening variable between participation and acceptance of change. Such an explanation would be consistent with the findings by Coch and French that employee participation resulted in much less hostility toward management. In the present data, there is also a marked association in the eight co-operative programs between participation in the program and feelings of common purpose with management ($r = .77$). When feelings of solidarity with management are held constant statistically, however, the correlation between participation through the co-operative program and acceptance of change drops only moderately (from .90 to .75).

It may be that there are aspects of attitudes toward management that were not measured, which may help account for the relationship found between participation and acceptance of change. Another possible explanation is that increased acceptance of change is due not so much to the more favorable attitudes toward management created by participation, but to the perception that the changes introduced are, at least in part, not arbitrarily imposed by management at all. Those employees who are well informed about the co-operative program and who participate in it (both actually and psychologically) should be more likely to see work changes as the product of joint consultation between management and employees.

CONCLUSIONS

The general question addressed by this paper is whether a program of labor-management consultation at an organizational level removed from the immediate work situation can have an appreciable impact on employee job attitudes. The results found at TVA cannot, of course, be generalized uncritically to all other programs of labor-management consultation and joint decision making. The results do, however, have some implications beyond the TVA setting. They suggest these conclusions:

1. The results clearly suggest that a vigorous employee participation program covering a large organizational unit can increase employee feelings of solidarity with the work organization and with management, and increase employee acceptance of work changes. They indicate further that these effects of a participation program can occur regardless of the degree of general satisfaction which employees feel about their job situation.

2. These data indicate that such a participation program will not be maximally effective in creating favorable work attitudes unless employees have some chance to have their opinions heard and heeded within their immediate work groups as well. Neither influence at the larger organizational level nor in the immediate work group occurs in a vacuum; attitudes toward the organization and toward changes introduced by management are affected by what happens on each of several organizational levels.

3. The association between employee influence on decisions and feelings of solidarity with the organization appears to be stronger among professional engineering personnel than among skilled but nonprofessional workers. This finding may indicate that attitudes toward the organization are improved by participation in decision making primarily among employees for whom such participation is seen as legitimate or as important to their occupational self-image.

4. While employee participation in organizational decisions brings more favorable attitudes toward management, increased acceptance of change does not appear to be due primarily to improved attitudes toward management. It may be rather that the greater acceptance of change found in units with a vigorous, well-publicized co-operative program is due largely to the feeling in such units that, although work changes are formally made by management, they are in fact the product of joint labor-management decision making. As such, they would be viewed less as imposed and more as mutual solutions to common problems.

FOOTNOTES

1. There is an extensive literature on this subject. A few noteworthy publications are: A. F. Sturnthal, *Worker's Councils: A Study of Workplace Organization on Both Sides of the Iron Curtain* (Cambridge, Mass.: Harvard University, 1964); T. McKitterick, *Workers and Management: The German Co-determination Experiment* (London: Fabian, 1953); F.B. Singleton and A. Topham, *Workers' Control in Yugoslavia* (London: Fabian, 1963); and D.L. Davis, *Formal Consultation—In Practice* (London: Industrial Welfare Society, 1962).

2. See *The Growth of Works Councils in the United States: A Statistical Summary*. (Special Report No. 32; National Industrial Conference Board, Inc., New York, 1925.)

3. See C. Riegelman, *Labor-Management Cooperation in United States War Production* (New Series No. 6; International Labor Office Studies and Reports, Montreal, 1948).

4. See, for example, G.S. Walpole, *Management and Men: A Study of the Theory and Practice of Joint Consultation at All Levels* (London: Jonathan Cape, 1944).

5. See D.L. Davis, *op. cit.*, for some managerial assessments of employee attitudes toward formal consultation in Great Britain.

6. This study was supported by the National Institutes of Health, under research grant M4514. Donald C. Pelz and Craig W. Allen collaborated with the author in the field work and in developing the questionnaire for the general study from which these data are drawn. Alison Clark assisted in preparing the paper, especially in programming the data for machine computation. The assistance of many persons at TVA is gratefully acknowledged, but the responsibility for the conclusions presented here is solely the author's.

7. Engineering employees are represented in negotiations with management by the TVA Engineers Association. This organization is a professional association rather than a union, but it performs the same function as do unions at TVA.

8. Reprint of talk given by H. Case, "Union-Management Cooperation in Action," at the Seventh Annual Valley-Wide Meeting of Union-Management Co-operative Conferences, Gatlinburg, Tennessee, March, 1956.

9. A small number of administrative section employees, chiefly women, included in the same co-operative program with laboratory employees were not sampled by our survey. A few power plant units composed of unskilled employees (e.g., janitors), were not sampled because pretests indicated difficulty in understanding the questionnaire. Some laboratory employees who are covered by the other power plant co-operative program were not included with other laboratory employees in the analysis.

10. Employees were assured that their individual responses would not become known to anyone at TVA, although their names were known to the researchers in order to match questionnaire and other data.

11. Scores on these various measures of interest and participation generally differ significantly among co-operative programs. The differences are especially large between engineering divisions, but significant differences among power plant programs are also found.

12. See M. Patchen, *Questionnaire Measures of Morale and Motivation* (Ann Arbor: Institute for Social Research, forthcoming monograph) for validity and reliability evidence for this measure and for a four-item measure of job motivation.

13. For data on the three-item scale shown here, see M. Patchen, "Questionnaire Measures of Employee Reactions to Their Jobs" (Ann Arbor: Institute for Social Research, July, 1963 [mimeo]). For validity and reliability data on an expanded six-item scale of interest in innovation, see M. Patchen, *Questionnaire Measures of Morale and Motivation, op. cit.*

14. An analysis of factors that affect job motivation and job interest is in progress as part of the larger project of which the work of this paper is a part.

15. A very similar question, rephrased in terms of a comparison between a specific private company and "other companies" was used in a private electronics firm in another phase of this project. Responses indicate that widespread perceptions of management and employees working toward the same goals are not limited to a government organization.

16. For data on the reliability and validity of this index, see M. Patchen, "Questionnaire Measures of Employee Reactions to Their Jobs," *op. cit.* For data on a seven-item index of identification with the organization, see M. Patchen, *Questionnaire Measures of Morale and Motivation, op. cit.*

17. C.G. Smith and M.E. Brown, "A Comparative Analysis of Factors in Organizational Control" (Ann Arbor: Institute for Social Research, August, 1964 [mimeo]).

18. See A.S. Tannenbaum, "Control in Organizations: Individual Adjustment and Organizational Performance," *Administrative Science Quarterly*, 7 (1962), 236-257.

19. The amount of change in their jobs (in the year prior to the questionnaire) which is reported by employees in each of the two engineering divisions is approximately equal; the amount of change reported in the main parts of power plants 1 and 2 are also approximately equal, with power plant 3 employees reporting somewhat less change; power plant laboratory 1 reported somewhat more change than laboratory 2 with laboratory 3 intermediate. Inspection of Figure 2 indicates that the amount of change experienced is not correlated with acceptance of change in these sites.

20. See M. Patchen, "Questionnaire Measures of Employee Reactions to Their Jobs," *op. cit.*, for data on the validity and reliability of this index. Since scores for acceptance of change cluster for work groups ($F = 1.62$; $p < .05$), the validity of group scores is probably greater than those for individuals. Also see M. Patchen, *Questionnaire Measures of Morale and Motivation, op. cit.*, for data on a five-item index of acceptance of change.

21. L. Coch and J.R.P. French, Jr., "Overcoming Resistance to Change," *Human Relations*, 1 (1948), 512-532. There are also a number of other studies that indicate that coercive methods produce resistance to influence attempts. See S. Zipf, "An Experimental Study of Resistance to Influence," (Unpublished Ph.D. dissertation, University of Michigan, 1958); J.R.P. French, Jr., H.W. Morrison, and G. Levinger, "Coercive Power and Forces Affecting Conformity," *Journal of Abnormal and Social Psychology*, 61 (1960), 93-101.

22. The ratio of employee representation in the programs covered here is very roughly as follows: engineering division I, 1 : 40; engineering division II, 1 : 25; power plant *A* programs, 1 : 20; power plant *B* programs, 1 : 8.

*Reed M. Powell is Dean, School of Business Adminis-
tration, California State Polytechnic University,
Pomona, California. John L. Schlacter is Assistant
Professor at Arizona State University.*
This article is reprinted with permission from the
Academy of Management Journal, *June 1971, pp.
165-173.*

Participative Management: A Panacea?

REED M. POWELL and JOHN L. SCHLACTER

In recent years the concept of participative management has become a focal point of interest among both scholars and practitioners of administration. Its acceptance has coincided with the increasing contribution of the behavioral science to managerial thought.

The appeal of the participative approach was suggested as early as 1937 by H.H. Carey [2, p. 44] in his definition of "consulting supervision" as the procedure whereby supervisors and executives consult with employees or their peers on matters affecting employees' welfare or interest prior to establishing policies or initiating action. From such beginnings the concept of participative management has grown into a full-fledged approach to administration affecting both patterns of organizational relationships and leadership style.

The appeal of this concept is many-sided. Participation viewed in Carey's sense can be construed as a comfortable rationale for the paternalistic manager. Applied in the modern interpretation it complements the political and social philosophies of democracy and individual self-actualization. Today, psychologists believe that participation enhances the learning process [1, pp. 117-132], and that a "democratic environment" may be more conducive to productive effort under certain conditions [10, pp. 115-156]. These and other alleged advantages serve to enhance the value of the participative concept.

However, the question must be raised, "Does the participative approach to management pay off in terms of job performance?" Research results in this area, while sometimes contradictory, suggest that the answer may be yes. An early study of participation, conducted by Coch and French at the Harwood Manufacturing Plant in Virginia, indicated that women allowed to determine their own rate of production improved their productivity significantly over that of a control group [3]. Subsequent research studies complementing these results validate the conclusion that positive evidence outweighs the negative or inconclusive findings of other researchers.

There does, however, seem to be a reason for concern relative to the methodology utilized in much of the research in the area of participation. Almost without exception, studies acknowledged to be of major significance have been performed within the environment of the corporation. Private industry has been the site of a variety of these behavioral experiments. The situation, then, is that in industry, particularly in our economic system, economic reward almost invariably accompanies improved performance. Economic reward is explicitly derived from incentive schemes, such as piece-rate systems, which directly link dollars paid to the number of units produced. Less direct are those systems which reward the individual economically for performance over some prior period, or for group effort, such as profit-sharing plans. An implicit economic reward is that which accompanies promotion for a job well done. In the environment in which research on participative concepts has been conducted, *it is quite impossible to divorce the effects of participation from the explicit or implicit economic incentive, which accompanies it.* While the participant may reap psychological benefits from participation, he is also well aware of the probability of economic reward [3, pp. 512-532].

The purpose of the present research is to contribute knowledge concerning the effect of participative management techniques in an environment different from the typical industrial setting and without economic incentives.

The research was conducted as a field experiment in a government organization in Ohio for a period of 5½ months. In lieu of control groups (because of the small number of people participating), historical data were compared with experimentally generated data in order to arrive at conclusions relative to the effectiveness of participative techniques.

The study specifically tested the impact of increased participation by field crews in the decision-making process. These crews were employed by the Operations Division of the Bureau of Traffic, Ohio Department of Highways. The six crews were allowed, with different degrees of participation, to perform the scheduling activity which determined their work routine for the coming months. The effect of this participation was noted in terms of changes in both productivity and morale.

The environment chosen for the study was unique because it was centered in public administration instead of industry. However, it was primarily important because of the absence of an economic incentive in the system. By law, no economic incentive could be provided. Moreover, promotion, an implicit economic reward, was granted on a seniority basis. Performance, for the most part, was recognized only if it deviated negatively from the standard.[1]

Participants in the experiment were members of two construction and four electrical crews responsible for the installation of all electric utilities for the state highway system (with the exception of those within city and municipality boundaries). The systems were comprised of signals, controllers, detectors, and general accessory equipment. The work itself, particularly for the electrical crews, was of a skilled and relatively technical nature.

Prior to the initiation of the experiment, each crew received from the Operations Division 1-month and 3-month schedules of work to be performed in the state. The schedules were subject to minor variations depending upon contingency situations. The crews were told essentially the jobs to perform, and when and how to get there. Participation was introduced into this setting by permitting the crews to become involved in developing the monthly (changed to bi-weekly for closer control) and tri-monthly schedules.

In order to refine further the experimental variable, participation, *three distinct degrees* of participation were employed. In first-degree participation, two crews worked indirectly in determining their work schedule by having their supervisor confer with Operations concerning the acceptability of the final schedule. A reasonable request for a change in the schedule would be considered. Second-degree participants conferred directly with a representative of Operations in developing their schedule from its inception, and third-degree participants assumed entire responsibility for the work schedules.

These changes in organizational procedure were introduced as a management directive, with no hint of the experimental nature of the undertaking.

Once the experimental setting was established, there still remained the problem of measurement. Determination of an accurate measure of productivity was critical. At first, the technical and rather broad nature of the jobs seemed to preclude finding such a measure. However, a careful study of basic activities involved in the effort of the crews exposed two distinct levels of activity permitting a statistical analysis of productivity change to take place. Moreover, once the relationship between the two levels of activity had been determined, a *net* productivity measure for jobs performed was obtainable. Crew productivity in the experimental condition was then compared to historical performance to determine if change had taken place which could be attributed to the introduction of the experimental variable. The approximate 6-month experimental period was compared with the *preceding* 6-month period, the prior *equivalent* 6-month period, and the preceding year.

The measure of change in morale after the introduction of the experimental variable took place in three ways. First, a questionnaire employing Herzberg's concepts of maintenance and motivational needs was administered prior to the experiment. The participants were informed that members of the Highway Department on all levels were participating. At the conclusion of the experiment, the questionnaire was again administered.

An indirect measure of morale was the amount of sick leave taken by employees. Therefore, crew records during the experimental period were compared with historical figures.

Finally, at the conclusion of the experiment, opinions regarding the morale of the employees were elicited from both their immediate supervisors and supervisors several levels above them.

RESULTS

In establishing the experimental participation variable, it was hypothesized that greater participation would result in increased productivity, and that the greater the participation permitted, the greater the increase in productivity would be. This did not prove to be the case.

The two crews participating at a first-degree level showed somewhat contradictory results. There seemed to be some improvement in the level of productivity obtained, although the improvement was *not* statistically significant.[2] Performance of the second crew was consistently lower, though not significantly.

When looking at second-degree participation, the results are also somewhat inconclusive. Again, one crew showed a positive, but not significant, gain while the second crew showed relatively little change.

Third-degree participants performed in a completely unexpected way. The performance of both crews was *consistently* poor in this case, with the performance of one crew being significantly so. In no case was the performance of any crew at any of the three levels of participation significantly improved when compared to data derived from the historical period.

In contrast to the experimental data regarding the productivity of crews operating in a participative setting, morale data *did* support to some degree the research hypotheses which stated basically that as participation increased, so would morale.

A nonparametric binomial sign test was applied to the "before" and "after" results of the attitude questionnaire. Although the first- and second-degree participants showed no significant change in morale, third-degree participants showed a marked improvement in their attitudes toward both the motivational and maintenance factors involved in their job performance.[3] Consistent with these results were the comments of supervisors who felt that morale of the crews as a whole had improved over the experimental period. Surprisingly, however, sick leave data indicate that during the period of the experiment, five of the six crews involved in the experiment *increased* their manhours absent per week. Despite this apparent ambiguity, there seems to be some evidence to indicate that morale of the crews did improve over that of the historical period.

An intriguing aspect of the combined morale-productivity findings is that the movement of productivity and morale was in opposite directions. Simply put, the often-accepted principle that increased morale leads to increased productivity was not supported by this research. The recently reported research by Stogdill appears to corroborate these findings [13].

DISCUSSION

There is some precedent in the literature for anticipating the results encountered in the present study. Lewin has pointed out the difficulty of introducing change into a natural field setting [9, p. 74], although this problem seemed to be successfully overcome in the present case. In addition, the experimental variable *was* visible, relevant, and work-related [11, pp. 326-327], and *excellent* cooperation was provided by Traffic Department personnel to insure the success of the experiment.

Neither was the Hawthorne effect a factor in this study. The crews maintained geographical separation during the course of the study, and at no time did any suspect that they were participants in a controlled field experiment.

Again, the influence of learning must be ruled out as a partial explanation of results, since trend analysis did not on the whole indicate increased productivity during the latter stages of the experimental period.

Finally, there is no reason to expect worker dissatisfaction with the experimentally introduced changes. In fact, almost without exception, the crew response was favorable [8, pp. 343-360].

There are several other possible explanations for the crew's behavior, however. Research has shown that some workers are simply not prepared to accept responsibility and prefer to perform in an atmosphere of authoritarian leadership [6, pp. 15-18]. This is particularly true if the worker feels easy about this dependency.

Closely related to this explanation is the finding that certain individuals seem to have low autonomy needs [9, p. 89]. These individuals cannot be expected to respond as positively to participative decision-making techniques as individuals with a high need for independence [14, p. 48]. Participative decision-making would simply not appear to contribute to the arousal of motivation in some persons [9, pp. 74 & 85; 14, p. 65]. Furthermore, even if participative decision-making did serve to motivate an individual, this in itself is no assurance that the change will be reflected in improved performance [5, pp. 143-157].

Another recent study [4, pp. 101-104] suggests that for change to be permanent, the change must be accompanied by both tension and a powerful influencing agent. While the influencing agent was present in the form of Central Office supervision in the present research, it is doubtful that any state of tension existed prior to or after the introduction of the experimental variable.

A different approach is taken by some authors, who emphasize that the use of behavioral incentives touch upon only one aspect of the total psychological and physical environment of the individual, and that to try to explain performance out of the context of the total system is useless [12, pp. 14 & 15].

One obvious factor not present in the research under discussion is the economic incentive usually present in an industrial environment. Few authors are willing to overlook the importance of this appeal in motivating individuals [9, p. 78]. It is difficult to avoid wondering what the impact of an economic incentive would have been in the present study, given the fact that over one-third of the participants scored highest in the economic interest area on an Allport-Vernon-Lindsey Personality Profile administered at the conclusion of the experiment.

Further support for the importance of economic considerations is obtained from data taken from the morale questionnaires. The two areas of greatest relative displeasure among the field crews dealt with the economic and personnel policies of the Highway Department. This, in turn, suggests possible lack of fulfillment of employer's maintenance needs. If this is the case, then theoretically one could not expect an incentive appealing to a motivational need to have much effect.

Other areas that offer a potential explanation for the experimental results relate to the particular environment of the experiment. One might hypothesize that the *level* of operations involved in the study (or in behavioral studies in general) may act as an intervening variable affecting the research, e.g., the response of employees to behavioral incentives may vary at different levels of the organization.

In the present study, the physical distance of the central office supervisors from the field crews in combination with the relative degree of autonomy possessed by the crews could have created an atmosphere of independence for which the crews were not psychologically prepared.

A final thought might be given to the environment of governmental administration in general. Is there, for example, something about this environment which mitigates against the application of behavioral incentives? Or, does the personality of the typical operative drawn to employment in public administration agencies differ in some basic manner from that of the typical industrial employee? What can be deduced from the fact that public administration agencies offer no economic incentive for productivity, an incentive usually found in industry and also in many of the studies purporting to show the positive effects of participative decision-making? These are a few of the questions raised by the findings of this research, and definitely represent areas for continuing research.

SUMMARY COMMENTS

This study lends some support to the theory that increased involvement of employees in the decision-making process results in higher worker morale. However, there was no such relationship in evidence between participation and productivity. The research suggests that while participative management techniques may produce involved, happy workers, it does not necessarily achieve productive results for the organization.

In the senior author's investigations into the promotion process, he has noted that there is more than a small degree of truth to the adage that "good guys come in last." It has been suggested that the old control-oriented, theory "X" manager is in process of being replaced by the new "concerned and involving" theory "Y" type executive.

Yet, following the promotion process within different firms, it is not uncommon to find the tough-minded, aggressive, control-oriented manager moving to the top. Results do count in business and the current emphasis upon management-by-objectives is seen by business leaders as an effective way to establish the rigorous standards necessary to obtain high performance.

It requires time, as well as energy and effort, for people to become involved. Participation stimulates increasing numbers of relationships and "interest-sharing" conversations among employees. It also results in the development of multiple and diverse objectives that people attempt to meet through work activities.

By their very nature, these conditions tend to hamper productivity. As a result of his investigation, Stogdill concluded that "a manager can choose whether he wants to maximize productivity or cohesiveness . . . if he prefers cohesiveness, he can be surrounded by loyal, happy workers but lose money on his operations" [13].

In another investigation recently completed under the senior author's direction, it was found that as group members become more interrelated and as their influence upon one another increases, the formal directive leadership pattern within the group erodes. The group members tended to neutralize the leadership thrust.

In all three research projects, the negative ramifications of participation and involvement upon the productive activities of the group were in evidence. The nature of the findings in these research projects does not suggest that the manager should abandon his attempts to involve his people as participants in the decision-making process and work activities. Instead, it points to the importance of the manager's being able to find that trade-off point between participation and morale on the one hand and high productivity on the other which gives him the best overall results.

To the student of management, the research findings suggest the complexities related to the problems of motivation and productivity. The previous stimulus-response approaches to motivation simply aren't satisfactory in explaining human behavior within work settings.

The study raises questions which would indicate that the case for participative management is not entirely closed. Perhaps it is time to look at the complexities related to different managerial styles and to carefully probe, through further experimentation, some of the questions raised by the research.

FOOTNOTES

1. Dialogues with Mr. Frederick Tarbox, Manager, Bureau of Traffic, Ohio Department of Highways.

2. Measured at the 1 percent and 5 percent levels of significance through the statistical analysis.

3. Significant at the 5 percent level.

REFERENCES

1. Allport, Gordon W., "Psychology of Participation," *The Psychological Review*, Vol. 53, No. 3 (May 1945).
2. Carey, H.H., "Consultative Supervision," *Nation's Business*, 25 (April 1937).
3. Coch, Lester, and J.R.P. French, Jr., "Overcoming Resistance to Change," *Human Relations I*, Vol. 1, No. 4 (August 1948).
4. Dalton, Gene W., Louis B. Barnes and Abraham Zalenznik, *The Distribution of Authority in Formal Organizations* (Boston: Harvard University Division of Research, 1968).
5. Friedlander, F., "Motivation to Work and Organizational Performance," *Journal of Applied Psychology* (April 1966).
6. Graham, Gerald H., "Theory X and Y in the Teaching of Management," *Collegiate News and Views*, Vol. XXII, No. 4 (May 1969).
7. Haire, Mason, *Psychology in Management* (New York: McGraw-Hill Book Company, Inc., 1964).
8. Lawrence, Paul R., "How to Deal with Resistance to Change," *Human Relations for Management*, Edward C. Bursk, ed. (New York: Harper and Brothers, 1956).
9. Lewin, Aaron, "Participative Decision-Making," *Organizational Behavior and Human Performance*, Vol. 3, No. 1 (1968).

10. Maier, Norman R.F., *Psychology in Industry* (Boston: Houghton-Mifflin Company, 1965).
11. Mann, Floyd C., and Franklin W. Neff, "Involvement and Participation in Change," *Psychology in Administration: A Research Orientation*, Timothy W. Costello and Sheldon S. Zalkind (Englewood Cliffs, N.J.: Prentice-Hall, Inc. 1963).
12. Marrow, Alfred J., David G. Bowers, Stanley E. Seashore, *Management by Participation* (New York: Harper and Row, 1967).
13. Stogdill, Ralph M., "Individual Behavior Group Achievement—A Behavioral Model of Organization," Paper presented at the annual meeting of the American Psychological Association (Washington, D.C., September 3, 1969).
14. Vroom, Victor H., *Some Personality Determinants of the Effects of Participation* (Englewood Cliffs, New Jersey: Prentice-Hall, Inc., 1960).

David G. Bowers is Program Director at the Center for Research on the Utilization of Scientific Knowledge, The University of Michigan. Stanley E. Seashore is Professor of Psychology and Assistant Director of the Institute for Social Research, The University of Michigan. *This article is reprinted with permission from* Administrative Science Quarterly, *September 1965, pp. 238-263.*

Predicting Organizational Effectiveness With a Four-Factor Theory of Leadership

DAVID G. BOWERS and STANLEY E. SEASHORE

For centuries writers have been intrigued with the idea of specifying predictable relationships between what an organization's leader does and how the organization fares. In our own time, behavioral science has looked extensively at this question, yet incongruities and contradictory or unrelated findings seem to crowd the literature. It is the intent in this paper to locate and integrate the consistencies, to explore some neglected issues, and, finally, to generate and use a network of variables for predicting outcomes of organizational effectiveness.

Leadership has been studied informally by observing the lives of great men and formally by attempting to identify the personality traits of acknowledged leaders through assessment techniques. Review of the research literature from these studies, however, reveals few consistent findings.[1] Since the Second World War, research emphasis has shifted from a search for personality traits to a search for behavior that makes a difference in the performance or satisfaction of the followers. The conceptual scheme to be outlined here is an example of this approach.

In this paper, the primary concern is with leadership in businesses or industrial enterprises, usually termed "supervision" or "management," although most of the constructs of leadership to be used here apply equally well to social groups, clubs, and voluntary associations.

Work situations in business organizations in a technologically advanced society typically involve a comparatively small number of persons who receive direction from one person. This is the basic unit of industrial society and has been called the "organizational family."[2] In this modern organizational family, there is usually task interdependence and there is frequently social interdependence as well. The ideal is that of a group of people working effectively together toward the accomplishment of some common aim.

This paper presents a review of the conceptual structure resulting from several programs of research in leadership practices, followed by a reconceptualization that attempts to take into consideration all of these earlier findings. In an attempt to assess the usefulness of the reconceptualization, it is then applied to leadership and effectiveness data from a recent study.

DIMENSIONS OF LEADERSHIP

It seems useful at the outset to isolate on a common-sense basis certain attributes of "leadership." First, the concept of leadership is meaningful only in the context of two or more people. Second, leadership consists of behavior; more specifically, it is behavior by one member of a group toward another member or members of the group, which advances some joint aim. Not all organizationally useful behavior in a work group is leadership; leadership behavior must be distinguished from the performance of noninterpersonal tasks that advance the goals of the organization. On a common-sense basis, then, leadership is organizationally useful behavior by one member of an organizational family toward another member or members of that same organizational family.

Defined in this manner, leadership amounts to a large aggregation of separate behaviors, which may be grouped or classified in a great variety of ways. Several classification systems from previous research have achieved considerable prominence, and are briefly described here.

Ohio State Leadership Studies

In 1945, the Bureau of Business Research at Ohio State University undertook the construction of an instrument for describing leadership. From extended conversations and discussions among staff members who represented various disciplines, a list of nine dimensions or categories of leadership behavior were postulated. Descriptive statements were then written and assigned to one or another of the nine dimensions, and after further refinement, 150 of these were selected as representing these nine dimensions and were incorporated into the Leader Behavior Description Questionnaire.

Two factor analyses attempted to simplify its conceptual framework further. Hemphill and Coons[3] intercorrelated and factor-analyzed group mean scores for 11 dimensions for a sample composed largely of educational groups,[4] and obtained three orthogonal factors.

1. *Maintenance of membership character.* Behavior of a leader which allows him to be considered a "good fellow" by his subordinates; behavior which is socially agreeable to group members.

2. *Objective attainment behavior.* Behavior related to the output of the group; for example, taking positive action in establishing goals or objectives, structuring group activities in a way that members may work toward an objective, or serving as a representative of group accomplishment in relation to outside groups, agencies, forces, and so on.

3. *Group interaction facilitation behavior.* Behavior that structures communication among group members, encouraging pleasant group atmosphere, and reducing conflicts among members.

Halpin and Winer[5] made an analysis using data collected from air-force crews, revising the original measuring instrument to adapt it to the respondent group. Only 130 items were used, with appropriate rewording, and the number of dimensions was reduced to eight. Treatment of the data indicated that five of the eight were sufficient for describing the entire roster, and the correlation of the 130 items with these five dimensions was regarded as a matrix of oblique factor loadings. These item loadings were then factor analyzed and the results rotated, producing four orthogonal factors.

1. *Consideration.* Behavior indicative of friendship, mutual trust, respect, and warmth.

2. *Initiating structure.* Behavior that organizes and defines relationships or roles, and establishes well-defined patterns of organization, channels of communication, and ways of getting jobs done.

3. *Production emphasis.* Behavior which makes up a manner of motivating the group to greater activity by emphasizing the mission or job to be done.

4. *Sensitivity (social awareness).* Sensitivity of the leader to, and his awareness of, social interrelationships and pressures inside or outside the group.

The Halpin and Winer analysis has been the more widely known and used. Because the investigators dropped the third and fourth factors as accounting for too little common variance, "consideration" and "initiating structure" have become to some extent identified as "the Ohio State" dimensions of leadership.

Early Survey Research Center Studies

Concurrent with the Ohio State studies was a similar program of research in human relations at the University of Michigan Survey Research Center. Approaching the problem of leadership or supervisory style by locating clusters of characteristics which (a) correlated positively among themselves and (b) correlated with criteria of effectiveness, this program developed two concepts called "employee orientation" and "production orientation."[6]

Employee orientation is described as behavior by a supervisor, which indicates that he feels that the "human relations" aspect of the job is quite important; and that he considers the employees as human beings of intrinsic importance, takes an interest in them, and accepts their individuality and personal needs. Production-orientation stresses production and the technical aspects of the job, with employees as means for getting work done; it seems to combine the Ohio State dimensions of initiating structure and production emphasis. Originally conceived to be opposite poles of the same continuum, employee-orientation and production-orientation were later reconceptualized,[7] on the basis of further data, as representing independent dimensions.

Katz and Kahn,[8] writing from a greater accumulation of findings, presented another conceptual scheme, with four dimensions of leadership.

1. *Differentiation of supervisory role.* Behavior by a leader that reflects greater emphasis upon activities of planning and performing specialized skilled tasks; spending a greater proportion of time in actual supervision, rather than performing the men's own tasks himself or absorption in impersonal paperwork.

2. *Closeness of supervision.* Behavior that delegates authority, checks upon subordinates less frequently, provides more general, less frequent instructions about the work, makes greater allowance for individuals to perform in their own ways and at their own paces.

3. *Employee orientation.* Behavior that gives major emphasis to a supportive personal relationship, and that reflects a personal interest in subordinates; being more understanding, less punitive, easy to talk to, and willing to help groom employees for advancement.

4. *Group relationships.* Behavior by the leader that results in group cohesiveness, pride by subordinates in their work group, a feeling of membership in the group, and mutual help on the part of those subordinates.

Differentiation of supervisory role corresponds in part to what the Ohio State studies refer to as initiating structure or objective attainment behavior, and clearly derives from the earlier concept of production orientation. Closeness of supervision, on the other hand, has something in common with maintenance of membership character, consideration, and employee-orientation, but also with objective attainment behavior, initiating structure, and production orientation. Employee orientation clearly corresponds to the earlier concept by the same name, while group relationships is to some extent similar to the interaction facilitation behavior and social sensitivity of the Ohio State studies.

In still another conceptualization, combining theory with review of empirical data, Kahn[9] postulated four supervisory functions.

1. *Providing direct need satisfaction.* Behavior by a leader, not conditional upon behavior of the employee, which provides direct satisfaction of the employee's ego and affiliative needs.

2. *Structuring the path to goal attainment.* Behavior that cues subordinates toward filling personal needs through attaining organizational goals.

3. *Enabling goal achievement.* Behavior that removes barriers to goal achievement, such as eliminating bottlenecks, or planning.

4. *Modifying employee goals.* Behavior that influences the actual personal goals of subordinates in organizationally useful directions.

Direct need satisfaction clearly resembles consideration and employee-orientation; enabling goal achievement seems similar to initiating structure or objective attainment behavior; structuring the path to goal attainment and modifying employee goals are probably closer to the Ohio State production emphasis factor.

Studies at the Research Center for Group Dynamics

Cartwright and Zander,[10] at the Research Center for Group Dynamics, on the basis of accumulated findings, described leadership in terms of two sets of group functions.

1. *Group maintenance functions.* Behavior that keeps interpersonal relations pleasant, resolves disputes, provides encouragement, gives the minority a chance to be heard, stimulates self-direction, and increases interdependence among members.

2. *Goal achievement functions.* Behavior that initiates action, keeps members' attention on the goal, develops a procedural plan, evaluates the quality of work done, and makes expert information available.

These descriptive terms clearly refer to broader constructs than consideration or initiating structure. Group maintenance functions, for example, include what has been termed consideration, maintenance of membership character, or employee-orientation, but they also include functions concerned with relationships among group members not in formal authority positions. This concept is in some ways similar to group interaction facilitation behavior in the Ohio State factor analysis of Hemphill and Coons.[11] Goal achievement functions seem to encompass what the Ohio State studies referred to as initiating structure and production emphasis or objective attainment behavior, and what early Survey Research Center studies called production orientation.

Mann's Three Skills

In subsequent work at the Survey Research Center built upon earlier findings, a recent classification, proposed by several writers and developed and operationalized by Floyd Mann,[12] treats leadership in terms of a trilogy of skills required of supervisors or managers. Although behaviors requiring particular skills and those skills themselves are not necessarily perfectly parallel, it seems reasonable to assume at least an approximate correspondence between the two. The three skills are:

1. *Human relations skill.* Ability and judgment in working with and

through people, including knowledge of principles of human behavior, interpersonal relations, and human motivation.

2. *Technical skill.* Ability to use knowledge, methods, techniques, and equipment necessary for the performance of specific tasks.

3. *Administrative skill.* Ability to understand and act according to the objectives of the total organization, rather than only on the basis of the goals and needs of one's own immediate group. It includes planning, organizing the work, assigning the right tasks to the right people, inspecting, following up, and coordinating the work.

Likert's New Patterns of Management

Rensis Likert of the University of Michigan Institute for Social Research, building upon many of the findings of the Survey Research Center and the Research Center for Group Dynamics as well as upon his own early work in the same area for the Life Insurance Agency Management Association, describes five conditions for effective supervisory behavior.

1. *Principle of supportive relations.* The leadership and other processes of the organization must be such as to ensure a maximum probability that in his interactions and his relationships with the organization, each member will, in the light of his background, values, and expectations, view the experience as supportive, and as one that builds and maintains his sense of personal worth and importance.[13]

2. *Group methods of supervision.* Management will make full use of the potential capacities of its human resources only when each person in an organization is a member of one or more effectively functioning work groups that have a high degree of group loyalty, effective skills of interaction, and high performance goals.[14]

3. *High performance goals.* If a high level of performance is to be achieved, it appears to be necessary for a supervisor to be employee-centered, and at the same time to have high performance goals and a contagious enthusiasm as to the importance of achieving these goals.[15]

4. *Technical knowledge.* The (effective) leader has adequate competence to handle the technical problems faced by his group, or he sees that access to this technical knowledge is fully provided.[16]

5. *Coordinating, scheduling, planning.* The leader fully reflects and effectively represents the views, goals, values, and decisions of his group in those other groups where he is performing the function of linking his group to the rest of the organization. He brings to the group of which he is the leader the views, goals, and decisions of those other groups. In this way, he provides a linkage whereby communication and the exercise of influence can be performed in both directions.[17]

Comparison and Integration

These various research programs and writings make it clear that a great deal of conceptual content is held in common. In fact, four dimensions emerge from these studies, which seem to comprise the basic structure of what one may term "leadership":

1. *Support.* Behavior that enhances someone else's feeling of personal worth and importance.

2. *Interaction facilitation.* Behavior that encourages members of the group to develop close, mutually satisfying relationships.

3. *Goal emphasis.* Behavior that stimulates an enthusiasm for meeting the group's goal or achieving excellent performance.

4. *Work facilitation.* Behavior that helps achieve goal attainment by such activities as scheduling, coordinating, planning, and by providing resources such as tools, materials, and technical knowledge.

This formulation is obviously very close, except in terminology, to that expressed by Rensis Likert and was, in fact, stimulated by it. Table 1 indicates how concepts from the various research programs relate to these four basic concepts of leadership. More important, however, is the fact that each of these four concepts appears, sometimes separately, sometimes in combination, in all but two (Katz, et al., 1950; Kahn, 1958) of the previous formulations listed. These four dimensions are not considered indivisible, but capable of further subdivision according to some regularity of occurrence in social situations or according to the conceptual preferences of investigators.

INDEPENDENCE OF LEADERSHIP AND POSITION

Traditional leadership research has focused upon the behavior of formally designated or recognized leaders. This is probably due, at least in part, to the historical influence of the hierarchical models of the church and the army. As a result, it has until recently been customary to study leadership either as an attribute of the person of someone who is authority-vested, or as an attribute of his behavior. More recently, attention has been paid to leadership in groups less formally structured, as illustrated by the work of Bass with leaderless group discussion, the work of Sherif, as well as some of the work of other researchers in the area of group dynamics.[18]

In the previous section, leadership was conceptualized in terms of four social-process functions, four kinds of behavior that must be present in work groups if they are to be effective. The performance of these functions was deliberately not limited to formally designated leaders. Instead, it was proposed that leadership, as described in terms of support, goal emphasis, work facilitation, and interaction facilitation, may be provided by anyone in a work group for anyone else in that work group. In this sense, leadership may be either "supervisory" or "mutual"; that is, a group's needs for support may be provided by a formally designated leader, by members for each other, or both; goals may be emphasized by the formal leader, by members to each other, or by both; and similarly for work facilitation and interaction facilitation.

This does not imply that formally designated leaders are unnecessary or

TABLE 1
Correspondence of Leadership Concepts of Different Investigators

Bowers and Seashore (1964)	Hemphill and Coons (1957)	Halpin and Winer (1957)	Katz et al. (1950)	Katz and Kahn (1951)	Kahn (1958)	Mann (1962)	Likert (1961)	Cartwright and Zander (1960)
Support	Maintenance of membership character	Consideration	Employee orientation	Employee orientation	Providing direct need satisfaction	Human relations skills	Principle of supportive relationships	Group maintenance functions
				Closeness of supervision				
Interaction facilitation	Group interaction facilitation behavior	Sensitivity		Group relationships			Group methods of supervision	
					Structuring path to goal attainment			
Goal emphasis		Production emphasis					High-performance goals	
	Objective attainment behavior		Production orientation		Modifying employee goals	Administrative skills		Goal-achievement functions
				Differentiation of supervisory role	Enabling goal achievement		Technical knowledge, planning, scheduling	
Work facilitation		Initiating structure		Closeness of supervision		Technical skills		

superfluous, for there are both common-sense and theoretical reasons for believing that a formally acknowledged leader through his supervisory leadership behavior sets the pattern for the mutual leadership which subordinates supply each other.

LEADERSHIP AND ORGANIZATIONAL EFFECTIVENESS

Leadership in a work situation has been judged to be important because of its connection, to some extent assumed and to some extent demonstrated, to organizational effectiveness. Effectiveness, moreover, although it has been operationalized in a variety of ways, has often been assumed to be a unitary characteristic. These assumptions define a commonly accepted theorem that leadership (if not a unitary characteristic, then a limited roster of closely related ones) is always salutary in its effect and that it always enhances effectiveness.

The pattern of the typical leadership study has been first, to select a criterion of effectiveness: sometimes a rating of overall effectiveness by superiors, at other times a questionnaire measure of "morale," on still other occasions a few measures such as output, absence, or accident rates. Next, an attempt is made to relate leadership to the criterion selected. When, in fact, a relationship is obtained, this is accepted. When no relationship or one opposite to that expected is obtained, the investigator often makes some statement referring to "error" or "further research."

It seems that a better strategy would be to obtain: (a) measures reflecting a theoretically meaningful conceptual structure of leadership; (b) an integrated set of systematically derived criteria; and (c) a treatment of these data, which takes account of the multiplicity of relationships and investigates the adequacy of leadership characteristics in predicting effectiveness variables.

In the present study an attempt is made to satisfy these conditions. A conceptual structure of leadership is developed, using empirical evidence. The four concepts of this structure are operationalized in terms of questionnaire items describing behavioral acts largely "loaded" on one or another of these constructs, and a systematically derived set of criteria of organizational effectiveness is obtained.

RESEARCH METHODS

Research Site

This study was conducted in 40 agencies of a leading life insurance company. These agencies are independently owned businesses, performing identical functions in their separate parts of the country. Only one or two hierarchical levels intervene between the regional manager, at the top of the hierarchy, and the sales agent at the bottom. The typical agency consists of an exclusive territory comprising a number of counties of a state or states. The regional manager ordinarily has headquarters in some principal city of his territory, and contracts with individuals to service the area as sales agents. He receives an "override" upon the commissions of policies sold by these agents, in addition to the full commissions from whatever policies he sells personally.

If geographical distance or volume of business is great enough, he may contract with individuals to serve as district managers. The district manager is given territorial rights for some subportion of the regional manager's territory, is permitted to contract agents to service the area, subject to the approval of the regional manager, and receives a portion of what would otherwise be the regional manager's override upon sales within his territory.

Although this is the usual arrangement, variations occur. Occasionally, for example, a territory will be so constituted as to prevent subdivision into districts. In these cases, the regional manager contracts directly with sales agents throughout his territory. In other cases, the territory is almost entirely urban, in which case the regional manager may substitute salaried or partially salaried supervisory personnel for district managers. In all cases, however, there are at least a regional manager and sales agents, and frequently, in addition, a district manager between these two parties.

In all, the company's field force comprises nearly 100 agencies. Of these, 40 were selected as being roughly representative of them all. Selection was made by company personnel, with an effort to select half of the 40 from the topmost part of the list of agencies ordered by performance, and the other half from among poorer performing agencies, omitting any having recent organizational disruption or change. Questionnaires were mailed out in April, 1961, to all contracted regional managers, district managers, sales agents, and supervisory personnel on full or part salary in these agencies; 83 percent were returned by June, 1961, for a total of 873 respondents.

Measurement

This report is concerned with 20 index measurements obtained through paper-and-pencil questionnaires, and 7 factorial measures of agency performance obtained from company records. A short description of each questionnaire variable appears in Table 2. These measures reflect perceptions of behavior rather than behavior itself, and are therefore no different from any other method of quantifying behavior: all involve the measurement of behavior, by some person and some mechanism. Close familiarity by the recipients of the behavior—and whatever systematic bias this introduces—is here considered as more desirable than the lack of information and large random error that an outside observer would very probably introduce.

In addition to these questionnaire measurements, the company provided some 70 measures of agency performance, which were then factor analyzed,[19] resulting in 7 orthogonal factors.

Factor I. Staff-clientele maturity. This factor reflects a difference in the kind of business produced by the agency attributable to the age and experience of the agent staff and the clientele that they reach. A high score reflects a high average premium per thousand, collected relatively infrequently, with very little term insurance or graduated premium life insurance, a small proportion of the business from new or young agents, and greater profitability from business already on the books.

TABLE 2
Content of Variables Used

Area	Description of questionnaire variable
Leadership* Support	Importance of morale
	Willingness to make changes
	Friendliness
	Conversational ease
	Opinion acceptance
Goal emphasis	Importance of competitive position
	Extra work effort
Work facilitation	Stressing standard procedures
	Offering new approaches
	Checking works vs capacity
	Emphasis upon meeting deadlines
Satisfaction†	With company
	With fellow agents
	With income prospects
	With regional manager
	With office costs
	With job
Need for Affiliation	Importance of being liked
	Importance of being accepted
Regional manager's expert power	Respect for regional manager's competence and good judgment
Classical business ideology††	Extent of agreement with statements of value and belief about nature of "best" economic society
Rivalry among agents	Extent to which some agents are trying to advance at others' expense

*Items in the leadership area were adapted from two sources: items used in the Ohio State studies and those used in previous Survey Research Center studies.

† 11 items, 6 satisfaction areas.

†† Items based upon conceptualization by F.X. Sutton, S.E. Harris, C. Kaysen, and J. Tobin, *American Business Creed* (Cambridge, Mass.: Harvard University Press, 1956).

Factor II. Business growth. This seems to indicate in fairly uncomplicated fashion the growth of business volume over the years immediately preceding the year of measurement.

Factor III. Business costs. Although the principal loadings are on variables measuring the costs per unit of new business, some minor loadings occur on variables relating to costs of renewal business. This factor, therefore, seems to be a business-cost dimension.

Factor IV. Advanced underwriting. This seems to be a factor measuring the extent to which there is emphasis by the agent staff upon advanced underwriting. A high score on this factor reflects a large average face value per life and per policy, comparatively large premiums per collection, a fairly high ratio of cases rejected, very little prepayment, fairly high costs, and high profitability of new business. A low score, of course, reflects a reverse pattern.

Factor V. Business volume. A fairly straightforward dimension measuring the dollar volume of new business done by the agency.

Factor VI. Manpower turnover. A measure of the extent to which there was a change in personnel within the agency during 1959. This factor loads most heavily on the ratio of terminations plus appointments to manpower, and on the ratio of terminations alone to manpower.

Factor VII. Regional manager's personal performance. This factor differs from those above by representing the performance of the regional manager, not of the agency as a whole. It seems to reflect the extent to which he is putting energy into agency maintenance and development, as against taking short-run gain. It is, perhaps, an age factor, related in some measure to the regional manager's distance from retirement.

Four of these factors are measures of performance in the usual sense; that is, a positive and a negative value can be placed at opposite ends of these continua: business growth, business costs, business volume, and manpower turnover. Factor I (staff-clientele maturity) and Factor IV (advanced underwriting) are descriptive, rather than evaluative,[20] and Factor VII is peculiar to only one person in the agency.

There are, therefore, within this study multiple-criteria measures, both of satisfaction, described earlier, and of performance. Although the use of multiple-criteria measures has become more common in recent years, it is still infrequent enough to make the study somewhat unique.

From the data that resulted, the following questions suggest themselves:

1. Are both mutual and supervisory leadership measures useful; that is, are there differential effects from the various leadership dimensions such that some criteria are associated with certain measures or combinations of measures and some with others?

2. In what way are mutual leadership measures related to supervisory measures?

3. How adequately may criteria of effectiveness be predicted from leadership measures as compared to other kinds of measures?

The reader should from the outset be reminded of several problems of the analysis. First, the analytic model used in this study assumes a particular causal directionality. Since the data are from a single period of time, this directionality cannot be proved. As an operating assumption, it must be either accepted or rejected by the reader, and the relationships otherwise interpreted by him. The assumption of managerial behavior as an organizational prime mover is, however, a common one. Second, since the model starts from assumptions about the nature of leadership, the analysis considers first the relationships of leadership characteristics to criteria of effectiveness. Third, since this is an attempt to locate possible precursors of effectiveness, the analysis then considers the relationship of nonleadership variables to effectiveness, paying serious attention only to those nonleadership variables that can reasonably be interpreted as causes of effectiveness. Fourth, not all of either leadership or nonleadership variables with statistically significant relationships are used to predict effectiveness measures; only the one or two of each category that is most highly correlated.

RESULTS

Relation of Leadership to Effectiveness

Table 3 presents the correlation coefficients of leadership measures with measures of satisfaction. Table 4 presents similar correlations of leadership measures to performance factors. These data indicate first, that the incidence of significant relationships of leadership to effectiveness is

TABLE 3
Correlation of Leadership with Satisfactions

| Leadership measure | Satisfaction with | | | | |
	Company	Fellow agents	Job	Income	Manager
Peer					
Support	.03*	.68	.39	.29*	.47
Goal emphasis	.37	.77	.26*	.42	.62
Work facilitation	.29*	.68	.34	.51	.45
Interaction facilitation	.31	.72	.30*	.42	.55
Manager					
Support	.31	.65	.35	.45	.86
Goal emphasis	.11*	.71	.09*	.43	.31
Work facilitation	.31	.61	.24*	.36	.41
Interaction facilitation	.30*	.67	.10*	.53	.78

*All others significant beyond .05 level of confidence, 2-tail

TABLE 4
Correlation of Leadership with Performance Factors

Leadership measure	Performance factor						
	I	II	III	IV	V	VI	VII
Peer							
Support	.26	−.02	−.27	−.21	.23	−.12	.27
Goal emphasis	.49*	−.05	−.45*	−.27	.15	.04	.04
Work facilitation	.33*	.14	−.41*	−.41*	.18	.00	.04
Interaction facilitation	.44*	−.13	−.44*	−.24	.11	.14	.05
Manager							
Support	.28	−.24	−.26	−.12	.25	.16	.10
Goal emphasis	.31*	.11	−.27	−.18	.41*	.03	−.19
Work facilitation	.43*	.13	−.37*	−.33*	.21	.16	−.12
Interaction facilitation	.42*	−.29	−.30	−.21	.13	.20	.01

* Significant beyond .05 level of confidence, 2-tail.

well above the chance level. Of 40 satisfaction-leadership coefficients, 30 are significant beyond the 5 percent level of confidence. Of 56 performance-leadership coefficients, 13 are significant beyond the 5 percent level of confidence. Second, the significant coefficients are not uniformly distributed throughout the matrix; instead, certain effectiveness criteria (e.g., satisfaction with income) and certain leadership measures (e.g., peer work facilitation) have many significant relationships, whereas others have few or none (e.g., performance factor VI). Third, significant coefficients are as often found in relation to peer as to managerial leadership characteristics.

For parsimony, the leadership characteristic with the largest coefficient in relation to each criterion measure is chosen as the analytic starting point in these matrices. To this is then added in turn each of the other significant leadership relationships by means of a two-predictor multiple-correlation technique. Because no r-to-z transformation of multiple correlation coefficients is possible, these cannot be compared with the original r value; therefore, seven correlation points are arbitrarily set as the criterion of significant improvement in prediction.[21]

It is apparent from Table 5, that, with two exceptions, adding other leadership characteristics that display somewhat smaller, but significant, correlations does not improve prediction. It is also apparent that peer goal emphasis plays a central role in this analysis: it is either the best predictor, or a significant additive, in five of the twelve cases.

Relation of Peer to Managerial Leadership

Before assessing the adequacy of leadership as a predictor of effectiveness, it seems advisable to answer the question posed earlier about the relationship between peer and managerial leadership. Table 6 presents the intercorrelation; all 16 coefficients in the table are statistically significant, indicating therefore that there is a close relationship between all managerial characteristics, on the one hand, and all peer characteristics on the other. Following the same method as that used for effectiveness, it appears that the best predictor of peer support is managerial support; of peer goal emphasis, managerial interaction facilitation; of peer work

TABLE 5
Improvement of Prediction of Criteria of Effectiveness by Addition of Other Significantly Related Leadership Characteristics

Effectiveness measure	Best predictor	Other measures improving prediction
Satisfaction with		
Company	Peer goal emphasis	None
Fellow agents	Peer goal emphasis	None
Job	Peer support	None
Income	Manager interaction facilitation	Peer goal emphasis
Manager	Manager support	None
Factors*		
I Staff-clientele maturity	Peer goal emphasis	Peer work facilitation
III Business costs	Peer goal emphasis	None
IV Advanced underwriting	Peer work facilitation	None
V Business volume	Manager goal emphasis	None

*Performance factors II, VI, and VII showed no significant relationships to leadership characteristics.

TABLE 6
Intercorrelation of Managerial and Peer Leadership Variables*

Managerial variables	Peer leadership characteristics			
	Support	Goal emphasis	Work facilitation	Interaction facilitation
Support	.59	.67	.52	.58
Goal emphasis	.54	.65	.72	.59
Work facilitation	.49	.63	.82	.66
Interaction facilitation	.55	.71	.62	.74

*All coefficients significant beyond .05 level of confidence, 2-tail.

TABLE 7

Improvement of Prediction of Peer Leadership Characteristics
by Addition of Other Managerial Leadership Characteristics

Peer measure	Managerial best predictor	Other managerial measures improving prediction
Support	Support	Goal emphasis
Goal emphasis	Interaction facilitation	Goal emphasis
Work facilitation	Work facilitation	None
Interaction facilitation	Interaction facilitation	Work facilitation

facilitation, managerial work facilitation; and of peer interaction facilitation, managerial interaction facilitation. With one exception, therefore, the best predictor of the peer characteristic is its managerial opposite number. Table 7 indicates that three predictions are improved by related managerial characteristics.

Assuming causation, one may say that if a manager wishes to increase the extent to which his subordinates support one another, he must increase his own support and his own emphasis upon goals. If he wishes to increase the extent to which his subordinates emphasize goals to one another, he must first increase his own facilitation of interaction and his emphasis upon goals. By increasing his facilitation of the work, he will increase the extent to which his subordinates do likewise, and if, in addition, he increases his facilitation of interaction, his subordinates will in turn facilitate interaction among themselves.

These data appear to confirm that there is in fact a significant and strong relationship between managerial and peer leadership characteristics. In general, the statement may be made that a forerunner of each peer variable is its managerial opposite number, and that substantial improvement is in most cases made by combining with this another managerial characteristic.

Adequacy of Prediction by Leadership Measures

Because this analysis has placed great emphasis on leadership constructs as predictors of organizational outcomes, it seems desirable to consider the extent to which prediction of these outcomes can be enhanced by the inclusion of nonleadership variables.[22] Table 8 summarizes the data on predictability of all criteria by nonleadership measurements. It seems likely from these data that some of the criteria may be much more successfully predicted using nonleadership variables than using leadership measures, that some others may be enhanced by using both, and that the predictability of still others is not improved by nonleadership characteristics.

The analysis at this point becomes somewhat complex, since relation-

TABLE 8
Prediction of Criteria by Nonleadership Variables

Criterion	Total no. of significant relations ($N = 214$)	No. of significant nonleadership variables	No. of significant nonleadership variables exceeding best leadership predictor	No. of possible causal variables*
Satisfaction with				
Company	56	52	33	23
Job	39	36	11	8
Manager	66	44	1	1
Fellow agents	56	34	0	0
Income	60	43	2	2
Factors				
Factor I	22	15	1	1
Factor II	19	19	19	17
Factor III	50	39	9	6
Factor IV	26	23	12	6
Factor V	19	17	5	1
Factor VI	17	13	13	0
Factor VII	11	9	9	0

*Based upon the judgment of the research staff.

ships exist not only between leadership or nonleadership variables and criteria, but also among leadership and among nonleadership variables. In effect, therefore, the search for the best predictive model turns into a rather complicated examination of various chains and arrangements of constructs. To simplify this procedure, each criterion is presented separately, diagramming for each a plausible and statistically optimal "causal" schema.

Figure 1a presents the relationships of leadership and nonleadership variables to satisfaction with the company and with income. This diagram indicates that supportive managers make more satisfactory arrangements about the office expenses of their agents, and that these arrangements, in part, lead to greater satisfaction with the company as a whole. In addition, as managers facilitate the interaction of their agents, the goals of the company and needs or aspirations of the people who work for it come to be more compatible, which also leads to satisfaction with the company and with income.

Figure 1b presents a similar chain of relationships to satisfaction with the job itself. This diagram is interpreted to mean that as agents facilitate the work for each other, less time is spent by agents in paperwork for specific clients. When this happens, when agents behave more supportively toward each other, and when the agents are, on the whole, higher in need for affiliation, there is greater job satisfaction. Figure 1c presents relationships to two criteria: satisfaction with fellow agents and volume of business. When agents emphasize goals among themselves, they become more satisfied with each other; and when this condition exists, an agency

FIGURE 1

Predicted measures: (*a*) satisfaction with company and with income; (*b*) satisfaction with job; (*c*) satisfaction with fellow agents; business volume; (*d*) satisfaction with manager; (*e*) business costs; (*f*) business growth.

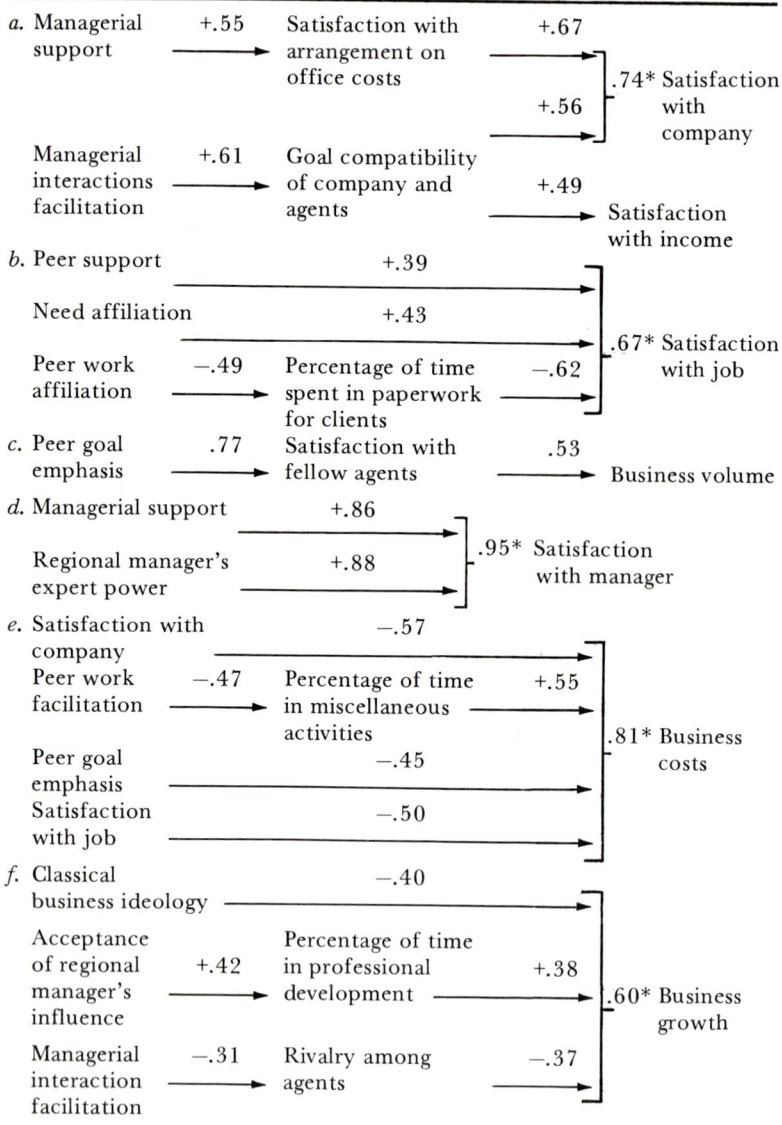

*Multiple correlation of variables listed against the effectiveness measure.

does a greater volume of business. Figure 1*d* shows very succinctly that agents are satisfied with their manager if he is supportive and knowledgeable. Figure 1*e* presents relationships to business costs in diagram form. Earlier diagrams showed the network of relationships associated with satisfaction with the company and with the job; here, these two satisfaction states are associated with lower business costs. In addition, as agents facilitate the work for each other, they spend a smaller proportion of their time in miscellaneous activities. When this occurs, and when agents emphasize goals to one another, costs are also lower.

Figure 1*f* diagrams relationships to business growth. The relationships presented in this diagram are less reliable than those presented in earlier figures. They are, as a group, somewhat smaller in size than those found in relation to other criteria already described. With this caution in mind, however, they can be interpreted as follows: business growth is high when the agent force does *not* hold to a classical business ideology; when regional managers, by accepting the opinions and ideas of their agents, encourage professional development; and when managers reduce rivalries among agents by encouraging their interaction. Far from stressing growth attained by competitive effort, this paradigm presents a picture of growth through cooperative professionalism.

Two additional performance measures of effectiveness present one significant, reasonable "causal" relationship each: staff-clientele maturity is greater when agents have a higher level of aspiration, and more advanced underwriting occurs when agents have a higher level of education. Although significant correlations were presented earlier in relation to these two factors, the reasonable interpretation of them is that the leadership measures are either effects or coordinates, not causes, of these descriptive rather than evaluative performance factors.

That no reasonable, significant relationships to manpower turnover are to be found is extremely puzzling. In most investigations of the effect of social-psychological variables upon organizational behavior, it is assumed that performance measures which are more "person" than "production" oriented will show the highest relationships to questionnaire measurements. In the present case this assumption is not supported. No variations of analysis that were attempted produced any noticeable change. An attempt was made to assess curvilinear correlations, but no improvement over linear correlation resulted. It was also thought that the factorial measure of turnover might be too complicated and that a simpler measure of proportion of terminations might be more productive. This also produced no noticeable effect. Apparently, manpower turnover in this particular company or industry is related to forces in the individual, the environment, or perhaps the organizational situation not tapped by the questionnaire measurement used.

It is not surprising that no correlations are found with the regional manager's personal performance. It is, as explained earlier, the weakest factor, and differs from the other factors in being descriptive of a single individual rather than of the agency as a whole. It may well be affected more by variables such as the regional manager's distance from retirement than by factors assessed here.

DISCUSSION AND CONCLUSIONS

To what extent have the data demonstrated the usefulness of the conceptualization presented at the beginning of this article? It seems reasonable to state the following:

1. Seven of the eight leadership characteristics outlined above in fact play some part in the predictive model generated from the data; only peer interaction facilitation seems to play no unique role.

2. Both managerial and peer leadership characteristics seem important.

3. There are plausible relationships of managerial to peer leadership characteristics.

4. The model is not a simple one of managerial leadership leading to peer leadership, which in turn leads to outcomes separately; instead, different aspects of performance are associated with different leadership characteristics, and, in some cases, satisfaction outcomes seem related to performance outcomes.

5. Some effectiveness measures are related to causal factors other than those tapped in this instrument.

6. The ability to predict outcomes with the variables selected varies from .95 to .00.

7. The role of leadership characteristics in this prediction varies in importance from strong, direct relationships in some cases (e.g., satisfaction with manager) to indirect relationships (e.g., business volume) to no relationship (e.g., advanced underwriting).

8. Leadership, as conceived and operationalized here, is not adequate alone to predict effectiveness; instead, additional and, in some cases, intervening constructs must be included to improve prediction. These "other" constructs are of several distinct types:

a. *Leadership-related.* Regional manager's expert power, regional manager's influence acceptance, and rivalry among agents.

b. *Work Patterns.* Percentage of time in miscellaneous activities, in paperwork for clients, in professional development.

c. *Personal and Motivational.* Education, level of aspiration, need for affiliation, goal compatibility of individual and organization, and classical business ideology.

FOOTNOTES

1. C.A. Gibb, "Leadership," in G. Lindzey, *Handbook of Social Psychology* (Cambridge, Mass.: Addison-Wesley Publishing Co., Inc., 1954), II, 877-917; R.M. Stogdill, Personal Factors Associated with Leadership: A Survey of the Literature, *Journal of Psychology*, 25 (1948), 35-71.

2. F.C. Mann, "Toward an Understanding of the Leadership Role in Formal Organization," in R. Dubin, G.C. Homans, F.C. Mann, and D.C. Miller, *Leadership and Productivity* (San Francisco, Calif.: Chandler Publishing Company, 1965), pp. 68-103.

3. J.K. Hemphill and A.E. Coons, "Development of the Leader Behavior Description Questionnaire," in R.M. Stogdill and A.E. Coons (eds.), *Leader Behavior: Its Description and Measurement* (Research Monograph No. 88, Columbus, Ohio: Bureau of Business Research, the Ohio State University, 1957), pp. 6-38.

4. The 11 dimensions were made up of the original 9, one of which (communication) had been subdivided, plus an overall leadership evaluation.

5. A.W. Halpin and J. Winer, "A Factorial Study of the Leader Behavior Description Questionnaire," in R.M. Stogdill and A.E. Coons, *Leader Behavior, op. cit.*, pp. 39-51.

6. D. Katz, N. Maccoby, and Nancy C. Morse, *Productivity, Supervision, and Morale in an Office Situation* (Detroit, Mich.: The Darel Press, Inc., 1950); D. Katz, N. Maccoby, G. Gurin, and Lucretia G. Floor, *Productivity, Supervision, and Morale Among Railroad Workers* (Ann Arbor, Mich.: Survey Research Center, 1951).

7. R.L. Kahn, The Prediction of Productivity, *Journal of Social Issues*, 12 (1956), 41-49.

8. D. Katz and R.L. Kahn, "Human Organization and Worker Motivation," in L.R. Tripp (ed.), *Industrial Productivity* (Madison, Wisc.: Industrial Relations Research Association, 1951), pp. 146-171.

9. R.L. Kahn, "Human Relations on the Shop Floor," in E.M. Hugh-Jones (ed.), *Human Relations and Modern Management* (Amsterdam, Holland: North-Holland Publishing Co., 1958), pp. 43-74.

10. D. Cartwright and A. Zander, *Group Dynamics Research and Theory* (Evanston, Ill.: Row, Peterson & Co., 1960).

11. Hemphill and Coons, *op. cit.*

12. Mann, *op. cit.*

13. R. Likert, *New Patterns of Management* (New York: McGraw-Hill Book Co., 1961), p. 103.

14. *Ibid.*, p. 104.

15. *Ibid.*, p. 8.

16. *Ibid.*, p. 171.

17. *Ibid.*, p. 171.

18. B.M. Bass, *Leadership, Psychology, and Organizational Behavior* (New York: Harper & Bros., 1960); Cartwright and Zander, *op. cit.*; M. and Carolyn W. Sherif, *An Outline of Social Psychology* (New York: Harper & Bros., 1956).

19. The factor analysis method used was that of a principal axes solution with varimax rotation.

20. It should be noted that these factors are interpreted by the authors on the basis of a single set of data. Data from other periods or other firms, as well as interpretations by life insurance experts, might differ from those presented here.

21. The actual multiple correlation values require much space and are therefore omitted here. Copies of these tables of multiple correlation coefficients may be obtained upon request from the authors.

22. Nonleadership variables comprised a large majority of the 214 items in the questionnaire.

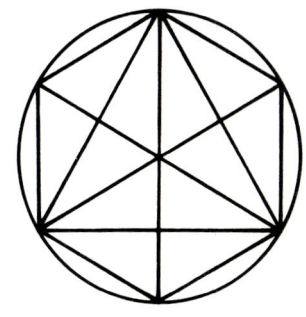

Part lll
Participative Practice
and
Implementation Techniques

Dr. Sorcher is a psychologist with the General Electric Company's Personnel Research Staff, specializing in social-industrial psychology. This article appeared in Personnel Administration, *September-October 1971, pp. 20-24 and is reprinted with permission of the International Personnel Management Association, 1313 East 60th Street, Chicago, Illinois 60637.*

Motivation, Participation and Myth

MELVIN SORCHER

Very frequently my telephone rings and there is an enthusiastic employee relations or manufacturing manager on the other end. He is interested in motivating a group of employees in his plant, and would like to try some of the ideas that he has read about on participative management. The manager explains that he is calling to check out some of his thoughts before he begins to apply them. I am quite pleased that he called for two reasons. First, his inquiry and interest indicate an awareness of the need to supervise employees in a somewhat different way than we have in the past. Second, it is good that he called because he is about to get himself into a situation which, at best, will probably not result in an improvement on present circumstances, and which, at worst, will be confusing and annoying to the employees, resulting in a detrimental effect on present performance.

No matter how gently one tries to explain this to the manager, it takes the steam out of his enthusiasm and confidence. This is regrettable. The manager probably placed the call for confirmation and encouragement for what he hopes to do. To learn that he is likely to be eaten by lions must surely be disappointing to him. To accept this idea, he must think differently than previously.

Most managers have read a good deal about the concept of participative management and employee involvement. Unfortunately, this literature often does more to mislead than to help because there is a wide gap between a conceptual understanding and the ability to put these ideas into practice. Too often the manager will fail to get the desired results, not because of inadequacy of conceptualization (his general ideas are good), but because of inadequacy of preparation, lack of skill, or naivete. Getting employees properly involved in their jobs is not something that most managers can easily bring about on their own, as simple as it may seem, or as simple and matter-of-fact as many writers make it seem.

Getting employees involved to their personal advantage, as well as to their company's benefit, requires skillful handling of people and situations. Management must, in addition, be willing to take some risk because there is no half-way point between participative management and autocratic management. Participative management requires *real* participation and involvement in activities and in decisions which management may be totally unwilling to give or unaware of the need to consider.

THE WRONG APPROACH

Typically, the manager who calls about this topic starts by describing the group he wants to motivate to higher performance. His approach is a reasonable one in view of the material available in the management literature. The best way to describe this approach is in the words of one manager who told me how he wanted to motivate his people:

"Well, I thought I would bring the foreman together with the group from the front end of the line. We would do this once a month in an hour of scheduled overtime. During this meeting, the foreman would present a problem to the group and tell them that since they know their jobs better than anyone else, they should try to solve the problem. Then, the foreman could sit back and watch the process move along toward solution of the problem."

Interestingly enough, this is how most managers describe their idea. They assume that by asking employees to sit down with the foreman, who asks them to solve a problem, the employees will be so delighted with the foreman's interest in their opinions that they will immediately work out a superior solution. Furthermore, many managers explain that one of the changes that they hope for is the opportunity to do a wider variety of operations. For example, they may suggest that six two-step operations be changed to three four-step operations. Employees are not likely to be pleased with this arrangement. There is little difference between a dull four-step job and a dull two-step job—especially when there is neither a change in pay nor a visible non-financial incentive (such as adequate recognition). In these cases, the manager's expectations of success are based on sheer myth, and the probability of an outcome that comes close to matching his expectations is remote.

Instead of hoping that employees will be motivated through horizontal job enlargement, the manager should be aware that employees can become more involved in their work if the incentive is a heightened sense of self-esteem. Second, allowing anything like one hour per month on scheduled overtime to deal with the concept of participative management is a waste of overtime pay. Nothing can be accomplished in this time—or even in several hours of scheduled overtime. The frequency of discussion between participants must be more often, as part of the employees day-to-day work, and not as an "extra." Moreover, when the foreman identifies a problem for his employees and then asks them to solve it, there is nothing new about this. Foremen do that all the time, and this alone does not produce employee involvement in the way that many managers would really like to consider the issue.

A BETTER APPROACH

The term "participative management" is not very useful since it has many different connotations and some people make narrow assumptions about it. There are, however, concepts that should be addressed by managers who are interested in **motivating their employees through true involvement**. These concepts require supervisory commitment to employee involvement, a basic trust in employees, and the willingness to take apparent risk (but perhaps not actual risk) when trusting employees, because there is no halfway point between mistrust (autocratic supervision) and trust (employee involvement).

BEGIN HERE

The task of motivating employees through involvement should not start off with the employees, which is the place where most managers plan to begin. It should begin with the supervisor of the employees who are the target of the motivation project. In fact, it should begin at least one step further back with the supervisor's manager because foremen will be responsive to expectations of their boss. If the foreman's manager is supportive in a different approach to supervision as a means of getting employees more involved in their work, the foreman is far more likely to follow this example. If the manager, however, is suspicious of deviations from traditional supervision, then the foreman will not change the way in which he supervises employees. A foreman cannot supervise in a manner which differs from his customary style unless he has a supportive and **encouraging boss**, no more than he can be a good foreman without a good boss. While a supportive boss is not a guarantee of success for a foreman, it is a necessary condition. Of course, a supervisor can use virtually *any style* he prefers and maintain some productivity. Performance, however, is likely to be much better if he is able to enhance the self-esteem of those whom he supervises. Therefore, the question of helping a supervisor and his manager to develop specific supervisory skills designed to enhance employee self-esteem is critical.[1] After the foreman is well versed in these new supervisory behaviors and he is aware that he has full support of his manager, it is time to turn to the employees themselves.

THE FIRST MEETING

Employees who constitute a functional or operational work group (i.e., a logical team) might be addressed in a meeting by the foreman's manager or by the foreman himself. In either case, both the foreman and his manager should be present. The functional or operational group of employees should probably number no fewer than 4 or 5 and no more than 12 to 15. Larger groups should be sub-divided to meet this size criterion. At this meeting, employees should be asked how they would like to try running a piece of the business by making decisions that were formerly made by management or by specialists.

The advantages and disadvantages of this should be discussed with the employees and employee concerns and hopes should be solicited. Management should make it clear that offering this opportunity to employees reflects confidence and trust in them. Very probably, employees will become enthused about the chance to do their own planning, scheduling and decision-making. Generally, the employees' reaction will be a mix of surprise, pleasure, anxiety, confidence, suspicion, and eagerness to begin.

During this first meeting the role of the foreman must be clarified. This can also be pursued at subsequent meetings. Since the supervisor and the employees operate in a reciprocal relationship, changing the role of the employees requires a role-change for the supervisor. One way to consider the new role of the supervisor or foreman is that he should be regarded by employees as an available resource rather than as a director of work. He must be available to meet with them, individually or in a group, whenever they wish. As a resource, he can provide them with information, instruction, and evaluation, as well as represent their needs or interests to upper management or to another parallel group.

Employees should be advised that they can take time during or after working hours to discuss and plan how they will meet and handle the job problems and demands of their revised roles. A meeting place should be available to them, and they should be encouraged to invite whomever they wish to these meetings as resources for them. For example, if they would like the foreman to be present, or, other members of the organization such as planners, quality control or methods people, the group or team should invite them, indicating the meeting time and place a day or two in advance.

CHANGING HATS

Initially, employees may start by identifying the problems from their perspective rather than the foreman identifying problems for them. Also, the employees should tour the plant to learn how the work they do affects the work of others if they are not aware of this or of the end product.[2] Employees might set their quality goals, plan some portion of their schedules,[3] or troubleshoot some of the job-related problems about which they and management are concerned.

With regard to the day-to-day activities of the group, the foreman should think of himself as a consultant to the group and try to change its past dependency relationship to him. His participation in a behavior "modeling" (i.e., skill training) program for supervisors will help him acquire the skills necessary to do this. Nevertheless, the foreman may be threatened by this arrangement since it may appear to him that he has lost his supervisory prerogatives and is no longer needed. On the contrary, he is more necessary than before, but must now spend his time servicing needs of his group rather than on troubleshooting, passing down supplies, and running errands. These personal needs of employees include recognition, information, and instruction. Perhaps his most important task is to run interference for his group, especially if it identifies roadblocks. This makes the foreman's job more difficult and more challenging, but in the beginning, he will be as uncomfortable with his revised role as the employees are uncomfortable with their new roles. The foreman's anxiety can be relieved, however, by proper support and counseling from his manager—which is the reason for beginning a program of employee motivation with at least the second level of management.

RISK v. REWARD POTENTIALS

By the end of the first meeting, employees should understand what management is proposing, how it differs from their customary work arrangements, and what advantages might accrue to both management and employees as a result of these changes. While they will at first be asked to concern themselves with some of the technical or production problems relevant to their work, they should be told that eventually they will be asked to determine methods and set time standards because their knowledge of the jobs will enable them to be more accurate than anyone else. Although even the strongest managers cringe at this prospect, only the best of them will give thorough and honest consideration to the idea.

This is a particularly important point: *management is telling the employees that they trust them and that they want them to run a piece of the business, but this trust will be fully evident only if management is willing to let employees really become involved in ways that are personally relevant to the employee, such as setting methods and time standards.* This will most likely require several meetings between management and employees before both become fully aware of their responsibilities.

Since management wants employees to do something for it (i.e., better performance), it must in turn do something for the employees or they will not reciprocate appropriately. For example, a supervisor can give employees the responsibility for planning or decision-making which, in turn, will make them feel better about their role as employees and raise their level of self-esteem. There are few substitutes for self-esteem as a motivational factor, but the supervisor must make this possible. Experience with these kinds of situations within industry has been quite good and, in fact, recent studies are very encouraging. In reality, management has little to lose, and much to gain. This is especially so in light of the many changes in the expectations of people coming to work in industry for the first time.

SOME SUGGESTIONS

Some points should be re-emphasized for the managers who want to become involved in activities designed to improve employees' motivation to perform through involvement. They must be sure to enhance the self-esteem of the employees involved, they must treat these employees as individuals, and they must show that they trust the employees. They can demonstrate this trust by letting employees set quality goals, determine methods, and by eventually letting them set time standards. Measurement of employees as a group will continue as usual, but employees will do a more effective job than the supervisor in monitoring the effectiveness of their own work, especially if employees have and want this responsibility. They, too, have a great deal to gain by this method of management, and it is unlikely that they will risk these gains. There is, in short, no halfway point.

CONCLUSION

Many behavioral factors are in the picture when we consider how to motivate people. The manager who wants to motivate employees should develop his knowledge and skill in applying the principles of behavioral science. This may require consultation with several different qualified resources, although relatively little consulting time would be necessary. Skilled resources can assist in identifying guidelines and potential roadblocks, while at the same time suggesting procedures for the manager to follow which will markedly increase his chances of success.

At the outset of a project aimed at improving motivation and work performance, supervisors should work with the consultant in developing effective methods. A tentative approach should then be reviewed with and critiqued by its target group, i.e., the work team itself. The team itself is probably in the best position to evaluate the potential effectiveness and possible roadblocks of an approach to motivation and performance improvement. Moreover, those plans which are developed and agreed upon should be frequently reviewed and adjusted by the work team so that maximum flexibility is designed into a "participative" approach.

Modified, and more adaptive, supervisory "styles" should be an outcome of a supervisor's success with the procedures developed through collaboration with a work team. To change one's supervisory style is not easy, but supervisors can definitely be helped to motivate employees. Management no longer has any alternative to facing this issue in an effective manner.

FOOTNOTES

1. Training supervisors to operate more adaptively in specific areas can be accomplished via the behavior "modeling" approach which is designed to increase the behavior repertoire of a supervisor. Rather than trying to change managerial style (an extremely difficult objective because of personality and environmental factors) a behavior modification program may provide a supervisor with the knowledge, practice and reinforcement of alternative, more adaptive behavior in a variety of situations relevant to his job.

2. Sorcher, Melvin, *Personnel Administration*, May-June 1969, pp. 40-48.

3. Sorcher, Melvin and Meyer, Herbert H., *Personnel Administration*, July-August 1968, pp. 17-21.

Gordon Zacks is President of R.G. Barry Corporation. This article is reprinted with permission from Innovation, *November 1970, pp. 50-56.*

How We Rebuilt Our Company

GORDON ZACKS

A great deal has been written about changing organizations—the need for change, the strategies for change, and so on; but I must confess to finding it often so abstract or theoretical that it leaves me with little of the guidance I need in solving my own problems as a day-in, day-out manager. I suppose it was because of this dissatisfaction that I allowed the editor from *Innovation* to talk me into describing an actual case history of change—in this case the significant change I have attempted to bring about at R.G. Barry.

Let me say at the outset that you will find here no neat blueprint for your own organization but, rather, a progress report on one company's far from perfect attempt to restructure itself. I believe, however, there are lessons in it for anyone who is suddenly faced—as I was in 1961—with the need to build an organization to meet the dynamic needs of our growing company. In order to understand better what I will say about the change, it is necessary to know a little about our company's history and the industry of which we are a part.

R.G. Barry started—as many companies do—with an idea. The year was 1946, and the idea was detachable shoulder pads for women's garments.

219

The idea's originator was my mother Florence Zacks. The first "production" of the shoulder pads took place in the basement of the private home of Mrs. Bessie Scott in Columbus, Ohio.

My father, who was then a merchandise manager at a major department store in Columbus, gave up his position to invest full time in the development of the fledgling business. The Zackses were joined by Mr. Harry Streim, whose knowledge of financing and sales, as well as his enthusiasm and faith, were an important early asset to the business.

The original idea proved viable and after the usual tribulations of a neophyte company the business began to prosper selling through notions departments of major department stores.

Just when we felt we were becoming established as a profitable little business the fashion designers of the world dealt our company a smashing blow. They abandoned the military look and the market for shoulder pads disappeared virtually overnight.

Fortunately, Mrs. Zacks had another idea about the same time—an idea that still forms the backbone of our business—the foam-soled, washable slipper. This item met the foot comfort needs of the many, many customers with tired, aching feet.

At the outset of the business it was the personalities of the partners—and not any "master plan"—that determined the way in which the company was organized.

My father controlled manufacturing and administration even though he had never been inside a factory in his life. Disliking detail work, letter writing, meetings, and written reports, he obtained all the information he needed by walking around and talking to people. In the course of this routine, he built up strong personal relationships with employees, while at the same time keeping abreast of what went on in the business. In this way we had quite an effective quality control system—it was my father who walked every day. We had an effective internal control system—it was my father who *saw* what was happening. And we had an effective personnel department—it was my father who listened every day. This added up to a company with a great feeling of family involvement.

The industry of which we are a part is a labor intensive industry. One of the reasons is that basic manufacturing technology has not changed significantly in the past 100 years. We are also in an intensely competitive industry because it takes only a small investment to set up a plant. My father instinctively realized that the only thing a competitor could not duplicate was the quality of the people in our company and the spirit with which they worked.

This paternalistic, informal method of management served well for some time. In 1961, however, it was apparent that to meet the expanding demand for our products new capital was necessary to expand our production capacity and build inventories to properly service our customers. The need was urgent if we were to defend against the competition emerging in the marketplace. It was at this point that we made the decision to offer stock to the public to raise the necessary capital for expansion of the business.

From sales of $4.6 million in 1961 we grew rapidly to sales of $8.3 million in 1964. During this period our company headquarters, manufacturing facilities, and administrative operations were located entirely within Columbus, Ohio. The sales offices in New York City were the only geographically separated segment of the business.

In 1965, with the acquisition of the Charles Bobst Shoe Company in Columbus, Ohio, and Dot & Peg Productions, in Chattanooga, Tennessee, it became apparent that the "management system" we had employed no longer adequately met our needs. It had become impossible to walk and touch and listen, and know what was going on, to communicate concern, to motivate, and to control personally. A system of informal management was no longer adequate.

Our problem in 1965 had become one of how to introduce professional management and still maintain a people-oriented climate within our business. Previously my father had known exactly how many pairs of slippers were produced each day without a manager having to fill in a form. There was control, but it was unstructured.

When you introduce formalized planning, which we needed badly by 1965, you also introduce formalized control, and that raises new questions for a manager: Does he trust me? Does he believe in me? Does he think I know my job?

We were concerned about this because of the conviction that conventionally organized businesses suffer a demotivation of people as the price of formal controls. But we felt we needed to introduce formalized planning, and this meant we would have to expect people to develop plans and then to control against plans. When this happens downward control is felt, and the downward control of a group by a supervisor can create tensions, anxieties, and resistance.

So, we were looking for a system that would give us the best of two worlds by establishing a formal control system while at the same time maintaining the unique style of our company.

Soon after we had defined what we were looking for, my father died, and I moved from the position of executive vice president to become president. I felt a compelling need to accelerate the development of a more compatible—and more formal—system of management. Even though we had been operating somewhat less informally for the previous several years, as long as my father was alive his presence had effectively influenced the climate of the business. I tended to operate differently, and being without experience in the job of president, I needed help.

At about that time I read *New Patterns of Management* by Rensis Likert of the Institute for Social Research, University of Michigan. In it I discovered an approach to building human organizations with which I felt comfortable. Likert's "System Four" style of management is characterized by a high degree of involvement in decision making by the very people that are going to be affected by the decision.

In 1966 I went to see Likert and asked him to help us build participative management in our company. After I explained my feeling that people, by and large, return trust with trust, he asked me "How do you behave? You say nice words and make nice speeches, but it is your behavior that must communicate your beliefs to others in your organization." Naturally, I thought my behavior demonstrated my trust in people. Nevertheless, Likert had someone observe me at work. At the end of the observation period he reported, "Mr. Zacks, we have observed you and want to advise you that your behavior is consistent with your beliefs about 20 percent of the time." Stunned, I asked him to be specific. Said Likert: "If you trust your managers, if you believe that you have men who are competent and who want to do the job right, why do you meet with them every week and review with them their areas of responsibility?" Dr. Likert pointed out that this behavior implies either that the manager is incompetent, or that I doubted his desire to do the job.

Likert also wondered why I had a monthly staff meeting with all the men who reported directly to me. At these meetings I reviewed with them what each had done or not done. He pointed out that this simply reinforced the lack of trust transmitted by the individual meetings.

Dr. Likert's criticisms set me thinking. Believing that what he said was right, I eliminated the individual meetings. I had to make my trust overt. I now rely on the men who report to me to bring to my attention any problems that can have a significant impact on the operations of the company.

The second point Dr. Likert made was that if a president believes he has able men he should use them as his advisers. They are there to help the president do his job. The president is not there to look over their shoulders. By the same token, the only items that can legitimately be put on the agendas of my staff meetings are matters that require a decision by the president. Of course, if any man feels he has a problem that he wants discussed at the staff meeting, he can bring it up, but it must be his initiative, not mine.

I realized that what we had been doing essentially was forcing each individual to justify his position and defend himself. I played judge, observing the men, trying to reconcile differences and get things going toward some sort of common goal.

The nature of our staff meetings has now changed. They are no longer operational review sessions in which we discuss orders and delivery position of each product line. These matters are now the concern of the divisions. At the same time as I redefined the jobs of the men reporting to me, I redefined my job as president. I learned that by managing the operations of the business I had been *operating* the business. As a result, I learned proper delegation of operating responsibility, and consciously sought to build a "team of advisers."

The first thing this team of executives had to come to grips with was a definition of the purpose, the scope, and the objectives of the company. We closeted the team away from the office for a series of six long meetings. Our sessions covered an enormous amount of ground. For instance, we spent one whole day discussing the scope of the business—whether we should be in the comfort footwear business or the washable footwear business. We decided on the former, and the implication was fundamental in terms of what we did with the company and with the divisions as they were set up. We then broadened our definition of scope to say that the business that we should be in is the innovating, manufacturing, and selling of comfort footwear for men, women, and children through all channels of distribution.

We also developed a statement of basic purpose that provided the framework upon which we were able to establish specific objectives for the current year (1966) through 1970. The basic purpose is the "constitution" for R.G. Barry and the source document against which we measure the appropriateness of each specific objective or goal.

It took many weeks to develop the team as a working unit so that it was able finally to formulate these objectives. The sessions were long and hardworking and we didn't get results without a struggle. It required an enormous commitment of time and energy, and at first there was terrific resistance. For example, one manager might say, "I can't be away for a week. We have a New York market to look after and I should be there." Another executive would say, "I can't be supervising manufacturing and taking off a week for talk."

The trouble was that these men had been managing their segments of the business as narrow-mindedly as I had been running my job. While I had been doing their jobs—the business of operating the company—they, in turn, had been doing the jobs of the men reporting to them. In other words, the control relationship that I had established had forced them to apply their efforts incorrectly. As a result, they had to steal time from operating the business if they were to plan the future. They hadn't developed the organization that would allow them to do this. I was very firm, however, in my insistence that we work as a team in planning the future.

In retrospect, I may have expected too much and demanded too much too fast. For a start, each man had to structure his job to provide time to meet the president's needs. Also, subordinates were not accustomed to the team process. I didn't explain to them what I was doing or how it would affect their own jobs. All I really said was "I need you, and even if we're going to suffer operationally, I think it will be worth it."

Because the team building process was new to us, we started off with very little idea of what makes it work. But gradually a few principles emerged. Perhaps the biggest problem was the tendency toward defensiveness on the part of the team member.

Certainly there has to be some controlled tension among members of a group for the group to be really creative. But tension doesn't necessarily mean conflict. It can well mean some form of anxiety or pressure to achieve a goal. A man must feel free to suggest an idea, regardless of how remote it may be. If a group doesn't have that, the defense mechanisms in a sensitive man may cause him to react by not submitting ideas.

One of our biggest problems related to my own style. An effective team leader should present problems to a team which the team then defines or refines, and hopefully, solves. The team is thus led through the process of identifying alternative solutions and evaluations. My personality, however, is such that I can't operate comfortably in that mode. I'm an enthusiastic guy. I would come in not with a problem but with a solution, and I would come in selling hard. That often resulted in a defensive reaction from the other members of the team. My behavior was interpreted as if I were saying, "Here's the answer, now what do you guys think of it. I'll accept your comments, but I've really decided that this is the way we're going to go." While some of my ideas were good, I was killing them with "over sell."

As a result, one of two things had to happen. Either I had to change what I was doing, or I had to persuade the members of the team that in spite of appearances I really wanted team problem solving and decision making.

I tried to change my behavior, but could not do it. So I gave up hope of making a change in my management style, and tried simply to persuade each member of the team that I had no "vested interest" in the ideas I was submitting. Even though I presented them in a positive, enthusiastic manner, I was not preempting an alternative solution. I told my team that I wanted to find the best solution to the problem. I said we should examine objectively the suggested solution, and develop alternatives. If the alternatives were better, we should go with them. I think that to a significant degree, the team accepted this approach and we made considerable progress.

In late 1967 it became apparent to both the team and myself that a functionally organized company could be a limiting factor on our growth. Members of my team insisted that there was insufficient time to fulfill adequately their functional responsibilities and at the same time devote sufficient attention to the topics introduced at the level of the president's team. I felt that I could not optimize the long-term profitability of the corporation without professional staff and operating advice. Having reached an apparent impasse, we began to deliberate about how our functional organizational structure might be affecting the ability to achieve our corporate goals.

Our plan for 1968 showed a $20 million year—four times the volume we had in 1962 when we had gone public—double the volume of 1965! Examining our long-range objectives, it became increasingly clear to us that we would be unable to achieve the results we wanted if all major decision making and interfunctional conflict had to be resolved at the top of the organization.

The conclusion we reached was to decentralize into operating divisions. This reorganization allowed our team more time to devote to tackling longer range opportunities and problems. More important, it permitted greatly expanded latitude for decisions and action at the operating unit level.

It is my observation that some of the greatest risks taken in business—or for that matter any organization—are those of a major reorganization. Old relationships are disturbed. People's perceptions with regard to the significance of the change vary considerably depending on their location within the new structure. The familiar becomes obsolete and a refamiliarization period occurs.

Businesses are really complex systems. A change in a portion of the system has an impact on other parts of the system. Sometimes the impact is immediate. Sometimes there is a significant time lag before the resultant impact occurs. It is frequently difficult to predict just how and when a change will affect the business system.

My entire team participated in designing and effecting the reorganization. The level of energy and commitment from this group was high. Not everyone was equally enthusiastic about the restructuring, but through the interaction process of the team mode true consensus on the reorganization was reached. We identified potential problems that might be encountered and worked out the necessary contingency plans.

Each executive reporting to me met, in turn, with his team and worked out the elements of the reorganization which affected their operations. In the same fashion, subunits were involved in the planning of the change.

Despite the fact that many people were involved with new responsibilities, new levels of risk, and new relationships, this change proceeded well. I attribute much of this success to the commitment produced in my staff through the team process.

With the members of my team now able to devote more time to long-range consideration, we began to examine our strengths, vulnerabilities and opportunities. As we saw it, the future was going to make many demands on our business—expensive demands.

The levels of education of the U.S. work force will continue to increase. The level of affluence in the country will increase. We concluded that it will become increasingly hard to find people who will accept employment on the frequently mundane tasks found in the apparel industry today. Foreign competition, we felt, will increase and improve in quality. It appears that our customers will continue to require increased and more sophisticated service and that pressure for larger markups will continue. To use the media of our times in advertising—TV—our products require a much larger expenditure than we had been able to make at our then current size.

The conclusion we reached was that we would need to continue growing rapidly if the business is to survive ten years from now. The larger sales base would give us funds to finance technological developments, organization development, data processing, systems capability, and television advertising.

At that time we were a $16 million company. We estimated that we would have to grow to $50 million and that became our objective. Today, I'm not sure that $50 million is big enough. I think the real figure is closer to $75 million, but at least we understood the order of magnitude of change that had to take place if we were going to provide for these capabilities internally.

We needed people and money. We hired a top-notch systems man, Dr. George Ornstein, who could transform our utilization of a computer from a high-class adding machine to a useful tool for management decision making. Dr. Ornstein can also help us build an integrated management information system that will upgrade our quality of decision making.

We resolved to grow through acquisition, as well as through active expansion of existing product lines. To head the acquisition efforts we recruited a group vice president, Merle Roberts. His initial assignment was to reorganize and develop two small divisions with sizable potential. His major responsibility, however, is to assist in acquiring new companies and in integrating and coordinating their activities with the rest of the corporation following acquisition. We also established a new market development department to identify and develop programs to exploit new marketing opportunities for our product lines.

These decisions resulted in three more people reporting directly to me, so that by 1969 I had a seven-man staff. Each of the members of my team is a highly capable individual with a proven record of accomplishment. The addition of three people to this group, however, changed the nature of the relationships and the team process.

A consequence of the expansion of the size of the team appears to be a loss of team effectiveness. We have searched for possible causes of impairment of the team process, and several factors appear to me to offer some explanation. First, the increased number of people means the interpersonal relationships are much more complex.

Second, the time framework within which team members work differs depending upon their specific area of responsibility. Operating division presidents are under pressure of current problems as well as those up to perhaps a year out. The president, on the other hand, must concern himself with the future five or even ten years out. To pull the division presidents away from the real live problems of today and ask them to sit down with the president and talk about what could happen five years from now is difficult.

Third, although we had a rewarding and productive experience in our first efforts at the team mode of management, we obviously have a great deal to learn about team behavior. None of us can be considered expert in either team leadership or team membership roles.

Despite the problems we have encountered, we believe team management provides us with better decisions, a higher level of commitment to the decisions, faster reaction time, better general coordination and communication. In addition, through the participation in top-level problem solving and decision making each member of the team has developed a broader perspective and understanding of the management process.

Utilization of the team process by second- and third-level management varies within the organization. In part, this depends upon the team leader's (or boss's) "natural" style of management. Each unit head within the corporation has the latitude to operate in his own style. We encourage him to use the team process, but we don't legislate its use.

At one plant the team process has been pursued in organizing the factory work force. This plant converts piece goods into finished footwear. Incoming material is laminated, cut, assembled by various sewing operations, packaged, and shipped to a warehouse. The plant manager implemented the team process with the people reporting directly to him. They examined the strengths and weaknesses of their operation, questioning everything they were currently doing. At that time the people involved in production operations were on a direct incentive system. To facilitate training operators, the assembly process was broken down to the shortest cycle time for each operation. Methods and rates were prescribed by industrial engineers, and inspectors checked 100% of the work of the production people. It had always been done this way and is typical of the industry of which we are a part.

The plant manager and his team asked themselves how well this approach to production fit our basic philosophy about people. We had been saying that people are our most important asset, that we trust people, that the individual on a job knows that job better than anyone else, that people want to do a good job, that people desire additional responsibility. Our behavior—which communicates much louder than words—seemed to communicate the opposite of what we were saying.

As a result of their self-appraisal, this team decided to organize the entire plant into work teams of 6 to 10 people. The piece rate system was replaced with a straight hourly rate system of pay.

The production teams were organized to assemble slippers completely from cut stock to finished product. In this way each person can readily identify with the end product. Team members were given the target of reducing the unit manufacturing cost, which is really what we are interested in—not just getting people to "work faster." Team members were also given an opportunity to influence the production flow, the methods used, and the quantity to be produced by the team. Time clocks were removed. The production teams became directly responsible for the quality of their production.

This was a major change for this plant. It took considerable time for people to accept the fact that this new approach to organization of the work around people was not just another "gimmick." As you would expect, some teams operate more effectively than others, but results to date indicate that involvement of people in production teams can result in lower unit costs.

We invested a lot of money to convert this plant to the team concept. On paper we've identified $170,000 worth of outlays which were expensed in 1969 that could be characterized as investments in capital equipment and in human resources. My guess is that the real cost was above $200,000. The benefits did not occur immediately. It was not until this year that it was apparent that our investments were beginning to provide a return. Our six-month figures indicate sales and profit for 1970 well ahead of the same period in 1969. It took considerable conviction and perseverance on the part of the plant manager and his team to carry through the conversion and make it work.

In reviewing the dynamics of the growth of R.G. Barry I can define certain stages of development. Each stage required fundamental changes in organization, formalization, and style of management.

Stage 1. Entrepreneurial. From 1947 through 1960 the management system and style were the extension of the personalities, and behavior patterns, of the partners in the business. The business was characterized by informality, few detailed reports, personal control and a paternal bent in relations between top management and other members of the organization. Decisions and plans were made by the partners.

Stage 2. Introduction of Professionalism. From 1961 to 1964, following the acquisition of additional capital, the business grew rapidly. Informal management and control failed to meet our needs as sales and production requirements expanded. We became aware that to compete and continue to grow we needed professional, technical help. Such staff departments as industrial engineering, quality control, personnel, and data processing were added. Formal organization structure and delineation of responsibilities occurred for the first time during this stage. Relationships became somewhat more structured but the "one big family" theme was emphasized. More formal control reports were instituted to provide better information to the president. All important decisions continued to be made at the top of the organization.

Stage 3. Geographic Decentralization. From 1965-1968 three small companies were acquired and a manufacturing plant was built in North Carolina. We found that former methods of planning and control could not be used effectively in a multi-division company, spread over five states. It placed new strains on the organization resulting, as I described earlier, in a decentralized organizational structure. This period was also characterized by introduction of more formal planning, better information systems, and improvement of management functions begun in the previous stage.

Real effort was made to encourage problem solving, decision making, planning and control to the lowest level in the organization where the information was available to permit action. During this stage an understanding of people as human resources began to emerge and paternalism faded as the company moved toward a more participative style of management.

Stage 4. Future Consciousness. In 1969 we became more acutely aware of the need to plan and organize to meet the changes in the market and the industry that can be expected in the future. Instead of a highly desirable condition, dynamic growth became a mandatory objective for the survival of our business in the future. The refocus at the top level led to introducing the more sophisticated management techniques that will be required for corporate survival in the years ahead.

There is a strengthening of conviction that participative management can provide greater responsiveness to change. With decentralized units able to make plans and decisions and control their operations without having to clear their actions with the top group, the organization should be much quicker on its feet.

Of course, these stages are not distinct. They overlap considerably and we didn't identify them as we proceeded from one to another. I find them helpful in reviewing where we have been and projecting future developments. I have also found these concepts helpful in examining the progress of other companies, particularly those we have considered for acquisition.

As I warned at the outset, this article is really an interim report. The final report will probably never be written as I see the company as an organism in a continual state of evolution, adapting to a changing environment and fighting for survival. Most important, we have been through the first rounds of adaptation and have learned that continual change is a fact of life for a viable company.

I believe that working in teams can be effective even though we have much to learn about the nature of team behavior. We believe, as Peter Drucker points out, that kingsize profits are the prize of the innovator. Innovations in the organization and management of the company may well prove to be our strongest profit producer.

Henry L. Tosi, Jr., is Visiting Associate Professor of Management, Graduate School of Business Administration, Michigan State University. Stephen J. Carroll is Associate Professor of Management, University of Maryland.

Henry L. Tosi, Jr., and Stephen J. Carroll, "Some Structural Factors Related to Goal Influence in the Management by Objectives Process," pp. 45-51, MSU Business Topics, *Spring 1969. Reprinted by permission of the publisher, Division of Research, Graduate School of Business Administration, Michigan State University.*

Some Structural Factors Related to Goal Influence in the Management by Objectives Process

HENRY L. TOSI, JR. and STEPHEN J. CARROLL

Management literature is filled with admonitions to increase the participation and involvement of subordinate managers in decision making. One of many techniques suggested for this purpose is management by objectives.

Management by objectives is a process in which the manager and subordinate together agree upon a set of activities, target dates, and goals which will be used as the criteria for the subordinate's performance evaluation. This may or may not involve high levels of subordinate participation. At one extreme, the manager may define performance criteria for his subordinates which the subordinate accepts. The boss may simply specify what results he expects and evaluate performance according to them. The other extreme is one of greater subordinate participation and involvement. Both the superior and the subordinate independently develop a set of goals for the subordinate, prior to meeting. They then meet to compare goals and target dates and through mutual exchange and interaction determine final priorities, target dates, and criteria for measurement. Most proponents of management by objectives at least implicitly suggest the latter as the most desirable and effective goal setting procedure because of the higher degree of superior and subordinate participation, involvement, and interaction.

There are some significant points which must be considered, however. Participation in goal setting means a reallocation, or redistribution, of influence over goals. When one participates, or is given the opportunity to do so, there seems to be a clear implication that he will have something to say about the factor or the problem in which he is involved. The most serious human relations problems probably occur in organizations where there is an incongruity between the verbalized level and actual level of subordinate influence, that is, participation may be a stated policy, but in practice it does not occur. Yet the question of increasing participation and influence is surely constrained by more than the willingness of the superior to delegate authority or relinquish power.

This research examines some factors which may affect the individual's influence over a set of performance goals. These goals were part of a more comprehensive management by objectives program. The program was instituted in a large manufacturing concern which had previously used a trait-oriented evaluation system. A change was made and the Work Planning and Review Program (hereinafter referred to as WPR) was instituted. The program called for managers to determine and specify, in conjunction with their boss, activities and projects for the following year, target dates for completion, and how performance is to be measured. These are called performance goals. The program also provided for self-improvement goals, or activities directed toward personal improvement.

Performance goals will be the focus of this research. First, the relationship between influence and some organizational factors such as functional area and organizational level will be examined. Secondly, the process by which the final determination of goals was reached, and its relationship to perceived influence will be studied. Interviews were conducted with fifty managers in the firm to determine their part in the goal setting process. These managers came from all levels, vice-presidents to foremen, and from all functional areas.

INFLUENCE MEASURE

The degree of influence over performance goals was determined by asking managers: Who had the most influence over the performance goals which finally ended up on your Work Planning and Review form? Responses were evaluated and grouped into one of three categories.

Category 1 is the case in which the *boss had greater influence*. These are instances in which the subordinate reported little or no participation or influence, and felt that his superior had specified the performance goals. The individual had little to say about the final statement of the goals. This was given an influence scoring value of one.

The second category of influence is one in which there was *mutual influence*. In this category are those cases in which the individual described the final form of the performance goals as resulting from a reasonably balanced discussion with his boss. The individual described this process as one in which there was essentially an equal, or only slightly unequal, distribution of influence. This category was scored two.

The third category was that in which the *subordinate felt he exerted the most influence.* Here, the boss had little to say about what should be included and what the final goals were. In these cases the subordinate felt he had the greatest degree of influence and control over the performance goals. This category value was scored three.

The scoring values were used in the development of an influence index. For each analytical category (function, level, and process) subclasses were broken out. These subclasses are simply the various groupings in the analytical category. For instance, in the analysis of functional area, the subclasses are marketing, production, finance, and engineering. In each subclass, the scoring values were multiplied by the number of managers reporting them. These were added and then divided by the total number of managers in that subclass. Differences in the index, which is a weighted average, could then be compared.

Organizational Unit

The influence index was constructed for each of the major functional areas of the firm. Executives were interviewed from the marketing, manufacturing, finance, and engineering divisions of the organization. Figure 1 shows the number of executives from each area and the influence index derived for each area.

As would be expected, the degree of influence is different for each major area. The influence index was highest (2.15) in the marketing division, which includes activities such as sales, distribution, and product service. This was not unexpected. Most of the individuals in this unit function, to a large extent, with others outside the boundaries of the firm. Since these interactions are external and cross the boundary of the organization, they may be less susceptible to control by the organization, and also be less predictable. Thus, higher level management would be more reliant upon those closer to the field for assessments of the realistic performance levels for both unit and individual.

The next highest influence index (2.0) was found in the finance and administration area. This is a highly technical and rapidly changing activity. The function is in the process of being reorganized. Many different demands are made on this unit by other sections of the organization. The firm is currently moving toward a more technically based computer information system. Under these conditions, there is probably greater reliance on those who have skills and capability in the technical areas. Since the area is new and highly technical, this precludes more precise specification of requirements from higher levels since they may not be generally aware of the potential from the area. It may be this fact which explains the higher individual influence level in finance.

The manufacturing division ranked third in the degree of influence (1.77). It seems logical that influence levels would be lower than marketing and finance, since activity is largely dependent on other units in the organization, particularly the marketing group. Manufacturing runs are determined by the sales forecasts and demands from the marketing sales force. The production system is such that lower level managers have little influence over it. Once the line starts running, there is little that the lower level manager can do to change its speed or to alter the content of the items being processed. Factors such as production procedures, schedules, and methods are some determinants of behavior within this unit. It follows, therefore, that the individual is likely to be more influenced by the system than he is able to affect it.

Finally, the R & D and engineering unit had the lowest influence index (1.55). One might have expected members of this unit to have the greatest degree of influence over their performance goals. However, closer scrutiny of the activities of this unit suggests other possibilities. In fact, the engineers work on applied projects which are product changes, adaptations, or innovations. These are usually specified by higher level management and invariably last for long periods. Obviously, when an engineer is committed to one of these, he has little to say about what activities and projects he

---

FIGURE 1
Perceived Influence Index
In Each Functional Area

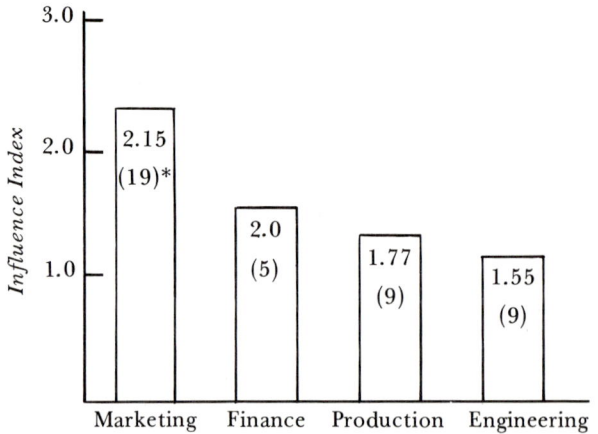

*Indicates number of managers interviewed who provided usable data.

will work on. This is determined for him. This is not to say, however, that the engineer does not have freedom. It may well be that he exercises a great deal of discretion in approaches to the project, but the projects and target dates, which form the backbone of the objectives system, are determined by others in the organization, not the individual performing the work.

Any student of organization would be quick to point out that the differences in the degree of influence may be more than a function of the climate induced by the behavior of key executives in the department rather than the technical parameters of a particular functional area. There is no question that these key managers have an important effect on the climate. On the other hand, one cannot avoid considering the importance of structural and technical differences. Certainly, one would expect the lower organizational levels in the marketing department to have a greater degree of influence over their performance goals than their counterparts in manufacturing.

Another phase of the research was directed at the differences in influence at different organizational levels. The influence index described above was constructed for each organizational level. Figure 2 shows the influence index and the number of executives in the sample at each level.

The relationship between level and influence was as expected. Those at the highest organizational level (vice-presidents) indicated the greatest degree of influence over their performance goals. Those at the next level (a group of managers commonly called directors) had a lower influence index (2.27). Those at the next lower level had an influence index of 1.59. Those at the bottom level had a slightly higher index (1.65). But the general trend of influence, as reported by the individual, still tends to decrease as organizational level decreases.

These results are generally consistent with conceptions of how organizations are structured. The manager's discretion area is narrower at lower organization levels and there is other evidence besides this study which indicates this is the case in other objectives programs. Raia[1] (1965) reported that the number of supervisors who were actively involved in goal setting decreased at succeedingly lower organizational levels. A lower percentage of managers at each succeeding level of the organization felt they were actively involved in the process. In this study, the managers were not asked whether they were actively involved, but how much influence they felt they had over the final goals on their review form. The same problem of participation and influence was examined in a slightly different fashion and the findings were consistent with those of Raia.

The traditional concept of organization structure and decreasing discretion areas at lower levels of the organization may impose a practical limitation on the degree of involvement and influence which one could expect to result from a management by objectives program. At lower levels, there is less discretion for subordinates; correspondingly, less influence.

Goal Setting Process

One of the main research questions treated the specific manner in which the goals were set. The objective was to find out how superiors and subordinates determined, negotiated, and agreed upon the goal levels and activities to serve as performance targets. Each manager was asked: How was the goal setting carried out? What happened first? Second? Next? Figure 3 shows the percentage of managers who reported different goal setting processes with their superiors and the general influence index for each process.

Process 1. The process with the highest levels of mutual involvement was designated as Process 1. Generally, the superior would first hold a department meeting where the unit goals and projects for the coming operating period were discussed. The subordinate would then, using the information from this general meeting, prepare a set of personal goals. At the same time the boss would independently prepare a set of goals and targets for the subordinate. Later they would meet to discuss these and

---

FIGURE 2
Perceived Influence Index
As Reported By Managers At Each
Organizational Level

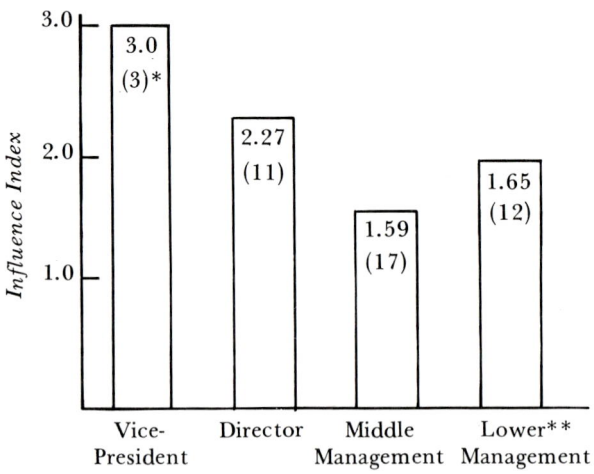

*Indicates number of managers interviewed
who provided usable data.
**Actually includes one more lower level,
combined here for ease of analysis.

arrive at some mutual agreement on the subordinate's goals. Twenty-eight percent of the managers reported this goal setting process.

Process 2. Here the boss was somewhat less involved. Goal setting usually began with an information meeting in which the general departmental and organizational objectives were discussed. Later, the subordinate prepared a set of goals and target dates. These were then given to the boss. Rather than preparing a set of goals for the subordinate, the boss edited and altered those which the subordinate prepared. When a meeting was held to discuss the goals, the basis for discussion was the subordinate's edited and revised goal statement. Approximately 21 percent of the managers indicated this type of goal setting occurred.

Process 3. Still another variant in the goal setting process was reported by 21 percent of the managers. First, the boss called a general meeting to discuss departmental objectives. From this, subordinates prepared individual goal statements. These were sent to the boss. However, contrary to the superior's involvement in Processes 1 and 2, the goal statements were accepted without any meeting or discussion. The subordinate did not have the opportunity to determine whether or not the goals were acceptable to his boss. He could only assume they were by the superior's silence.

Process 4. This was the most boss-centered of all. The subordinate was simply informed about the objectives program. The boss and the

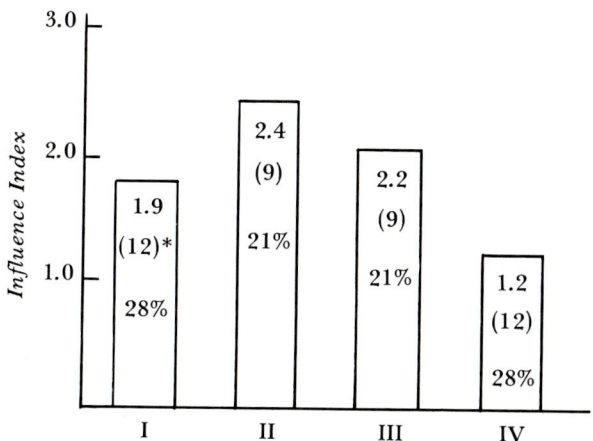

FIGURE 3
Influence Index As A Function
Of The Goal Setting Process

*Indicates numbers and percentages of managers reporting a particular type of goal setting process.

subordinate met, at which time the subordinate was given a set of goals which the boss prepared for him. The subordinate had little to say about the goals and target dates set for them. Twenty-eight percent of the managers reported this goal setting process.

Perceived Influence

As would seem to be the case in the various processes described above, the subordinate's perception of influence on performance goals varied with the approach taken. The influence index was constructed for each process. This index is assumed to be an indication of individual involvement and influence. This influence index for the different goal setting processes is also shown in Figure 3. The lowest index (1.2) is for Process 4, where the goals were prepared by the superior. Process 1, in which there were the highest levels of mutual involvement and preparation, had the next lowest index (1.9). While there is much more subordinate involvement than in Process 4, the superior is still seen as having slightly more influence than the subordinate. In Process types 2 and 3, the influence index was 2.4 and 2.2 respectively. In both, the subordinate felt he had greater influence than his boss over the goals set. This certainly seems reasonable. In types 1 and 4 there is more superior involvement and physical presence. Meeting types 2 and 3 tend to be more subordinate dominated; apparently the boss is less involved. The perceived influence over goals may be related to superior presence and action. The more he does, the greater his felt influence and the less influence the subordinate feels he has. This is consistent with cultural perceptions of the superior-subordinate relationship in organizations. Perhaps the subordinates are reporting influence as they believe it ought to be. That is, the boss should have more to say about subordinate goals than the subordinate does. This may be heightened when the superior is more physically present and involved in the goal setting process.

A set of organization factors is described here which may significantly affect the implementation and use of management by objectives. How the goal setting process occurs is also examined. Both are practical limitations which affect the degree of perceived subordinate influence over his goals.

All too often managers at all levels and in all functions are prodded to use management by objectives. If the degree of influence is a function of the activities, organization, work structure, and level of a particular unit, then the effect of these constraints must be considered. Influence may be determined not only by leadership style but also by organizational and technological constraints.

CONCLUSIONS

Influence is the critical factor in the process. Management by objectives requires a change in the distribution of influence. We may increase involvement, participation, and influence by enlarging the number of discretionary areas of a subordinate. Or, more realistically we might attempt to obtain all the potential involvement possible within the constraints of organizational considerations, some of which we have already mentioned. We would certainly not expect the production foreman to define the allocation of production facilities to various products when this is generally handled by a production scheduling unit, but he could perhaps have some influence in deciding how to achieve the allocation goals.

Factors such as organization level and organizational unit, which seem to be related to the subordinate's perception of the degree of influence, are less susceptible to change and manipulation by management. Organizational assignments and the structure of some jobs are difficult to alter. These constraints must be treated and accounted for. It may be possible, however, to change the interpersonal relationship between a boss and a subordinate if goal setting can be handled in a different manner. Yet, that process itself may be a function of both personal and organizational factors, also very difficult to change.

To introduce a program of objectives may be to change the subordinate's expectations about participation and involvement. If the managerial personalities and the organization structure are incompatible with redistribution of influence so as to preclude this redistribution, a condition is created which enhances dissatisfaction with the objectives approach. This may be generalized to a broader set of organizational conditions, increasing general dissatisfaction with the organization.

Implementing management by objectives requires effort to analyze existing organizational conditions and make a conscious decision to operate within those constraints or to attempt to alter them. Either strategy is time consuming. In the case of the first, it means an intensive organizational analysis and structuring a specific program to fit that organization. Under these conditions, limited levels of subordinate participation and involvement may be appropriate. This, however, may be the most short-sighted of the two alternatives. Yet, to change the structure of the organization and top management orientations to use management by objectives effectively may well require not only the process of policy change and revision, but it may necessitate the development and implementation of a complex organizational change process which may be painful and time consuming.

FOOTNOTES

1. Anthony P. Raia, "Goal Setting and Self Control," *Journal of Management Studies* I-II (February, 1965), 34-53.

Frank A. Heller is at the University of California at Berkeley. Gary Yukl is at Sacramento State College. The authors wish to express their appreciation to Professors Selwyn Becker, Vaughn Blankenship, and Lyman Porter for helpful comments on an earlier draft of this paper. This article appeared in Organizational Behavior and Human Performance, *August 1969, pp. 227-241 and is reprinted with permission of Academic Press, Inc.*

Participation, Managerial Decision-Making, and Situational Variables

FRANK A. HELLER and GARY YUKL

Over the last ten years, the literature on management and administration has reflected a growing interest in the subject of managerial decision-making. A number of frequently appearing terms such as "participation," "power equalization," and "democratic leadership" refer to an important and controversial aspect of managerial decision-making, namely the extent to which it is shared by the manager's subordinates. There are a number of different decision-making procedures that managers, or for that matter, any formal leader, can use. Some procedures involve a great deal of subordinate influence, and others exclude the subordinate altogether from the decision-making process. Although there is no widely accepted typology or model for classifying the decision behavior of managers, there does appear to be wide acceptance of the general concept of a continuum of subordinate influence along which various decision procedures can be ordered.

Probably the most influential decision-making typology was introduced in the pioneering study by Lewin, Lippitt, and White (1939) who described three leadership styles: "democratic," "authoritarian," and "laissez faire." Authoritarian leaders made nearly all of the decisions themselves, whereas laissez faire leaders allowed the subordinates to make all the decisions (a style not appropriate for business organizations). Democratic leaders made their decision jointly with their subordinates. In retrospect, this categorization, which clearly reflects the influence of political theory, may have been an unfortunate one. In subsequent research there was a tendency to focus upon democratic and autocratic styles, when in fact, other equally important decision styles are also used by managers. This tendency to conceptualize managerial decision-making in terms of two widely divergent styles is still evident today (Sales, 1966; Davies, 1967; Lowin, 1968), despite appeals for more differentiated and well-defined theory (Leavitt, 1962; Strauss, 1963; Argyris, 1964).

Various other social scientists have also proposed systems for classifying managerial decision-making or for describing the amount of subordinate influence. March and Simon (1958, p. 54) suggested a continuum of supervisory styles ranging from "decisions made by the supervisor and communicated to the worker without prior consultation" to "decisions made on the basis of free and equal discussion." In the same year, Tannenbaum and Schmidt (1958) described a scale of leader behavior with seven differentiated styles of decision-making. Likert (1961 and 1967) has elaborated four styles of managerial decision-making, each corresponding to one of his four theoretical approaches to organizational management. In addition, Likert (1961, p. 242) mentioned a twelve point scale for describing the amount of subordinate participation that occurs when organizational change is introduced. Blake and Mouton (1961) have proposed a system for evaluating the amount of weight an individual exerts on a decision made by himself and a subordinate, measured on a "power spectrum." Strauss (1963) has differentiated between decisions made by managers alone, decisions made jointly by managers and subordinates, and decisions which the manager permits the subordinate to make on his own. Blankenship and Miles (1968) have developed a questionnaire which takes into account three stages in the process of making organizational decisions and attempts to find the organizational locus for each of these three stages.[1] Finally, other writers, including Argyris (1964) and Tannenbaum (1962), have proposed systems for describing the amount and distribution of influence and control in the organization as a whole.

Despite the basic agreement that various decision styles represent different degrees of subordinate influence and participation, there has been little attempt to develop and apply measures based on a complex typology of decision procedures. The measures that have been used in field research to date are simple rating scales indicating the degree of overall subordinate influence as computed by some averaging procedure. While this type of participation index is useful, the exact pattern of decision procedure used by a leader may be more meaningful. A further weakness of most previous measures is the failure to assess managerial decision behavior in relation to specific, typical organizational decisions. Finally, although there has been much discussion in the literature of the constraints and demands placed on the leader by his situation (e.g., Tannenbaum and Massarik, 1961) a systematic investigation of the relation between situational variables and leader decision-making has not been undertaken. The small number of studies that have related situational variables to decision-making (surveyed briefly by Bass, 1967) strongly support the proposition that a leader's situation substantially limits and shapes his decision behavior, but further research is clearly needed.[2]

In view of these various omissions from the research literature, the purpose of this article is threefold. The first objective is to present a meaningful model of decision procedures that incorporates the best features of earlier systems for classifying managerial decision-making along a continuum of subordinate influence. The second objective is to describe a method of measuring (by self report) how often a leader uses each of these decision procedures to make typical leadership decisions and, in general, how much subordinate participation is allowed. The final objective is to analyze the responses to these questionnaires by a variety of different leaders in order to identify the influence of various situational variables on the leader's use of the decision procedures. The situational variables include the following: authority level in the organization, span of control, job function, staff-line position, length of time in present position, and type of decision.

THE DECISION BEHAVIOR MODEL

The amount of subordinate influence in decision-making within a formal unit of the organization can be viewed as a continuum ranging from no subordinate influence to complete subordinate influence. Figure 1 shows the hypothesized relationship between the influence continuum and five decision procedures that have been found to be relatively clear and meaningful for managers. These decision procedures were defined in behavioral terms and can be briefly summarized as follows.

Own Decision without Explanation refers to decisions made by a manager without any prior consultation with his subordinates (consultation with persons at a higher or equal authority level in the organization is not excluded).

FIGURE 1
Relation of Decision Styles to the Influence Continuum

LOW SUBORDINATE INFLUENCE   HIGH SUBORDINATE INFLUENCE

Own decision without explanation	Own decision with explanation	Consultation	Joint decision making	Delegation

Own Decision with Explanation refers to decisions made without prior subordinate consultation but adds a formal post-decision explanation of the reasons for the decision; this may induce the manager to take into account any known subordinate preference before he makes the decision (Bass, 1967).

Prior Consultation refers to decisions made only after consultation with one or more subordinates. The manager makes the decision himself, but his decisions will usually reflect some subordinate influence.

Joint Decision-making is a process of consensus formation in which one or more subordinates participate and some determination of the majority position is made. Although the manager may occasionally overrule the majority, more often than not the majority view is accepted.

Delegation refers to decisions that the manager allows subordinates to make on their own. A report on the decision may or may not be requested, and although the manager can veto the subordinate decision, he seldom does so.[3]

Until more sophisticated scaling methods can be applied, the precise location of the five decision procedures on the influence continuum is not possible. The two scoring procedures that were used on the present scale will be described in the section on methodology.

METHODOLOGY

The leaders used in the research included 82 senior managers in 15 large West Coast companies, 28 first-line supervisors and 72 second-line supervisors from three of these companies, and 21 student leaders from a large university. The student leaders were elected and appointed officials of traditional student organizations. Information was obtained from the senior managers by a combined questionnaire and discussion approach (Heller, 1968). Information from the rest of the sample was obtained by means of mailed questionnaires; the average response rate for the survey was 90 percent.

Leader decision-making behavior was measured by three similar questionnaires, which will be referred to as Forms A, B, and C. Form A was a one-item questionnaire requiring the leader to indicate what percentage of his decisions was made with each of the five decision procedures.

Form B had eleven decision items involving specific decisions which are appropriate for senior managers. If a manager was not usually responsible for making one of the decisions he was asked to indicate that it was not applicable and to go on to the next item. Otherwise, he was to indicate what percentage of the time each of the five decision procedures was used by him to make that kind of decision. Of course, if a manager used only one procedure to make a given decision, then he could put 100 percent next to that style; if he used more than one of the procedures, the percentages could be distributed to reflect the relative frequency of use for the five styles.

The eleven items in Form B can be subdivided into two classes of decisions, EMP and SUB. The term EMP refers to decisions that in some way involve the employees of the manager's subordinates. An example of an EMP decision is: "The decision to give a merit pay increase to one of your subordinate's employees." SUB decisions involved only the immediate subordinate himself. An example of a SUB decision is: "The decision regarding what targets or quotas should be set for your subordinate(s)." This SUB-EMP classification did not stand out in the wording of the questions.

Form C had eighteen decision items consisting of decisions that most leaders must make. For each decision item, the leader was required to select which of the five decision procedures he was most likely to use to make that particular kind of decision. The eighteen items in Form C can be divided into two categories of decisions. The categories correspond to the distinction that is often made between task and maintenance functions of leaders. Task decisions are those that involve planning and execution of the group task. An example of a task decision is the following: "The decision how to schedule the various tasks that need to be performed." Maintenance decisions involve personnel matters (e.g., promotion, pay), discipline, and preservation of subordinate satisfaction and cohesiveness. An example of a maintenance decision is: "The decision as to which subordinate to recommend for promotion or appointment to a position outside of your group."[4]

Relative frequency scores for the five decision procedures were obtained from Forms A and B but not from Form C. In the case of Form B, the average percentage score for each decision procedure was calculated using the percentage scores (for that procedure) from the eleven decision items. Average percentage scores were also calculated separately for the EMP and SUB decision categories. An index of the average relative degree of leader and subordinate influence was obtained from all three forms. This index, referred to as Decision-centralization, enabled leaders to be ordered with respect to how much influence they allow subordinates. In order to facilitate the computation of Decision-centralization, the five decision procedures were assumed to be separated by equal intervals on the influence continuum, and scale scores of 1, 2, 3, 4, and 5 were assigned (Delegation = 1, etc.). With Form C, each item was scored in terms of the scale value of the decision procedure selected by the leader. The mean of the eighteen items provided an index ranging from 1 to 5 (high Decision-centralization means low subordinate influence). A comparable index was obtained from Forms A and B by multiplying the average frequency scores by the scale values (1 to 5), summing these products and dividing the sum by 100.

Only a moderate amount of internal consistency was expected for Forms B and C, since a variety of different types of decisions was purposely included in these questionnaires. Item-total correlations were calculated for Form C, and of the eighteen items, seventeen had an item-total correlation of .40 ($P < .01$) or better. Although all three forms were not administered to every leader, there was some overlap of method in order to test for method comparability. Decision-centralization scores for Form A correlated .55 ($P < .01$) with Decision-centralization scores for Form C. For Forms A and B, Decision-centralization scores correlated .71 ($P < .01$). Re-test reliability for Form B with an interval of seven weeks was .82 ($P < .01$).

Information regarding the situational variables other than type of decision was obtained from straightforward questionnaire items and from organization records. The term *situational* is used, for want of a better term, to describe a mixed group of variables. Two of them, namely, authority level and span of control, are usually called structural variables.

In interpreting the results in the next section, certain limitations in the design of the study should be borne in mind. Perhaps the most important limitation is that in a correlational study of this nature, no conclusions about causality can be made. A second limitation is that three different questionnaires were used on four samples of leaders; while the questionnaires were found to be reasonably well intercorrelated, the design makes it impossible to present exactly the same information for all four samples. Thirdly, Forms A and B were used to obtain Decision-centralization scores (Tables 1 and 2) as well as percentage scores distributed over the influence continuum (Figure 1, Tables 3, 4, and 5). Percentage scores probably simulate very accurately the real managerial choice situation, but the scale is limited by the fact that the choices must add up to 100. As a consequence, the correlations between situational variables and the five decision styles are not entirely independent of each other. This is not likely to be a major problem, however, if conclusions are based on the overall trends rather than on individual correlations or *t*-tests. Finally in the present study, the effect of the intercorrelations between the situational variables is not eliminated. However, the intercorrelations are generally small.

RESULTS

1. The means and standard deviations of the Decision-centralization scores for the four groups of leaders are presented in Table 1. An analysis of variance indicated that there were significant differences among groups with respect to Decision-centralization ($F = 8.73$, $P < .01$). For the three groups of industrial leaders, the higher the leader was in the authority hierarchy, the less centralized was his decision-making. Student leaders tended to be more permissive in their decision-making than the industrial leaders. The difference between the four groups can be seen more clearly in Figure 2. The most preferred decision style among student leaders was Joint Decision-making. Senior managers used Prior Consultation most frequently. Second-line supervisors used Prior Consultation and Own Decision with Explanation more often than the other three styles. First-line supervisors used Own Decision with Explanation most frequently. This pattern of results is not surprising considering the differences between the leadership roles for the four groups of leaders. Blankenship

TABLE 1
Decision-Centralization Means and Standard Deviations
for Four Types of Leaders[a]

Type of leader:	Mean	S.D.	N
Student leaders	2.98	.42	21
Senior managers	3.14	.52	82
Second-line supervisors	3.26	.37	72
First-line supervisors	3.66	.53	29
$F = 8.73, p < .01$			

[a] Note: Data is from Questionnaire B and C.
High scores imply decision-centralization.

FIGURE 2
Pattern of Decision Making for Four Groups of Leaders

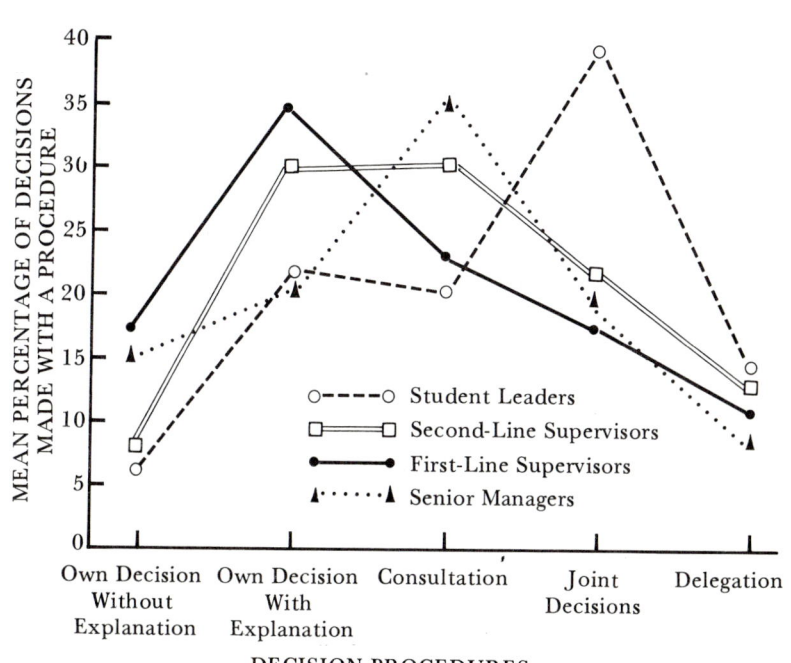

and Miles (1968, p. 119) have recently reported the finding that senior levels in a hierarchy involve their subordinates in decision making more than managers at lower levels. Factors such as the nature of their subordinates' task, the capacity of the subordinates to contribute to the decision process, and expectations regarding the proper amount of subordinate influence probably all contribute to the tendency of leaders at higher authority levels to allow greater subordinate influence.

2. Functional specialization is also related to the style of decision-making that will be selected. The sample of senior managers could be divided into six managerial functions: production, finance, sales, purchasing, personnel, and nonspecialized "general" management.[5] Table 2 presents the mean and standard deviation of the Decision-centralization scores for these six groups of managers. The six functions appear to form three clusters. Production and finance managers tended to use centralized decision styles, whereas nonspecialized "general" managers and personnel managers tended to be the most permissive. Managers of purchasing and sales units occupied an intermediate position on the influence continuum. An analysis of variance indicated that the mean Decision-centralization scores for these three clusters of managers were significantly different ($F = 3.84; P < .05$).[6] The differences in decision styles are most likely related to the nature of the task performed by the manager's department. The degrees of freedom available to managers in the tasks performed in the finance and production departments are probably fewer than in the case of the relatively unprogrammed jobs in the personnel and "general" management fields. Also, there is evidence that production divisions are under greater pressure than non-production divisions (Fleishman, Harris, and Burtt, 1955, pp. 98-99).[7] The extent to which programmed jobs restrict the meaningful possibilities of participation, has been pointed out in the literature, but particularly in relation to low level jobs (Leavitt,

TABLE 2
Decision-Centralization Means and Standard Deviations
for Six Management Functions[a]

	Function:	M	S.D.	N
High Centralization group	Production	3.43	.40	15
	Finance	3.36	.66	11
Medium Centralization group	Sales	3.16	.82	8
	Purchasing	3.06	.45	7
Low Centralization group	General	2.98	.39	17
	Personnel	2.96	.39	8

F for the three functional groups = 3.84, $p < .05$

[a] Note: Data is from Questionnaire B.
High scores imply decision-centralization.

1965, p. 1166; Strauss, 1963, p. 71). The present finding would suggest that the concept may also operate at very senior levels (see also Lefton *et al.*, 1966).

3. The distinction between line and staff is another way of classifying managers by function. Although many of the senior managers could not be clearly classified as line or staff managers, it was possible to differentiate 26 managers whose primary function was to implement and control managerial policy (line) from 16 managers whose major function was to advise and recommend on policy matters. The mean and standard deviation of the Decision-centralization scores for line managers were 3.18 and .55 respectively. The mean and standard deviation of the Decision-centralization scores for staff managers were 2.93 and .32 respectively. Although the line managers were expected to be less permissive in their decision-making, the difference between means was not significant (t = 1.61).[8]

4. Information about span of control was available for all of the industrial leaders, but first line supervisors were omitted since their subordinates were workers rather than supervisors and the variance in their span of control was extremely small. Span of control ranged from 2–16 subordinates for second-line supervisors and from 1–14 subordinates for senior managers. The relation between decision-making behavior and span of control for these two groups of leaders can be found in Table 3. When group size or span of control increases, decision procedures such as Consultation and Joint Decision-making become less feasible since they

---

TABLE 3
Correlation between Span of Control and the Use of Five Decision Procedures by Managers and Second-Line Supervisors[a]

	Span of Control:	
Decision procedure:	Senior manager	Second-line supervisors
Own decision without explanation	.33[c]	.00
Own decision with explanation	−.09	.34[c]
Consultation	−.20	−.14
Joint decision-making	−.10	−.10
Delegation	.22[b]	−.12
	N = 82	N = 72

[a] Note: Data is from Questionnaire A and B.
[b] $p < .05$.
[c] $p < .01$.
The five correlations for each sample are not independent because ipsative scoring was employed.

require considerable time-consuming interaction and communication between group members. These time pressures could lead us to expect three alternative approaches to decision-making when span of control is large. The leader could make the decisions by himself; he could decentralize; or he could centralize some decisions and decentralize others. Table 3 shows that both senior managers and second-line supervisors tended to centralize their decisions when the span of control was large. However, only senior managers used delegation as a second time saving procedure, thereby demonstrating greater flexibility.

5. The relation between a leader's decision-making behavior and the amount of time that he has occupied his leadership position is shown in Table 4. The correlations in this table are consistent with the differences in decision behavior found for the three authority levels (see Table 1). The longer they have been in their job, the greater is the tendency for first and second-line supervisors to shift from permissive to directive decision procedures. In contrast, the senior managers tend to use more delegation as their length of tenure increases. It would appear that the better the lower level leaders get to know their job and subordinates, the less inclined they are to share decision-making, perhaps because there is a real or felt difference in skills between the lower level leader and his subordinates. On the other hand, as the senior managers get to know their subordinates better, some of the decision-making responsibility is handed over to them completely. This would suggest that the managers gain confidence in their subordinates' ability, or that they have been able to train them to carry out a wider range of tasks.

TABLE 4
Correlation between a Leader's Time in Present Position and his Use of Five Decision Procedures[a]

	Leader's time in present position		
Decision procedure:	First-line supervisor	Second-line supervisor	Senior manager
Own decision without explanation	.45[b]	.38[c]	.08
Own decision with explanation	.06	−.01	−.07
Consultation	−.16	−.10	−.12
Joint decision-making	−.22	−.04	−.03
Delegation	−.19	−.17	.39[c]
	$N = 29$	$N = 72$	$N = 82$

[a] Note: Data is from Questionnaire A and B.
[b] $p < .05$.
[c] $p < .01$.
The five correlations for each sample are not independent since ipsative scoring was employed.

TABLE 5

Comparison of Decision Procedure for Two Types of Decisions
$N = 82^a$

Senior managers decision procedure:		Percentage of time the procedure is used		
		Mean percentage	S.D.	t
Own decision without explanation	EMP	7.1	16.1	$4.58\,p < .001$
	SUB	20.9	24.1	
Own decision with explanation	EMP	12.2	17.9	$3.70\,p < .001$
	SUB	30.7	24.0	
Consultation	EMP	41.4	31.7	$-3.18\,p < .01$
	SUB	30.4	21.2	
Joint decision-making	EMP	27.1	27.3	$-6.27\,p < .001$
	SUB	16.0	21.9	
Delegation	EMP	12.0	19.5	$-5.39\,p < .001$
	SUB	2.1	5.3	

[a] Note: Data is from Questionnaire B. EMP = Decisions concerning employees working under the subordinate of the leader. SUB = Decisions concerning the immediate subordinate of the leader.
The five t-tests are influenced by the ipsative nature of the scale which adds up to 100%; however, they indicate trends.

6. The nature of the problem requiring a decision also appears to be related to the leader's decision-making behavior. The findings presented in Table 5 suggest that leaders vary their decision behavior according to the hierarchical locus of the problem. The two centralized decision styles are used more frequently when the problem relates to their immediate subordinates (SUB decisions). On the other hand, leaders tend to use one of the three influence-sharing methods when the problem to be decided involves persons two levels down the authority hierarchy (EMP decisions). The difference in the choice of style between EMP-SUB problems is highly significant. This finding is consistent with the notion that the authority structure represents functional specialization and delegation of responsibility. A manager would not need lower level supervisors if he had to make *their* decisions for them. On the other hand, the figures in Table 5 indicate that most managers continue to play an important part in the making of EMP decisions.

7. For first and second-line supervisors, a different kind of distinction was made with respect to the nature of the problem. Decision-making dealing with task problems was compared to decision-making dealing with group maintenance problems by the use of Form C. The mean and standard deviation of Decision-centralization scores for the task decisions were 3.05 and .53, respectively. The mean and standard deviation for the maintenance decisions were .62 and .36, respectively. A t-test indicated that the means were significantly different ($t = 9.20$, $P < .01$). Apparently the supervisors were more willing to allow subordinate participation in

making task decisions than in making maintenance decisions. Perhaps this is because many maintenance decisions, especially those involving personnel matters or discipline problems, do not lend themselves easily to decentralization, even though some discussion with subordinates will often be necessary.

DISCUSSION AND CONCLUSIONS

The results of the present study support the thesis that the amount of influence a leader allows his subordinates changes with six of the seven situational variables studied in this research. More specifically, the results show that sharing of decision-making with subordinates was greatest under the following conditions:

- When the leader was a senior manager rather than a supervisor or foreman.
- When the leader was an elected or appointed student leader rather than an industrial leader.
- When the leader was a personnel manager or a general manager, as opposed to managers of sales, purchasing, production, or finance divisions.
- When the leader had a small span of control.
- When a first or second-line supervisor was newly appointed to his position.
- When a senior manager had been in his position for a considerable amount of time.
- When the decision involved persons more than one level down in the authority hierarchy.
- When the decisions were concerned with task matters rather than with personnel matters, discipline, or morale.

As has been pointed out earlier, recent reviews of the literature on participation (Sales, 1966; Lowin, 1968) show clearly that the majority of previous studies have been concerned with broad overall relations between participatory behavior and other variables. In their view, this research has been indecisive. There are probably three reasons for this. Firstly, previous investigators have not taken into account the variety of decision styles commonly used by managers. Secondly, specific decisions of the kind typically confronting leaders have not been used in scales measuring decision behavior. Finally, "the mediating conditions which shape the effect of participatory decision making" have been largely ignored (Lowin, 1968, p. 99).

The five point decision continuum and the measuring scales which were used in this research appear to lend themselves to a study of how leaders adapt their decision-making to the needs of the situation. These questionnaires could also be used to investigate the relation between leader decision-making and group performance. Furthermore, the situational variables found to be related to leader decision-making in this study are potential mediators of the relation between participation and group performance. These situational variables and others like them will be useful for determining the parameters of feasibility for participation in different kinds of organizations.

FOOTNOTES

1. Scale B to be described later was influenced by the business decision categories used in the Blankenship and Miles (1968) questionnaire.

2. On a broader front, but excluding decision-making, Porter and Lawler (1965) have reviewed studies supporting the relation of structural variables to attitudes and job performance in business organizations. In Europe, there have been several sociologically oriented studies on the effect of structural variables (Woodward, 1965; Pugh, Hickson, Hinings, and Turner, 1968); and sociotechnical systems (Trist, Higgins, Murray, and Pollock, 1963). These studies also exclude decision-making at the plant level.

3. Several of the decision procedures could be further subdivided within the range of the continuum. In particular, different degrees of delegation are possible in terms of the time span of a manager's review and the probability of revoking any given decision. There is a slight and possibly superficial resemblance between *delegation* and *laissez faire* leadership. However, delegation does not represent passive leadership and, although subordinates are given some freedom, the area of choice is usually delineated and constrained.

4. Copies of the various scales can be obtained from the authors.

5. General management is not usually considered to be a separate function. In the present sample, the term nonspecialized "general" management was used to describe all managerial positions in control of divisions or sections which do not have specialized functional responsibility. These managers were at the same level of seniority as the functional managers.

6. The F-test for the six separate functions was not significant.

7. Heller, in a 1968 study now being analyzed, used a scale of job constraints. Preliminary analysis suggests that the degrees of freedom available to managers differ with their task function in a way comparable to the findings of Fleishman *et al.* (1955, p. 98).

8. Since the direction of relation between the situational variables and the dependent variable was not always clearly specified beforehand, the significance tests of all product-moment correlations and "Student's" t-tests, are two tailed.

REFERENCES

Argyris, C. *Integrating the Individual and the Organization*. New York: Wiley, 1964.

Bass, B. Some effects on a group of whether and when the head reveals his opinion. *Organizational Behavior and Human Performance*, 1967, *2*, 375-382.

Blankenship, V., and Miles, R. Organization structure and managerial decision behavior. *Administrative Science Quarterly*, 1968, *13*, 106-120.

Blake, R., and Mouton, J. *Group Dynamics: Key to Decision Making*. Houston, Texas: Gulf Publishing Company, 1961.

Davies, B. Some thoughts on organizational democracy. *Journal of Management Studies*, 1967, *4*, 270-281.

Fleishman, E., Harris, E., and Burtt, H. Leadership and supervision in industry. Ohio State University Studies, Bureau of Educational Research Monograph No. 33. Ohio State University, Columbus, Ohio, 1955.

Heller, F. Group feed-back analysis: A method of applied research. Paper presented at Western Psychological Association meeting. San Diego, March 1968. Mimeographed, University of California, Berkeley. To be published *Psychological Bulletin* 1969.

Leavitt, H. Unhuman organization. *Harvard Business Review*, 1962, July-August, 90-98.

Leavitt, H. Applied organizational change in industry: structural, technological and humanistic approaches. In J. March (Ed.). *Handbook of Organizations*. Chicago: Rand McNally, 1965.

Lefton, M., Dinitz, S., and Pasamanick, B. Decision making in a mental hospital: real, perceived and ideal. In Rubenstein, A.R., and Haberstroh, C. (Eds.) *Some Theories of Organization*. Homewood, Illinois: Dorsey Press, Revised Edition, 1966.

Lewin, K., Lippitt, R., and White, R. Patterns of aggressive behavior in experimentally created "social climates." *Journal of Social Psychology*, 1939, *10*, 271-299.

Likert, R. *New Patterns of Management*. New York: McGraw-Hill, 1961.

Likert, R. *The Human Organization*. New York: McGraw-Hill, 1967.

Lowin, A. Participative decision-making: a model, literature, critique and prescription for research. *Organizational Behavior and Human Performance*, 1968, *3*, 68-106.

March, J.G., and Simon, H.A. *Organizations*. New York: Wiley, 1958.

Pugh, D., Hickson, D., Hinings, C., and Turner, C. Dimensions of organization structure. *Administrative Science Quarterly*, 1968, *13*, 65-105.

Sales, S. Supervisory style and productivity: a review. *Personnel Psychology*, 1966, *19*, 275-286.

Strauss, G. Some notes on power-equalization. In H. Levitt (Ed.). *The Social Science of Organizations*. New York: Prentice-Hall, 1963.

Tannenbaum, A. Control in organizations: industrial adjustment and organizational performance. *Administrative Science Quarterly*, 1962, *7*, 236-257.

Tannenbaum, R., and Massarik, F. Participation by subordinates. In Tannenbaum *et al.* (Eds.). *Leadership and Organizations.* New York: McGraw-Hill, 1961.

Tannenbaum, R., and Schmidt, W. How to choose a leadership pattern. *Harvard Business Review*, 1958, *36*, 95-101.

Trist, E., Higgins, G., Murray, H., and Pollock, A. *Organizational Choice.* London: Tavistock Publications, 1963.

Woodward, J. *Industrial Organization: Theory and Practice.* London: Oxford University Press, 1965.

Mr. Lee is Professor of Management in the College of Business Administration at Ohio University. This article is reprinted with permission from Harvard Business Review, *March-April 1971, pp. 20-28, 157-159.* Copyright © *1971 by the President and Fellows of Harvard College, all rights reserved.*

Behavioral Theory vs. Reality

JAMES A. LEE

Most behavioral theorists have "known" for years how an organization and its management style should be changed to bring about tremendous improvement in morale and productivity. Executives, managers, and administrators who have been exposed to Modern Human Resource Management theories appear, at least to the theorists, to have adopted their "findings" almost not at all.

And the question is: Why?

The purpose of this article is to answer this question. The reasons, in my view, are quite simple and straightforward. But because of the approaches of many behavioral theorists and training consultants, most managers have been placed in such a defensive position that to argue effectively against Modern Human Resource Management would be tantamount to shooting Smokey the Bear for sport.

A typical example of apparent management rejection, as it appears to some behavioral theorists, is in the introductory chapter of a recent book containing excerpts from the writings of most Modern Human Resource Management theorists:

"Recently one of the authors of this book proposed a management development program to a major American corporation. Human behavior in organizations was to be the subject of the first week, new decision-making tools the second, and business and society relationships the third. The latter two weeks were accepted, the first rejected rather strongly—with an oath about having had enough human relations! Of course, this may reflect one chief executive's opinion, but it does seem symptomatic of the suspicion and perhaps cynicism that characterizes management's view on the subject of human relations. 'Not useful,' 'too fuzzy,' 'theoretical,' 'soft,' 'not operational' are all responses we have received to pleas for consideration of behavior."[1]

One must admit that the reasons just given are not pieces of a carefully prepared rationale. Because they appear flippant and somewhat unrelated, however, they cannot be brushed aside as evidence of simply a bad decision by a single unenlightened executive.

I propose to provide here a useful rationale that will account for the rates at which Modern Human Resource Management theories can be found in application. My purpose is not to provide executives with a better list of reasons for rejecting proposals for Modern Human Resource Management training. I believe, however, that if *real* causes of the resistance are not carefully analyzed, there is little chance for increasing the use of what is known today about organizational behavior motivation.

MHRM THEORIES

At the outset, my definition of Modern Human Resource Management should be explained in some detail. By MHRM, I refer primarily to the overlapping theories and concepts of behavioral theorists such as Douglas McGregor, Frederick Herzberg, Chris Argyris, Rensis Likert, Robert Blake with Jane S. Mouton, and Abraham Maslow. Consider:

☐ McGregor described two sets of contrasting assumptions about man and his attitudes toward his work. The Theory X assumptions (man is lazy, needs watching and prodding), and Theory Y assumptions (workers seek responsibility and are capable of self-control) are now part of management jargon.

☐ Herzberg's work, focusing on worker motivation, pointed up "hygiene" factors (working conditions, fringe benefits, and so on) as essential but not motivators, and the real motivators (responsibility, achievement, and so forth) as the key to improving worker performance.

☐ Argyris' theories are concerned with the effects of organizational life on individual motivation. He has developed organizational structures and control systems designed to help build consistency between organizational and individual goals.

☐ Likert has developed four organizational model systems. His System 1 manager could be said to be a Theory X type, and his System 4 manager, a group consensus seeker, is not far from holding Theory Y assumptions.

Likert has also proposed a human-assets inventory approach involving the management of people with at least the same care and concern as the management of land and other material resources.

☐ Blake and Mouton provided the theory that integrated the work of McGregor, Likert, and others. Their 9,9 manager (people and output oriented) is similar to a System 4 or Theory Y manager, while at the opposite corner of their grid is a 9,1 manager who is primarily concerned with output but not particularly concerned with people.

☐ Maslow, a theoretical psychologist and father of the "need hierarchy" concept (a dynamic model of Aristotle's soul hierarchy), has suggested that efforts to motivate workers must be consistent with the theory that a satisfied need does not offer opportunities for motivation. Higher order needs must be acknowledged as motivators as lower order needs are fulfilled.

Modern Human Resource Management as used here, then, is an abbreviated summary of these theories which, in general, hold that (a) managers should trust their subordinates to be more responsible in the performance of their jobs; (b) managers should permit the subordinate to participate in the making of his own job; and (c) managers should replace much of the mechanistic structure, characteristic of most institutions, with an organic approach to organization.

Before beginning with an analysis of the resistance to wholesale adoption of MHRM approaches, let me point out that over the years managers *have* changed in the way they approach human resource management. Their changes have been necessarily integral with the cultural changes in Western societies (more on this later). For training directors, consultants, theorists, or anyone who would contemplate influencing an organization's management to adopt MHRM applications, however, I suggest beginning with a quick review of the list of obvious possible reasons for resistance shown in Exhibit 1.

It should be noted here that top management's willingness to experiment is to be commended, even though many such organizational experiments fail or offer questionable results. The risks can be quite high compared with experiments using college sophomores or tiny work-force units.

All of the accompanying rationales shown in Exhibit 1 suggest or point directly to the need for a system approach as the only useful avenue for further exploration and application. Since managerial behavioral change is primarily a function of cultural change, it is implicit that subordinates must change integrally with superiors and that this subsystem is part of a subculture which must change and which is part of a total culture which must also change.

All MHRM theory I have ever seen or heard is addressed to only one element (management) in the culture, as though it were independent. (Where is the Theory Y for nonmanagers—"Trust your boss to do the right

EXHIBIT 1
Reasons for Resistance to MHRM

From sociology and anthropology[a]
    ○ A society is a semistationary integrated unit.
    ○ The introduction of a new element affects other elements.
    ○ Many elements in the culture must be changed to accommodate the new element.
    ○ This reordering process is a very slow one.

From industrial case analysis[b]
    ○ Most behavioral science is focused on human motivation and group behavior without fully accounting for the technical environment which circumscribes, even determines, the roles the actors will play.
    ○ Such abstractions as motivation, interaction, and authority do not take place in a technical vacuum.

From research in industrial administration[c]
    ○ The link between technology and organization persists in spite of, rather than because of, conscious behavior or deliberate policy.
    ○ Therefore, analysis of situational demands is necessary before organization appraising is attempted.
    ○ This analysis would also lead to an increased understanding of the personal qualities and skills required in different industrial situations.

From social psychology[d]
    ○ Perception is functionally selective.
    ○ Beliefs and culturally acquired attitudes about leaders and followers play a significant role in determining the nature of this selectivity and tend to determine the meaning of these perceptions.
    ○ The new data available to an individual but contradictory to his beliefs and attitudes may not be fully perceived or may be assimilated in such a way that the basic beliefs are not changed (lip service to MHRM, for example).

From applied behavioral science[e]
    ○ A person's leadership style reflects the individual's motivational and need structure.
    ○ It takes several years of intensive psychotherapy to effect lasting changes in this structure.
    ○ A few hours of lectures and role-playing are not the equivalent of intensive psychotherapy.

From experimental application in industry
    (representative examples only)
    ○ The well-known Western Electric studies revealed, among other things, that it was possible to increase worker production up to 40%. From an operational standpoint, however, this would have required a prohibitive increase in overhead. Also, the special assignment nature of the work environment (Hawthorne effect) could not be maintained on any large-scale basis.[f]
    ○ The Ohio State University Studies indicated that human relations

Exhibit 1 continued

training (with role-playing, group discussion, etc.) had no measurable effect on plant behavior after return to work. "The results clearly indicated that the foreman is more responsible to the day-to-day climate (subculture) in which he operates than to any special course of training he may have been given." (Parentheses added.)[g]

○ A Southern California company that had experimented with a number of MHRM techniques reversed its style, letting go senior executives in the process. Financial difficulties were blamed for dropping the experiment.[h]

○ A major chemical company had a sizable department staffed by specialists in organizational development who were well schooled in MHRM theories and well supported by top theorist-consultants. This department no longer exists as such, and its manager has moved to another company not known for its avant garde MHRM practices.

a. William F. Ogburn and Meyer F. Nimkoff, *Sociology* (New York, Houghton Mifflin Company, 1946), pp. 880-882.
b. Robert H. Guest, *Organizational Change: The Effect of Successful Leadership* (New York, Irwin-Dorsey Press, 1963), p. 4.
c. Joan Woodward et al., *Industrial Organization: Theory and Practice* (London, Oxford University Press, 1965), p. 74.
d. David Krech and Richard S. Crutchfield, *Theory and Problems of Social Psychology* (New York, McGraw-Hill Book Company, 1948), pp. 190-192.
e. Fred A. Fiedler, *A Theory of Leadership Effectiveness* (Urbana, The University of Illinois, 1967), p. 248.
f. Mason Haire, "Some Problems of Industrial Training," *The Journal of Social Issues*, Summer 1948, pp. 44-45.
g. Edwin A. Fleishman, Edwin F. Harris, and Harold E. Burtt, *Leadership and Supervision in Industry: An Evaluation of a Supervisory Training Program*, Monograph No. 33 (Columbus, Ohio, Bureau of Educational Research, Ohio State University, 1955), p. 94.
h. *Business Week*, March 20, 1965, pp. 93-94; see also Vance Packard, "A Chance for Everyone to Grow," *Reader's Digest*, November 1963, pp. 114-118.

---

thing"—or for the engineer—"Trust the worker to have useful ideas of his own"—and what behavioral scientist is writing to the union leaders urging them to trust corporate management to be fair and honest?)

Cultural Changes

The first step in the analysis requires that one accept an anthropologist's view of a culture or subculture as an integrated unit. If we hold this point of view, we can eventually arrive at the conclusion that most MHRM theories are only *descriptions* of cultural changes taking place in institutional subcultures in certain Western societies. Once seen in this light, the varying rate of adoption of techniques springing from these theories begins to make sense.

Cultural or societal change in Western countries is usually uneven. The factors influencing this change are not present to the same degree everywhere in the culture at the same time. Therefore, there are a few subcultures or semiencapsulated groups changing less slowly than others. The general *direction* of this change appears to be more or less the same, however, and there is enough evidence available for me to describe certain aspects of it in terms of moving either *toward* or *away from*.

Toward:
○ More autonomy for individuals in institutional settings.
○ Greater demand for information affecting autonomy, health, and security, and increased ability to get this information.
○ Wider participation in institutional planning and decision making.
○ Greater dependence upon individual's judgment in institutional task performances.
○ More widespread recognition of the potential power of the nonmanager to effect institutional goal attainment.
○ More response to the law of the situation.
○ More self-evaluation with the implicit discipline of the task.
○ More organic organizational structures.

Away from:
○ Elitism (blood, class, or technical).
○ Mechanistic organizational structures.
○ Sacredness of management rights and institutional policies and procedures.
○ Formal discipline based upon position authority.

There can be no isolated cause of these directional changes, of course. However, the causal whole can be described by my listing its most important elements: technological, economic, family, and educational.

Technological changes. In the past 70 years in the United States, few work tasks have not been changed radically. The nature of individual tasks in certain industries (electronics, space, R&D, chemical) has resulted in altered behavior that has begun to produce changes in attitudes toward work performance and the roles of superiors. The increased proportion of complicated work cannot be supervised in the same manner as could the simple tasks of a previous period.

Certain technologies have severely altered intra-institutional worker density and the nature of worker controls. (Compare a machine-paced mass production work environment with that of a modern refinery or chemical processing operation.)

Communication and transportation changes have made available more information and opportunity for escape from immediate subcultures.

Economic changes. Increased affluence, partly a function of technological changes, has altered the early need of the young to work. It has made possible educational gain throughout society. The family has been radically altered (see next part) due to a combination of technological and economic changes. Increased independence and mobility of individual members of society is due at least in part to increased affluence.

The family. There can be little doubt that the family is the most powerful single environmental force in shaping the personality structure, social response patterns, values, and attitudes toward work, authority, and autonomy.

There is also little doubt that this root social institution is changing. The increased absence of both parents from their young for longer periods (divorces, separations, and work), the reduced need for interdependence for economic survival, the increased freedom from drudgery in the home, and the relatively private use of leisure time cannot help but change the family. Moreover, since many parents have the knowledge and time to consciously raise their children according to some philosophy (Spock, Freud, the Existentialists, la Leche, and others), it is unreasonable to expect the family to remain stable.

Because the family is the nuclear social unit, roles and power relations changes can be seen reflected in the larger institutions in the society. The mother (traditional roles: suckle, teach, comfort) has begun a new role with a new "authority" in relation to the father (decide, discipline, direct) whose position of authority has been diluted. The children (learn, work, obey) who have more knowledge and better education, are needed very little for the family's economic survival and are gaining autonomy and power in the family earlier. These changes also appear in larger social roles and relationships comparable to those of the family: government (suckle, teach, comfort), business (decide, discipline, direct), and workers (learn, work, obey).

The results of family changes reflected in the wider culture are obvious: the power relationships between government, business, and labor are mirror images of the changes that have taken place in the individual family. For a long-range prediction of major institutional power relationships, one should now observe the family carefully.

For example, when the children begin to take greater license with the mother, one should expect (a few years later) the unions of government employees to begin to exert greater pressure on the government.

Other results should also be obvious: attitudes toward work, drudgery, authority, and autonomy affect employee motivation. And as these changes reach the organizational setting through workers, the pressures thus generated change managerial behavior.

Educational changes. Teaching philosophies and methods have focused more on the individual. During a child's most formative period, his teachers are more often women than men. Democratic approaches to school administration and classroom activities have altered individual role conceptions. A greater proportion of the population is educated at all levels.[2] People are more interested in information now that more of them know how to use it.

All these important elements are obviously interrelated. They are abstracted here only for the purpose of elaborating on the causes of the cultural changes that affect behavior in organizational settings. Another thing is obvious: *the manager does not have much direct control over these changes.*

Which of the causal factors are within the manager's control?

Education of the work force can be effected (directly but only slightly) by two methods: (1) tuition refund and training programs, and (2) changes in the work technology (through product or production method changes) that will force a replacement of some of the work-force population.

Technology of the work can be affected by changes in products or methods of production. These changes, however, are not conscious managerial choices for MHRM purposes but are dependent on many factors (e.g., markets and economics).

The family, of course, is almost completely outside the direct control of management. If at all, management indirectly affects this institution through the hiring of more wives and mothers.

Another indirect effect has been the reduction of family worry over financial catastrophe through health and life insurance plans. The role of the wife-mother has been altered, therefore, because in lower- and middle-class families in Western countries, she was often the primary force influencing the "saving for the rainy day" behavior. Today's increased affluence is also outside any immediate control by the manager. Only through the overall increases in national productivity does the manager influence the standard of living which in turn alters the social institutional environments.

'Vanguard' Institutions

A few institutional populations are affected more than others by these cultural changes. Roughly, in order of their change rate, they are:

○ Research and development institutions.

○ Many government departments.

○ Certain quarters of the space, aeronautics, electronics, and chemical industries.

○ Certain quarters of the utility industries.

One can hardly miss the government thread running through most of the list, although given the government's increased role in the protection of the individual over the past 50 years (labor legislation, civil liberties, individual rights, and so on), this is hardly surprising.

Behavioral scientists will appear to have had more success with their management seminars in the institutions just listed. Failures occur more often in industries whose success depends little on the coordinated efforts of affluent professionals and highly educated technicians who are in the forefront of cultural change in our society.

Therefore, the adoption of Modern Human Resource Management will necessarily be slow simply because manpower management style is almost completely intertwined in the system of cultural values. These values are in turn a function of technological, economic, family, and educational changes that alter behavior.

As the economic, family, and educational changes have an impact on behavior, of course, so will they change the manpower management styles, with or without much help from seminars offered by behavioral scientists. These cultural values will change not as a direct result of these scientists' findings.

Rather, quite the opposite is closer to the truth: as the culture changes, so will the scientists, their findings, and their seminars. The history of management theory is replete with subculturally and self-referenced contributors. Consider:

O *Niccolo Machiavelli* (1469-1527) who was exiled by a conquering family before writing *The Prince*, which was designed to show how power should be gained and held.

O *Adam Smith* (1723-1790) who was professor of moral philosophy for eight years before publishing *The Theory of Moral Sentiments*, and worked 2½ years as private tutor to the stepson of the Chancellor of the Exchequer, Charles Townshend, before writing *Wealth of Nations*.

O *Thomas Alva Edison* (1847-1931), the inventor's inventor, who on several occasions devised machines for the specific purpose of replacing troublesome workers.

O *Frederick W. Taylor* (1856-1915), a laborer and shop worker of unusual intelligence, who devoted his life to efficiency in shop methods and tooling.

O *Mary Parker Follett* (1868-1938), primarily associated with social work institutions, who emphasized the role of the group in satisfying needs, in realizing individual potential, and in decision making.

O *James David Mooney* (1884-1957), author of *Principles of Organization* in 1926, who was an engineer, a vice president of General Motors, and a 20-year reserve military officer, and who emphasized the need for all organizations to be hierarchical.

O *Chester I. Barnard* (1887-1961) who was president of New Jersey Bell for 21 years (1927-1948) and whose writings emphasized the role of communications in management.

The vast majority of the behavioral theorists today are professors, whose strong autonomy needs and antiauthoritarian bias govern much of their research approach and ideal model-building.[3] They bounce their theories off other faculty members and students, who are well known to have similar needs and biases; they use students for subjects for some of their studies, and they arrive at a recommended work environment in the image of the ideal university.

Among the theorists, Douglas McGregor (if not his zealous followers) must be considered an exception. On the eve of his retirement as President of Antioch, he wrote:

"Before coming to Antioch I had observed and worked with top executives as an adviser in a number of organizations. I thought I knew how they felt about their responsibilities and what led them to behave as they did. I even thought that I could create a role for myself which would enable me to avoid some of the difficulties they encountered.

"I was wrong! It took the direct experience of becoming a line executive and meeting personally the problems involved to teach me what no amount of observation of other people could have taught.

"I believed, for example, that a leader could operate successfully as a kind of adviser to his organization. I thought I could avoid being a 'boss' . . . but I couldn't have been more wrong."[4]

Most MHRM theories, then, are self- and subculturally referenced. They have been given to us in some detail. Most, however, are descriptions of what is fairly standard practice in a few small subcultures in the vanguard of cultural changes in most Western societies. Theorist-consultants have studied attempts to produce change in a few socio-industrial subcultures. They have reported all the temporary successes and few, if any, of the failures.

The southern California company mentioned earlier in Exhibit 1, which used everything from T-groups to complete self-determination of production process and control, was described by Vance Packard as "a chance for everyone to grow," and was the subject of several evangelistically designed cases registered with the Harvard Case Clearing House.[5] No follow-up cases have been prepared telling the rest of the story, which was available as early as 1965. (One of the MHRM-oriented "let-go" vice presidents visited the Harvard Business School at that time, looking for a job.) Yet these cases are still being used by organizational behavior faculty in business schools!

The major chemical company (also cited in Exhibit 1), with the organizational development department that was hailed in business news media, was similarly the subject of business cases, but follow-up studies and cases marking the elimination of the department are conspicuously lacking.

Managerial Approach

If the managers and the theorists are not directly responsible for cultural change, then what value is there in all the research and theory? Considerable, in my opinion, if a reasonable change rate (with limits that we do not yet know how to alter significantly in specific operational environments) can be accepted.

Here, then, is an eight-step approach for managers that would make maximum use, however meager the actual results, of our knowledge of human behavior in organizations.

First, avoid all theory suggesting that managers alone can, by conscious design, change enough to become the major direct change agent of organizational behavior. If managerial tasks can be altered to produce behavior in the desired direction, it is worth a try.

Consider this example: if a manager seems to avoid utilizing known or suspected talent under his supervision, *ask* him what his people think about a certain problem. This can be done only after he has been assured that the better his people are, the better he is.

Here is another example: if a particular manager needs to learn to delegate more of his work but glues himself to his operation, his superior officer can give him specific tasks that take him physically away from his operation before sending him to management seminars on "how to delegate."

Second, if a major organizational change is needed, top management should double a behavioral scientist's estimate of the time required and triple its own. Subcultures change more slowly than everybody realizes.

For example, a large U.S. corporation with a holding company history and style figured that a new president and a few new staff vice presidential appointments at corporate headquarters would lead to integration in a few years. When integration failed to take place, corporate management was so disappointed that it replaced this president with one who left the new cadre of corporate headquarters vice presidents to quit or find some busy work.

Another major American corporation utilized the most well-known behavioral scientist consultants available and an internal team of organizational development people in an effort to integrate an old holding company. They made good progress, but not fast enough to satisfy the board. Every time the president would make an effort to accelerate the integrative process, flak from within the system would undermine his position. A bad year for earnings now and then further undermined his efforts because in some quarters it was attributed to his change program. He is still suffering from poor judgment of the *rate* at which he could produce change.

Third, determine the need for organizational changes in terms of performance in relation to company objectives—and not because of measured attitudes, fashions, or the opinions of behavioral scientists. Look for *behavioral* changes necessary to achieve the organizational changes, which, in turn, will enable the company to attain its organizational objectives. Begin with organizational and individual incentives to change behavior through fairly straightforward but well-publicized policy changes and reward system changes.

For example, a division of a major mining company needed to adapt to closure threats from the U.S. Bureau of Mines because of its accident record. All supervisory and middle-management personnel job descriptions were rewritten to incorporate accident prevention responsibilities, performance appraisal forms were rewritten to conform, and supervisory management training programs were launched to teach accident prevention techniques.

The evidence that these took top management initiation and support was unmistakable. The accident frequency, severity, and compensation per each $100 of payroll were cut by some 90% within three years. The division's cost per ton mined was the best of all its domestic operations.

Fourth, study the organization to determine if integration efforts have resulted in a single management cadre over several different technologies. Specifically, mines, mills, smelters, and fabricating units require different types of managements, attract different kinds of people, and usually require different policies. Attempts to integrate them on a management and policy basis can produce unnecessary problems.

For example, a large light-metal mining and processing division of a major corporation is certain its productivity can be increased. It has been studied to death by top MHRM people who have ignored the varieties of technologies (and subcultures) under one roof. Its single union has as much trouble with influence as does management. The executive style (because of historical promotional streams) represents mostly only one of the three technologies, as does the corporate headquarters management.

No one in management or among the MHRM people is considering any short- or long-range plan that recognizes the differences in the subcultures formed by the technologies of a mill, smelter, or fabricating unit. The company, given its locked-in capital investment, would probably be better off to have three separate, relatively autonomous managements with three sets of local policies and a plan for replacing, over time, the one union with two or three unions.

Conglomerates should study their organizations to determine if acquisitions have resulted in a single management cadre with a single policy system over several different technologies. Remember, different tasks attract different people who glue themselves together and respond as groups with needs for different policies and incentives.

Fifth, do not attempt significant change unless most top people are prepared to introduce adequate tension along with a powerful change agent or two.

This point is illustrated by the experience of a machinery manufacturer's president who attempted to bull his way through a difficult labor negotiations year representing a major change in the corporate labor relations approach. Most top people nodded approval, but, when the chips were down, they undermined the whole strategy by subtle foot-dragging so as to avoid the production of tension below them.

The president should have taken more care to look behind their apparent agreement with the strategy. He could have done this by discussing in detail, and in advance, the course of negotiations as each projected stage produced probable alternatives to be faced in carrying out the planned strategy.

If too many such alternatives were to emerge, he could have dropped his plan. It also follows that perceived radical shifts in strategy would be tested thoroughly by the top people because they had, at least instinctively, a good feel for an impractical change rate.

Sixth, determine, with the help of behavioral scientists if necessary, a readiness for change diagnosis. This should include an assessment of rate readiness as well as a priority of changes in order of the likelihood of success.

Thus, if a company needs to begin in earnest to integrate blacks into supervisory or management cadres, it should have a long-range plan devised with the help of social scientists. Be wary of any short-range plan that promises to achieve real integration objectives. (Also beware of any plan that looks like it will have blacks "sitting near the door.")

If a readiness diagnosis indicates that rank-and-file supervisors will openly resist the plan, hold off the plan while a readiness program is undertaken. Get social scientists' help with the readiness program and with the plan to follow. Remember, though, that both of you likely will err in the direction of impatience.

Seventh, ask a behavioral science consultant, in specific terms, *how* any proposed change in managerial behavior or style will be accomplished. Whether his choice is T-groups, role playing, or ignorance removal, ask him to include follow-up studies at least six months after the training period to test the program's effectiveness.

Eighth, remember that there is scant evidence that attitudes can be changed, and then behavior. There is a mountain of evidence that "belief is shown in the willingness to act." Strive for changes in behavior. The attitudes will follow for behavioral scientists to come around and measure.

IN SUMMARY

In this article, I have attempted to point out why there are differential rates of the application of Modern Human Resource Management techniques, and that these rates are relatively unrelated to the direct efforts of behavioral science theorists. Managerial style or behavior has been shown to be integral to social subsystems and, therefore, cannot be changed in a vacuum. Managers, as integrated parts of subcultures, change their behavior primarily in response to changes in their subculture (work environment), after which measurable changes in their attitudes and values take place.

Attention, then, must be focused on the *total* system in which they operate before any changes should be attempted. This examination must be done with the full knowledge that technological, educational, economic, and family elements are responsible for altering behavior that produces managerial style changes.

If an obvious gap indicates the need for managerial changes, search for means of focusing on a task that can result in the desired managerial behavior changes. Examine thoroughly the evidence that such a gap, when closed, will help the organization achieve its objectives.

I have also pointed out that most behavioral scientists are more observers and describers of cultural, and therefore managerial, change than causes of it. . . .

FOOTNOTES

1. David R. Hampton, Charles E. Summer, and Ross A. Webber, *Organizational Behavior and the Practice of Management* (Glenview, Illinois, Scott, Foresman and Company, 1968), p. 5; see also *Studies in Personnel Policy No. 216* (New York, National Industrial Conference Board, 1969), for results of a survey of opinions of management in over 300 companies regarding the impact of various behavioral theorists.

2. In 1920, 17% finished high school compared with 80% today, and over half of our high school graduates enter college, compared with 20% in 1940.

3. See Peter P. Gil and Warren G. Bennis, "Science and Management: Two Cultures," *Journal of Applied Behavioral Sciences*, Vol. 4, No. 1, 1968, in which case analyses of a group of behavioral scientists and industrial managers were compared, yielding an easy identification of the effects of the scientists' antiauthoritarian bias.

4. *Antioch Notes*, Vol. 31, No. 9.

5. "A Chance for Everyone to Grow," *Reader's Digest*, November 1963, pp. 114-118.

Lawrence L. Steinmetz is a faculty member in the Graduate School of Business, University of Colorado, and Charles D. Greenidge is assistant to the president, Larson Industries, Inc., Minneapolis. This article is reprinted with permission from Business Horizons, *October 1970, pp. 23-32. Copyright© 1970 by the Foundation for the School of Business at Indiana University.*

Realities That Shape Managerial Style: Participative Philosophy Won't Always Work

LAWRENCE L. STEINMETZ and CHARLES D. GREENIDGE

The typical businessman, whether he is a line executive or line foreman, has been exposed to so much "current" managerial theory that he is incapable of thinking about employees and their work attitudes except in terms of the highest dignity of mankind. The reader is invited to assess his own tendencies in this area by taking the test contained in Figure 1. The odds are that he will score somewhat higher than the average score of 38.5. Experience in using this questionnaire with some 2,000 managers in various business seminars has shown that the average score for managers on the questionnaire is 41.5 (s = 3.6). This figure is significant at the .01 level. The hypothetical population mean of 38.5 was suggested as being representative of the general population as a result of a survey of 200 "average people"–people not in managerial or supervisory positions. This difference from the general population means that the average manager is more in favor of "nondirective," "participative," or "consultative" management.

The typical trainer of managerial talent, whether he is a line supervisor-trainer or an executive consultant, may delight in the fact that managers are becoming "enlightened," that on a simple test they can intuitively give

FIGURE 1
Assumptions About People

	Strongly Disagree	Disagree	Agree	Strongly Agree
1. Almost everyone could improve his job performance quite a bit if he really wanted to.	____	____	____	____
2. It is unrealistic to expect people to show the same enthusiasm for work as for their favorite leisure activities.	____	____	____	____
3. Even when encouraged by the boss, few people show the desire to improve themselves on the job.	____	____	____	____
4. If people are paid enough money, they are not likely to worry about such intangibles as status or individual recognition.	____	____	____	____
5. Typically, when people talk about wanting more responsible jobs, they really mean they want more money.	____	____	____	____
6. Being tough with people normally gets them to do what is expected.	____	____	____	____
7. It is difficult to get employees to assume responsibility because most people do not like to make decisions on their own.	____	____	____	____
8. The best way to get people to do work is to crack down on them once in a while.	____	____	____	____
9. It weakens a man's prestige whenever he has to admit to a subordinate that the subordinate has been right and he has been wrong.	____	____	____	____

10. The most effective supervisor is the one who gets the

Figure 1 continued

results management expects, regardless of the methods he uses in handling people.

11. It is too much to expect that people will try to do a good job unless they are prodded by their boss.

12. The boss who expects his employees to set their own standards for superior performance will probably find they do not set them very high.

13. If people do not use much imagination and ingenuity on the job, it is probably because few people have much of either attribute.

14. One difficulty in asking subordinates for ideas is that their perspective is too limited for their suggestions to be of much practical value.

15. It is only human nature for people to do as little work as they can get away with.

SCORING: Plus 4 = each "strongly disagree"; plus 3 = each "disagree"; plus 2 = each "agree"; and plus 1 = each "strongly agree."

The original source of this questionnaire is not known to the authors. It has, however, been developed and refined over the past six years by the authors into its present form in order to measure the different assumptions that supervisors hold concerning the attitudes of their subordinates toward work.

"right" answers. He might worry that the right answers are not right enough (college seniors frequently average above 50 as a group on the same questionnaire), but, nevertheless, he will probably feel that we are making strides in the right direction.

On the other hand, a minority group of managerial trainers—the authors included—are not delighted by this turn of events. In fact, our experience has shown that this circumstance does nothing more than indicate the root source of many of the trials and tribulations experienced by managers. This is especially true for owner-managers of smaller enterprises, and lower- and middle-level managers in the larger corporations. But before one can understand why the tendency toward participative, nondirective management reflects a fundamental problem emerging in our business society, he must first understand why managers can score as they do on such a test.

REASON FOR CONFUSED BEHAVIOR

The theory of industrial humanism has all too often been interpreted to mean "that *all* people have a higher order of needs," that man must find fulfillment on the job," and "that man works because he has ego motives, security motives, curiosity, creativity, and the desire for new experiences." It is easy for the manager to agree with such statements; they are noble, and noble statements are currently popular. Furthermore, we would like to believe that all people possess (at least in latent form) the same fine attributes identified with the successful in our society. Herein, however, lies the problem: the successful person (who does possess such traits) erroneously believes that others possess them. Unfortunately, the successful people in our society are also in a position to issue mandates designed to bring forth these latent attributes and hidden qualities in others (via the process of orders and training prescribed for subordinate managers).

Consequently, despite their high ideals and unquestioned sincerity, these crusaders for industrial humanism commit a fatal error. They overlook the fact that, while many people agree with their ideas and give them support, those who agree with their position are people already committed to that point of view and, therefore, are lending moral support for an indefensible position.

Examples of such errors in thought and the outcome of such thinking are common. The student who fails an exam has no difficulty convincing another student with a failing grade that the exam was unfair (and therefore should have the results discarded); the clergyman has no trouble convincing a Christian that Christianity is the best religion (and therefore should be embraced); and managerial consultants have little trouble convincing top-level executives (people who like to work) that working is fun and desirable (and will be appreciated by all). But the student has trouble convincing the professor, the clergyman has trouble convincing the Buddhist, and the managerial consultant has trouble convincing the lower-level manager who would rather play golf or go fishing, or who has people working for him who would prefer to golf or fish.

Therefore, it must be recognized that the reason for the high scores recorded on the questionnaire, the reason why executives generally accept the notion of participative management, and the reason why managerial trainers teach participative management is because they all believe it. However, the problem is not in their believing it or in the way that they practice or teach it. The problem lies in their proselyting others to accept their beliefs and in their attempts to force their subordinates to live with these ideals. In short, today's lower- and middle-level management trainee is suffering because he is being told by his consultant, trainer, educator, or boss that he must be a participative manager *because the consultant, trainer, educator, or boss is, and because such practices have been successful for him.*

The problem is further complicated by the fact that conventional wisdom tells the management trainee that he should practice the Golden Rule. Unfortunately, this rule has validity only in those circumstances where the person being managed—the employee—has the same outlook toward working as does the manager. Doing unto others as one would have others do unto him is not necessarily the rule that results in profitable and workable management. Participative management may work when the manager is supervising highly motivated people, but in the·event that the subordinate has a different outlook toward working (perhaps he just does not like it), the Golden Rule is inapplicable and must be substituted with the far more altruistic rule (called the Rule of Human Realism) of doing unto others as others would have done unto themselves. In other words, employees can only be managed in terms of what they are, not in terms of what we would have them be.

RULE OF HUMAN REALISM

How does the Rule of Human Realism differ from the traditional Golden Rule? The important difference is that the enlightened manager looks beyond himself and what supervisory practice would work with him; he looks at his employees as individuals and tries to understand their work attitudes. He refuses to accept the popular notion that participative management is the magic potion for all employee groups just because it has been successful with some groups, and he finds it personally appealing.

Several writers in recent years have attempted to establish some guidance toward such enlightened managerial thinking. Presthus, for example, has set down some of the differences that can be found between managerial attitudes toward work and subordinate attitudes toward work.[1] These differences are summarized in Figure 2, but basically can be described as (1) the ascendant viewpoint (which represents the outlook of the typical manager); (2) the indifferent outlook (which represents the frame of reference of most rank-and-filers); and (3) the ambivalent attitudes (which represents the outlook of many low-level managers and aspiring managers-to-be). It is not, however, so important that we label these groups as it is that we understand the attitudes which they express toward working and necessarily, therefore, the managerial style to which they will best respond as a result of their attitudes toward work.

Different Attitudes Toward Work

The assertion that people have different views of work is not new. McGregor made clear the fundamental dichotomy years ago. What is

FIGURE 2
Differences in Work Attitudes

Ascendants

Identify closely with the company
See failure as reflecting personal inadequacies
Want feedback from superiors
Engage in ritualistic behavior to conceal resentments
Want power for its potential influence
Tend to be procedure and rule oriented
Place personal success above acceptance by coworkers
Have high visibility drive
Go down hard when they fail.

Indifferents

Withdraw from identification with the company
Prefer not to compete for rewards
Avoid ego involvement with the company
Gravitate toward off-the-job satisfaction
Reject those who strive for success and power
Demand individual treatment and recognition
Get upset by anything not routine
Frequently depreciate the things they produce
Seek immunity to discipline by joining unions and otherwise identifying with immediate work group
Tend to have satisfactory interpersonal relations
Usually adjust (slowly) to change.

Ambivalents

Creative but anxious about the work
Tend to rise to marginal positions and have limited career opportunities
Cannot reject a promotion even if they do not want it
Tend toward the neurotic
Always want change from the status quo
High intellectual interests but low interpersonal skills
Subjective, withdrawn, and introvertive, and given to displays of anger and temper
Make it a rule to resist rules and procedures
Have idealistic and usually unrealistic career expectations
Avoid psychological involvement with the company
Tend to feel that success comes from luck and is a denial of talent, wisdom, or morality
Usually are out-of-step in the company
Reject fellow workers and what they view as compromises accepted by them in their relationships to the company
Become disturbed by the fact that they are successful (if they do get a promotion)
Tend to display a compulsive interest in the job in an effort to gain recognition
Are poor decision makers.

---

discouraging is that those who have attempted to implement the ideas have all too frequently looked at the "right" and "wrong," rather than the "best," at least in regard to relating such ideas to managerial behavior styles. It is heartening to note, however, that many managerial theorists of current vintage have begun to look for the best and have begun to identify the differences between people, their outlooks toward work, and how these differences should help determine a manager's leadership styles. For example, in an effort similar to Presthus', McClelland talks about what he calls the self-motivated achiever and how to develop him, and Myers carefully dichotomizes between what he terms the motivation-seeking and the maintenance-seeking employees. In the same vein, Schachter talks of the affiliation motive, and Dubin talks about employees with an indifferent attitude toward work.[2] For our analysis, we will follow Presthus' writings simply because he not only differentiates between the "I like work" and "I don't like work" attitudes that McGregor first wrote of, but he throws in a third person, the ambivalent, who says he likes work but really has mixed emotions toward it. We will examine the nature of these attitudes toward work, and explain why these people need to be managed differently and why the Rule of Human Realism is a better rule for the manager to apply in deciding how to manage his employees.

The Ascendant Personality

The ascendant personality is the stereotype of the successful man. He is continually striving for success and has high upward mobility. In Jennings' terms, he is a mobile manager.[3] He identifies closely with the company and his job, and has a morbid fear of failure, particularly personal failure. He is sensitive to how he is doing and what his superiors think of his performance. He tends to vent his emotions on inanimate objects, is rather ritualistic in his behavior (particularly in making efforts to conceal resentment against others), desires to be in a powerful position, is rule- and procedure-oriented, and has a high visibility drive.

More important, from a managerial style standpoint, he does not take failure easily and tends to place personal success before group acceptance. He devotes little or no effort to being popular among his peers or subordinates, and feels little sense of conflict in requiring compliance with company rules and regulations, even when it is obviously the unpopular thing to do. He is a poor loser and takes failure miserably, partly because he wants so desperately to succeed, but mainly because his feelings of failure are always deepened by the fact that he has no one to commiserate with because he saw no need to cultivate friendships on the job. In fact, it is common for him to be subjected to a variety of "I told you so" reprisals from colleagues he alienated in his struggle for success.

The Indifferent's Outlook

The characteristic behavior pattern of the indifferent is that he withdraws from company participation, not particularly wishing to be identified with the job or the company. He is not inclined to compete strongly for reward, nor is he inclined to share in either the ownership or profits of the company. He tends to seek off-the-job satisfactions and categorically rejects the value system of success and power that the ascendant personality embraces.

Typically, of course, he wants individual treatment and recognition, and only pays lip service to getting ahead. He rejects the striving and self-discipline of the ascendant, does not expect to accomplish much (because he does not think he is particularly capable of accomplishing anything), does not try hard, and tends to fail (by ascendant standards). Comfortably for him, however, he does not feel particularly disappointed at his failure because he never really thought he could succeed anyhow. According to Harman, he jealously guards his own time and clearly differentiates between his work time and his personal time.[4] He feels worried and threatened by anything on the job that is not routine, and, more significant, tends to depreciate the things which he produces.

The indifferent personality will usually seek immunity to discipline by identifying with his immediate work group (usually in a union), but he does have one particular saving quality in his behavior pattern. Because of his strong affiliative drive, he tends to have sound interpersonal relationships with his coworkers and, as a rule, will adjust to almost any working circumstances. (These two points are important, because it must be recognized that most of his motivational drive at work is to pursue friendships and good home relationships; because of his disinclination to compete, he offers no real threat or challenge to anyone.)

The indifferent seldom antagonizes his coworkers because they are, like him, noncompetitive. Of course, the ascendant personality may look with disdain upon the noncompetitive attitude of the indifferent because he (the ascendant) perceives the indifferent as being lazy. The indifferent, however, does not react with antagonism because he is disinclined toward antagonizing anyone. He may view the ascendant as a "kook" with an unremitting desire to work and fail to understand his drive, but he usually will not deliberately refuse to cooperate with the boss or any other ascendant.

The Ambivalent's Outlook Toward Work

A third classification of employees' viewpoints toward working is what Presthus terms the ambivalent. The ambivalent person is one who is both creative and anxious about doing his job. Perhaps he will generate ideas, but he is afraid to implement them because of possible consequences of such actions. The ambivalent personality usually will rise only to marginal positions within the organization and will tend to have limited career opportunities because of his general reluctance to fully commit himself to doing the job at hand, particularly if the job requires that he assume responsibility for the results.

The unfortunate thing about the ambivalent is that he wants so much to be successful that he is unable to reject a promotion and sometimes, by default or reason of seniority, finds himself in a managerial position that he is mentally ill-equipped to handle. Because of his attitude of both loving and hating the job, the ambivalent's attitude tends to become neurotic, and frequently he will display flashes of anger and temper and/or become subjective, withdrawn, or downright introverted in his relations toward others on the job.

The mental anguish experienced by the ambivalent leads him to resist rules of the organization and yet, at the same time, he dreams of his possible successes in the organization. He becomes easily and quickly frustrated with his job, and such frustration increases his "psychological distance" from the company. Usually, the ambivalent feels that real success within the organization (in view of the fact that he achieves only moderate success) is more a function of having done something illegal, immoral, or unethical, rather than having worked hard to get ahead. This is because he truthfully believes he too has worked hard.

Frequently the ambivalent's attitude toward work causes him to be out of step with the rest of the organization and, in fact, the ambivalent many times becomes antagonistic toward his coworkers (particularly if they are envied ascendants). The ambivalent is almost always poor at decision making; sometimes he is unable to render a decision. His unhappiness with his job and his performance causes him to win, at best, the antipathy of the indifferent and the disdain of the ascendant personality who sees the ambivalent as a snivelling wishful thinker and day-dreamer who fails to perform.

About the only saving grace of the ambivalent, but one which makes him valuable to the organization, is the fact that because he is articulate in his discontent and tends to have high intellectual interests, he may become the agent of change within the organization. An ascendant may grasp and implement an idea generated by the ambivalent, who, of course, is afraid to initiate any action—good or bad—and resents the ascendant for "stealing" his idea. He is totally unaware that, left to him, the idea would have died on the vine.

Impact on the Organization

By definition (assuming that most promotion decisions are based upon qualifications, prior job performance, and extrapolated job performance), the ascendant personality will rise to the top in any organization. Figure 3 shows the distribution that might be expected of ascendants, ambivalents, and indifferents in a hierarchical structure of a small organization consisting of twenty people. The organization is headed by an ascendant, as is the entire second level of management.[5] (McClelland, for example, suggests that people with high achievement needs—an ingredient of personality in the person we call the ascendant—are the ones who tend to start and run successful small businesses and otherwise get ahead.)

These ascendants, in turn, manage some ascendants, but also some

FIGURE 3
Expected Distribution of Types of Employees

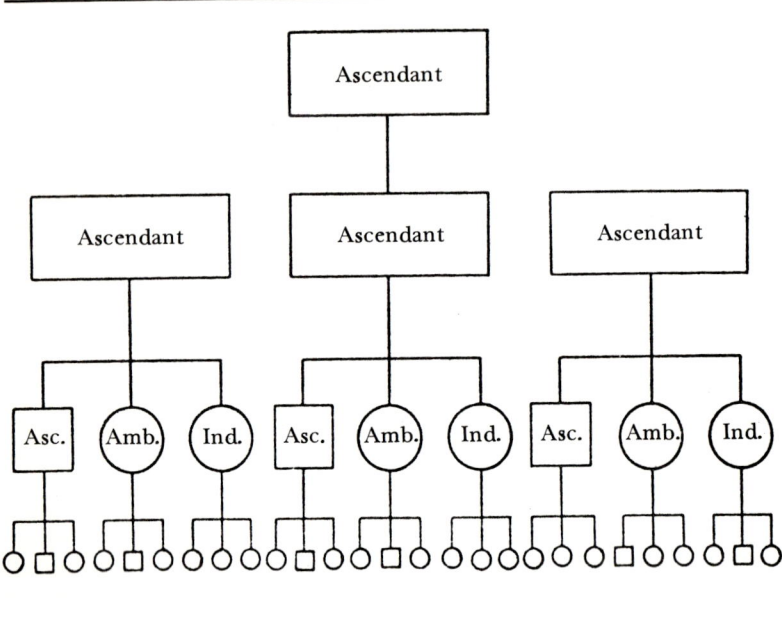

Key: □ = Ascendants
O = Ambivalents and indifferents

ambivalents and some indifferents. The lowest level in the organization is composed of mostly indifferent and ambivalent personalities (although some "coming" ascendants are included in the group). This distribution is consistent with the estimates of McClelland and others that perhaps 10 to 25 percent of our population have a high achievement-ascendancy orientation and tend to rise to higher positions in organizations or develop their own.

TOP MANAGEMENT—THE SAFETY ZONE

The implications for top management of this short organizational chart should be obvious in Figure 3. Top levels of management are in an ivory tower and are reasonably safe (particularly in the large organization) in making the assumption that most all the people immediately reporting to them are, or have been, achievement-ascendant oriented and, therefore, could be managed in a System 4 or Theory Y fashion, if that is what is desired.[6]

The lowest level of management, the line foreman or supervisor, however, cannot make such a broad sweeping assumption. To be sure, some people will display initiative, drive, and creativity at work. But it is just as sure that some people will not, and herein lies the difficulty and challenge to the line supervisor and middle levels of management. While upper-middle and top-level managers for the most part will be managing ascendant-oriented people, people who can be trusted to follow their own lead and work toward organizational goals, the mix or percentage of indifferent and ambivalent personalities will be far larger in the lower levels of the organization.

As a result, great caution is required upon the part of lower-level managers attempting to apply participative techniques. The nature of the job for these managers becomes one of recognizing that successful management at these levels is apt to be a function of applying the right style of supervision with the right subordinate in any given situation and not one of applying *the* style of supervision. The lower-level manager must recognize that there is no "right" style; the best style might be Theory X or Theory Y; systems 1, 2, 3, or 4; hard-nosed or not hard-nosed; nine-one, one-nine; or anywhere in between. It is foolhardy for managers at these levels to make any categorical assumption as to the suitability of a given leadership style.

Top levels of management must also be aware of this phenomenon and quit proselyting their junior executives. In fact, they must also recognize that, even in their personal leadership beliefs, they may need to reshape their thinking. Once it is recognized that there are, in fact, different outlooks toward working—ascendants, indifferents, and ambivalents—and that people can change from one basic orientation to another no matter what their level in the organization, a pat managerial style may not be in order. For example, a man may be ascendant oriented and rise to a lofty position in an organization while he is still young and vital. In his later years, he may develop an ambivalent or indifferent outlook toward work. Therefore, the style of leadership he will best respond to at different times may change.

Furthermore, a mixture or combination of the various outlooks and a mixed type may require a still different leadership pattern. Finally, some recent research conducted by these authors indicates that man's motivational drives may undergo significant change as he ages, discovers what he is successful or ineffectual at doing, and decides whether or not his talents are being effectively utilized in his given job.[7]

Academic, consultative, and upper-level management proselytism may be doing more harm than good in the area of training lower-level managers in leadership techniques, behavior, and strategems. The mere fact that people are people is the basis for such a statement, but broad classifications of the types of attitudes toward work help emphasize this point.

The article is intended to highlight the fact that consultants and theorists have entirely too much in their favor when preaching their message of participative management to top-level managers. The problem is that top-level management—the people in a position to decide what kind of training should be given to lower and middle levels of managers—are, for the most part, themselves ascendant-oriented and are susceptible to management styles founded on the notion that "work is fun." Consequently, they make the grave error of embracing these ideas and end up projecting their motivational drives (and their concomitant behavior patterns and perceptual outlooks) to their subordinates.

Unfortunately, such projection is unwarranted and increases managerial and supervisory headaches; it forces many lower- and middle-level managers to learn and apply inapplicable (if not harmful) tools of management. This is not to say that all people dislike work, or that participative or consultative management is applicable in all cases. However, in accordance with the Rule of Human Realism, a significant understanding of rational human behavior and attitudes toward work is a far more reasonable and healthy outlook for supervisors when it comes to the question of adopting an appropriate leadership style or styles.

FOOTNOTES

1. Robert Presthus, *The Organizational Society* (New York: Alfred A. Knopf, Inc., 1962). See, especially, Chapters 6, 7, and 8.

2. David McClelland, "Business Drive and National Achievement," *Harvard Business Review*, XL (July-August, 1962), p. 99; Scott Myers, "Who Are Your Motivated Workers," *Harvard Business Review*, XLII (January-February, 1964), pp. 73-88; Stanley Schachter, *The Psychology of Affiliation* (Stanford, Calif.: Stanford University Press, 1959); and Robert Dubin, *Human Relations in Administration* (2nd ed.; Englewood Cliffs, N.J.: Prentice-Hall, Inc., 1961).

3. Eugene Emerson Jennings, *The Mobile Manager: A Study of the New Generation of Top Executives* (Ann Arbor, Mich.: Bureau of Industrial Relations, University of Michigan), 1967.

4. Samuel Harman, *Psychology for Managers: Frustration and Conflict* (Los Angeles: The Management Health and Development Corporation, 1968).

5. The example is an expected example, and may not be the case in any given circumstance. Ascendants usually rise to the top but, upon reaching any given level in the organization, may become ambivalent or indifferent. It must also be recognized that any person is usually a mixture of the three types; rarely does the pure ascendant, indifferent, or ambivalent personality emerge.

6. At this point, the authors do not wish to be interpreted as flatly advocating System 4 or Theory Y management at the top levels of management, if for no other reason than because they are not yet convinced that nondirective management in its purest form is feasible or desirable. The reason for this is that the achievement-ascendant oriented personalities, being so competitive, may not work well as teammates, may need to "build fences" around their areas of accomplishment to feed their high visibility drive, and may not respond at all well to the various participative managerial styles frequently advocated, such as System 4 or Theory Y.

7. Lawrence L. Steinmetz, "Age: Unrecognized Enigma of Executive Development," *Management of Personnel Quarterly*, Vol. 8, No. 3 (Fall, 1969), pp. 2-12.